CONTENTS

"Existentialism is worth revisiting at intervals for the help it may offer with themes of contemporary interest"

—(Cooper, 1990: vii)

POST-EXISTENTIALISM
AND THE PSYCHOLOGICAL THERAPIES

POST-EXISTENTIALISM AND THE PSYCHOLOGICAL THERAPIES
Towards a therapy without foundations

Del Loewenthal

KARNAC

First published in 2011 by
Karnac Books Ltd
118 Finchley Road
London NW3 5HT

British Library Cataloguing in Publication Data

A C.I.P. for this book is available from the British Library

ISBN-13: 978-1-85575-846-9

Typeset by Vikatan Publishing Solutions (P) Ltd., Chennai, India

Printed in Great Britain

www.karnacbooks.com

PERMISSIONS

We wish to acknowledge permissions from the following:

Cayne, J. & Loewenthal, D. (2008). The between as unknown. *Journal of Philosophical Practice*, 3(3): 322–332.

Greenwood, D. (2008). A case of counseling with a person diagnosed with dementia. *Journal of Philosophical Practice, 3 (3)*: 333–342.

Loewenthal, D. (2007). *Case Studies in Relational Research*. Basingstoke: Palgrave Macmillan, 245–250.

Loewenthal, D. (2008). Introducing post-existential practice. *Journal of Philosophical Practice, 3(3)*: 316–321.

Loewenthal, D. (2009) (editorial). Ideology, research and evidence in the psychological therapies. *European Journal of Psychotherapy and Counselling, 11(3)*.

Loewenthal, D. & Snell, R. (2008). The learning community and emotional learning in a university-based training of counsellors and psychotherapists. *International Journal for the Advancement of Counselling, 30 (1)*: 38–51.

Stamp, R. (2008). A re-examination of the case of Lola Voss. *Journal of Philosophical Practice, 3(3)*: 353–361.

Notes on the Chapters

Chapters Two, Three, Four, and Five are developed by permission of the publisher from articles that originally appeared in *Philosophical Practice: Journal of the American Philosophical Practitioners Association (APPA)*, 3.3, October 2008.

Chapter Eight is developed by permission of the publisher from an article that originally appeared in the *International Journal for the Advancement of Counselling*, 30.1, March 2008.

Chapter Nine is developed from a book chapter "Relational research, ideology and the evolution of intersubjectivity in a post-existential culture", from *Case Studies in Relational Research*, by Del Loewenthal (2007), with permission of Palgrave Macmillan.

Del Loewenthal
London
May 2011

ACKNOWLEDGEMENTS

My thanks to so many people: first, to my co-authors Julia Cayne, Tom Cotton, Dennis Greenwood, Patrick Larsson, Robert Snell, and Rhiannon Thomas, all from the Research Centre for Therapeutic Education, Department of Psychology, Roehampton University, UK, for the joy of working with them. A particular thanks to Mick Cooper, for taking an interest in this post-existential project and taking the time to write his delightful and generous foreword. My thanks also to Joanna Gee and Rhiannon Thomas for their invaluable assistance in helping bring this book together.

I would also like to acknowledge at least those organizations and in particular the people from them who, over the years, have invited me to speak, the results of which have led to the contents of this book. The organizations include: The American Psychological Association; Auckland University of Technology, New Zealand; The British Psychological Society; Centre Source, Paris, France; OISIE, University of Toronto, Canada; University of British Columbia, Canada; University of Malta; University of Seattle, USA, and W. K. Kellogg Battle Creek, USA (for a Faculty Fellowship).

Further thanks to those on our Thursday evening Advanced Practitioner Programme on Post-Existentialism. The company of this company has been invaluable to me in the development of this book. The current members include: Erik Abrams, Philip Bailey, Betty Bertrand, Gillian Brooks, Onel Brooks, Julia Cayne, Tom Cotton, Geraldine Dawes, Jo Eastwood, Anastasios Gaitanidis, Elena Gil-Rodriguez, Anne Guy, Denise Ham, Richard House, Razwana Jabbin, Baraheh Khah, Anne Laungani, Del Loewenthal, Darren McClounan, Sharon O'Driscoll, Stephane Preteux, Sue Saxby-Smith, Susan Stephenson, Di Thomas, Val Todd, Christine Wells, Mags Whittle, Neil Worman, and Rafia Yousuf (further thanks to Onel Brooks for the conversations, particularly regarding Chapter Seven).

The above group and its forerunners has been meeting weekly for over ten years (before 2004 at the University of Surrey), and previous members included: Carolyn Armstrong, Philip Channer, Tom Davey, Rose Gallagher, Angela Gillard, Dennis Greenwood, Liz Hammond, Vivien Issany, Mary Lawes, Lynn Mansfield-Osbourne, Alistair Parkes, Jayne Redmond, Theresa Rose, Mary Sharpe, Robert Snell, Celia Sturgeon, Maureen Taylor. This group, as with others of the Centre for Therapeutic Education, so ably administered by Helen McEwan.

Whilst of course taking responsibility for the contents of this book, I would like to acknowledge at least some of the conversations I have had along the way: Stuart Wheatley from the Henderson Hospital and John Heron from the Human Potential Research Project at Surrey University for introducing me to therapeutic communities and humanism. Gaie Houston, Pat Milner, and Brigid Proctor at South-West London College for training me as a counsellor. Emmy Van Deurzen and David Smith, then from Regent's College for introducing me to existentialism. Steve Gans, John Heaton, and Chris Oakley from the Philadelphia Association and Ben Churchill from the Guild of Psychotherapists for introducing me to both continental philosophy and psychoanalysis.

I would also like to thank Oliver Rathbone and Lucy Shirley for their support and encouragement in writing this book.

Most of all, I would like to thank, besides my family (my wife Jane and children Lola, Lucy, and John-Louis) and those named above, my students and patients for what has emerged over the last thirty years, starting with the first course at the Wolfson Rehabilitation Centre in Wimbledon with the help of Madelyn Brewer, Val Magner, and, shortly afterwards, Steve Gans (who amongst other things introduced me to the work of Levinas).

In writing this book, the greatest controversy amongst us has been whether to put the word "post" in front of "existentialism" and "phenomenology". I hope, as argued in this book, for the most part, it is found helpful.

Dr Julia Cayne is a Senior Lecturer and Programme Coordinator for the MSc in Counselling and Psychotherapy at the Department of Psychology at Roehampton University. Her PhD research, carried out at the Research Centre for Therapeutic Education through the University of Surrey was funded through an ESRC studentship, and considered how to research the unknown by questioning how psychotherapists learn about the unknown. These two issues continue to provide a focus for her ongoing research in terms of the implications of post-existential, post-phenomenological thought for research methodology, as well as how it might inform the problematic of the relationship between the known and the unknown. She is also interested in phenomenological research through the use of reverie. She has a private practice offering psychotherapy and supervision in south-west England.

Tom Cotton is a psychotherapist and film-maker with a special interest in phenomenology and the construction of narrative. Tom studied Fine Art Film and Video at Central Saint Martins College (1996–1999) before working in the film industry. Later, he gained an MSc in Psychotherapy and Counselling at Roehampton University (2004–2008) and continued his studies there over the course of a two-year Advanced Practitioner programme (2008–2010). He is currently researching his PsychD thesis carried out at the Research Centre for Therapeutic Education, Roehampton University, "An exploration of whether psychotherapy is helpful or not for those who have received a diagnosis of schizophrenia", and recently directed a half-hour documentary, *There is a Fault in Reality*, which explored three people's experiences of "schizophrenia". Tom also works in a therapeutic community for people experiencing psychosis and is a UK delegate for Phototherapy Europe.

Dr Dennis Greenwood is Principal Lecturer in the Department of Psychology, Roehampton University, and is currently Chair of the Universities Psychotherapy and Counselling Association and former member of the Board of Trustees for the United Kingdom Council of Psychotherapy. His research interests have focused on working with people suffering with dementia and exploring the works of continental philosophers such as Emmanuel Levinas. His doctoral research was on the possibility of psychotherapy with a person diagnosed with dementia, and this was recently published. He has also published articles in a wide range of professional journals.

Dr Patrick Larsson has completed his training as a Counselling Psychologist at Roehampton University, where his doctoral dissertation, carried out with the Research Centre for Therapeutic Education, explored counselling psychologists' constructs and experiences of working with clients diagnosed with "schizophrenia" using a critical discursive psychology approach. He previously worked with Camden and Islington NHS Foundation Trust as a recovery worker with individuals diagnosed with "schizophrenia" and is currently employed by the Priory Group and Richmond and Twickenham Psychological Therapy Service. His interests include critical perspectives on psychology and counselling, and pursuing further research concerning the epistemology and ontology of counselling psychology.

Professor Del Loewenthal is Director of the Research Centre for Therapeutic Education, Department of Psychology, Roehampton University. He is also in private practice as a psychotherapist and counselling psychologist in Wimbledon and Brighton. He is founding editor of the *European Journal of Psychotherapy and Counselling* (Routledge) and former Chair of the United Kingdom Council for Psychotherapy Research Committee. His publications include *Critically Engaging CBT* (co-edited with Richard House, 2010, PCCS Books), *Childhood, Wellbeing and a Therapeutic Ethos* (co-edited with Richard House, 2009, Karnac Books), *Case Studies in Relational Research* (2007, Palgrave Macmillan), and *Post-Modernism for Psychotherapists* (co-authored with Robert Snell, 2003, Sage). He is currently writing *Phototherapy and Therapeutic Photography in a Digital Age* (Routledge).

Dr Robert Snell is an analytic psychotherapist (London Centre for Psychotherapy); he also has a background in existential therapy. He is an Honorary Senior Research Fellow at the Research Centre for Therapeutic Education, Department of Psychology, Roehampton University, London. His first career was in art history. He is the author of *Theophile Gautier: A Romantic Critic of the Visual Arts* (Oxford University Press, 1982) and the co-author, with Del Loewenthal, of *Postmodernism for Psychotherapists: A Critical Reader* (Routledge, 2003).

Dr Rhiannon Thomas is a psychotherapeutic counsellor in private practice. She has previously worked as a counsellor in a school for children diagnosed with learning and behavioural difficulties and has just completed her PhD, carried out at the Research Centre for Therapeutic Education, Roehampton University, on language and experience, with particular reference to the experience of psychotherapy of mothers with children diagnosed as having a significant language delay.

Post-existentialism and the psychological therapies: towards a therapy without foundations

Mick Cooper

From an ethics of care, existentialism emerged. Kierkegaard, Rosenstock, Buber, Sartre ... all the great existentialists, each in their own way, challenged the increasing technologization, mechanization, and systematization of human being that they witnessed around them. Each of them called for a return to an understanding of human being *as* its being: the particular, unique, concrete being-in-the-world of each human existence. An existence that, as Buber (1964, p. 64) puts it, can be squashed flat "as a boy violently spreads out a rosebud" by the forces of scientism and modernist "progress".

Yet existentialism, too, has the potential to do violence to the very existence that it strives to retrieve. When it calls, for instance, for human beings to "stand naked in the storm of life" (Becker, 1973, p. 86) or to courageously mark out their individuality by facing their ownmost being-towards-death (Heidegger, 1962), it risks re-introducing the very same system of norms, expectations, and "truths" that it had set out to overcome.

In this respect, post-modernism can be understood as existentialism turned back on itself. It is a way of thinking about human being that consistently strives to side-step the pull towards systematization and reification—existential or otherwise. Post-modern thought challenges us to stay open to the unpredictability and ineffability of being-in-the-world: to an otherness that can never be fully defined.

Paradoxically, however, even post-modernism has the potential to be brandished as a final, definitive truth; as an interpretative framework through which the Others' concerns and experiences become transformed into "narratives" and "discourses". And it is important here to note that, in the vast majority of instances, clients do not come into therapy unhappy with their "life narratives" or "discursive understandings". Rather, they come to therapy with problems located in the discourse of "the real" (Cooper, 1999): *real* worries, *real* concerns, *real* pain and suffering.

For psychotherapists, counsellors, and psychologists who wish to engage with their clients in deeply respectful, non-dogmatic ways, therefore, the space between existentialism and post-modernism provides an inordinately fertile ground. It is a space in which the client's lived, phenomenologically experienced concerns can be attended to, but within a spirit of "unknowing" and a deep respect for the "unstable, ambiguous and temporary" (Loewenthal, this volume). It is a space in which norms can be side-stepped, but also norms about norms—in which the whole encounter between truth and uncertainty can be held with a care for both certainty and uncertainty.

This is the ground that Del Loewenthal and his colleagues furrow in *Post-Existentialism and the Psychological Therapies: Towards a Therapy without Foundations*. Through a series of stimulating, challenging, and accessible essays, they outline the boundaries of this "post-existential" ground; discuss the theoretical, empirical, diagnostic, and training perspectives that emanate from it, and illustrate it with case examples and case analyses. Throughout, the book holds open this "space between" as a realm of possibility and unknowing: an opportunity for reflection, consideration, and mystery, without the fixed answers and certainties that can foreclose dialogue. And while the book is subtitled *"Towards a Therapy without Foundations"*, one of its most important contributions may be to contribute to the development of a psychotherapeutic perspective that is rooted in Levinas's ethics of care. It calls us back to the heart of the therapeutic enterprise—the capacity to help an Other fully realize their Otherness—through a willingness to stand alongside them in uncertainty, unknowing, and the inevitable incompleteness of Being.

CHAPTER ONE

On the very idea of post-existentialism

Del Loewenthal

This book is for individual and group psychological therapists: counsellors, psychotherapists, psychoanalysts, psychologists, and arts and play therapists, whether they be integrative, humanistic, pluralistic, psychodynamic, existential, systemic, or cognitive behavioural, who want to start with practice. I am therefore proposing the possibility of exploring the psychological therapies at the start of the twenty-first century, in a way that is in contrast to the prevailing culture that has led to the increasing dominance of approaches such as cognitive behavioural therapy (CBT) (which start with theory and are increasingly being manualized). Though what is ultimately being criticized in this book is any theoretically driven model.

An attempt is made to offer a space where we might still be able to think about how alienated we are through valuing existential notions such as experience and meaning, whilst questioning other aspects such as existentialism's inferred narcissism and the place it has come to take up with regard to such aspects as psychoanalysis and the political. The post-existential would also include the post-phenomenological, where, for example, Merleau-Ponty's notion of being open to what emerges in the between (Merleau-Ponty 1962), as well as his notion of embodiment, would be given primacy over Husserlian notions

1

of intentionality. As a result, questions such as those of mystery, an unknown and an unconscious, and the non-intentional can be re-examined. A third element to be explored will be the extent to which we might consider more recent ideas—for example, those of Saussure, Levinas, Derrida, Foucault, Lacan, and Wittgenstein (as explored, for example, in Loewenthal & Snell 2003)—without becoming too caught up in them. It is hoped that by having a possible space to explore what some would now call our "wellbeing", theoretically through post-ex-istentialism, and methodologically through post-phenomenology, that this can provide a loose base, without concerns of any further gener-alization, for a greater possibility of accepting, rather than escaping, who we are.

This book, in developing one way of starting with practice, raises fundamental questions about the nature of knowledge in the psycho-logical therapies and the implications for what might be meant by theory, research, and indeed practice. The rest of this chapter starts to put the case for post-existentialism as another possibility, which is in contrast to the work on existential psychotherapy as developed by May (1950), Yalom (1980, 1989) in North America, and Van Deurzen (1997, 2005) and Spinelli (2005) in the UK. Yet, in other ways, this book is putting the case for a contemporary return to the existentialism of those such as Heidegger and Kierkegaard. One way of distinguish-ing post-existentialism from existentialism and post-modernism may be provided through a comparison between Buber and Levinas (see Chapter Two). Further, post-existentialism may be seen to question issues of practice, theory, and research (see Chapter Four), exploring such problematics of staying with an unknown (see Chapter Three) and the inter-relationships of language and experience (see Chapter Five). Post-existentialism may also be seen, in part, as a development of the work of R. D. Laing (see Chapter Six for interviews with Laing's col-leagues, particularly with reference to the pioneering therapeutic com-munity Kingsley Hall). Further questions that may be examined will include how one may provide therapy to a client with a diagnosis of schizophrenia from a post-existential perspective, within the emerging profession of counselling psychology (Chapter Seven); and, how one may provide a psychological therapeutic training from a post-existential perspective with particular reference to both the place of psychoanal-ysis and working therapeutically in groups (see Chapter Eight). This book also explores an overview of research in post-existentialism in the psychological therapies in relation to ideology and inter-subjectivity (see Chapter Nine), questioning whether post-existentialism could enable a return to giving a primacy to practice (see Chapter Ten).

Why post-existentialism?

The name "post-existentialism" is tentatively being put forward in an attempt to describe a potential cultural moment whereby the psychological therapies can at least start with practice. To give such a name, albeit to a particularly loose mixture of cultural influences, is done with much trepidation and is not meant to name yet another school. However, such a branding is with some reluctance presented as it is considered necessary to counter the hegemony of training technicians as psychological therapists (a term used here to include counsellors, psychotherapists, psychoanalysts, psychologists, art and play therapists) to oil the wheels of our increasingly dominant managerialist culture (see, for example, Loewenthal 2010) This book expresses one way of starting with practice and then considers the implications, rather than the applications, of theory. A position is taken, more akin to Wittgenstein, that theory as such cannot provide a foundation for the psychological therapies (Heaton 2010). In giving a primacy to practice, various notions of phenomenology come closer to this, something that most psychological therapists would associate with existentialism, though most contemporary readings of existentialism are considered dated, hence the name "post-existentialism".

Whilst at least starting with practice (and hopefully continually attempting to return to it) is associated with ordinary language, both this and how we consider it is already mediated by the language of our contemporary culture. In working therapeutically, the psychological therapist may find that certain ideas/theories come to mind when working with a client/patient. This is regarded as very different to starting with such theories as a frame-up. This book attempts to explore how various authors can hopefully enable a thoughtful return to practice. As mentioned, the term "phenomenology" could be thought to come closest to what is being considered here. However, there have been attempts to discredit phenomenology from Foucault and others that have led this term to be less prominent in more recent cultural developments. Though it is argued here that practice is always the basis of our work, it will always be problematic to describe this through words such as "phenomenology" and "tacit knowledge"—another attempt to conceptualize the essence of practice.

It is also argued that by linking phenomenology with developments in structural linguistics, it is possible to consider the political in terms of chains of signifiers. It would also appear that phenomenologists, alongside most psychological therapists, do not seem adept at political consideration outside their immediate training institute. There is a further suggestion in this book, that we consider the term "post-phenomenological" to both free us of some of phenomenology's previous connotations whilst continuing, for example, with the notion of what emerges in the between (Merleau-Ponty 1962). It is recognized that in construing the names "post-existentialism" and "post-phenomenology", this is not ordinary language and that attempting to put the case of using these terms, to stay with practice and ordinary language, is at best a paradox. It is, however, hoped that if "post-existentialism" is considered as a temporary device, then the benefits in attempting to return to at least starting with practice will outweigh the hypocrisy.

Following Laing (1965) and others, I have previously used the term "existential-analytic" to describe a practice which might have been seen to originate from the Greek concept of Pyrrhonian scepticism. However, "existentialism" seems increasingly stuck in its self-centredness, and "analytic" appears to increasingly imply a frame-up whereby psychological therapists are meant to be able to diagnose and treat patients in terms of an unconscious as if they were modern medical doctors. Existentialism was therefore losing its original meaning of being "astonishing", and analysis was appearing less a practice of thoughtfulness and more the reverse through the application of technologies. Something else therefore appears to be needed so that one can explore what emerges in practice between psychological therapist and patient/ client.

We appear to be in a managerial culture in which CBT is the therapy of choice. CBT has numerous variants, but its fundamental assumption is to change the way we think from where we find ourselves. This taking our minds off what comes to us can be useful but, as has been argued elsewhere (House & Loewenthal 2007; Loewenthal & House 2010), is disastrous as an overall approach for a culture, as it means we can never come to our senses. What if we want to allow thoughts to come to us? There are arguments that we are unable to allow such thoughts, either because of, for example, existential anxieties such as death, or psychoanalytic anxieties as signified by the Oedipal complex. So how could one be with a psychological therapist who, rather than lead us to stop thinking, might enable us to work through that which blocks our thinking so we can breathe more easily? Such a practice, which might include what Kierkegaard (1944) has described as education through "dread" (whereby one might find it hard to breathe, in order eventually to breathe more easily), could start with meaning, but in contrast to manualized psychological therapies might be more influenced by Heidegger's notions of being in the world with others (Heidegger 1927). Yet how could one consider such a space in contrast to those who start with theory, which would potentially allow for other developments in our cultural practice such as psychoanalysis, structural linguistics, and post-modernism without starting with them as the theory?

Post-modernism can be seen to consider the person not as a "subject" but decentred and "subject to" (Loewenthal & Snell 2003). One important example of this, following the work of Saussure (1959), is that we are subject to language—an example of a cultural development of potential interest to anyone involved in a talking cure. Another currently particularly important figure is Levinas, as he suggests that if we are to consider our being, then we need to try and start not with such self-centredness that sets up the world so that everything returns to us, but instead be strong enough to first consider our responsibility for others (Levinas 1961). Such examples of postmodernism may have the potential for us then to think of meaning without excluding questions of an unconscious, but in a way that counters the consumerist managerialist forces in our society (Loewenthal 2010), which are relentlessly destroying our communities, particularly for our children (House & Loewenthal 2010), and for ourselves.

Post-existentialism is therefore an attempt for us to experience our alienation in the hope that we may still be able, individually and collectively, to do more about it. Further, it is an attempt to consider a potential cultural practice that, in contrast to what are theory-driven therapies, considers psychological therapy as essentially subversive: personally, in not excluding thoughts; and politically, in terms of our relationship with others.

"Post post-modernism" would be another term that could have been used. Post-modernism is considered to have made important contributions in opening up possibilities for the psychological therapies, yet to stay with it might mean we would be unable to communicate with anyone! Post-existentialism is therefore in some ways a return to Heidegger's questions of being-in-the-world-with-others, exploring meanings in their specific contexts, without ignoring the work of the post-modernists, the psychoanalysts, or the political.

When previously writing about post-modernism for psychotherapists (Loewenthal & Snell 2003), we were careful to attempt not to create a post-modern practice. In writing *Post-Existentialism and the Psychological Therapies*, the temptation has again been avoided (just!) to call for a post-existential psychological therapy. Instead, it is hoped that by naming a post-existential cultural moment, this can inform the myriad of existing therapeutic approaches/schools.

Therefore, it is hoped this book may identify a way of challenging a dominant discourse in revitalizing previous approaches by, in some way, going back to where we are coming from. In this sense, as Lyotard (1984) points out, the word "post" does not only mean "after". Further, it is an opportunity for me to put in one volume revisions of my previous writings on post-existentialism together with chapters written specifically for this book. Other than my colleague Robert Snell, I have written some of the chapters with my doctoral students at our Research Centre for Therapeutic Education (both at Surrey University and, subsequently, Roehampton University, UK), many of whom are now colleagues. Hopefully, our struggles to find such a way will inspire others to develop further, particularly questioning what is meant by psychotherapeutic research and developing the political, a practice that can enable us to be thoughtful, both individually and collectively.

Finally, there is yet another response to the question "why post-existentialism?" The first time I gave a talk on this subject at an international conference was when I was invited to speak at the American Psychological Association annual conference in Hawaii in 2004 and presented a paper called "Post-Phenomenology". Afterwards, as I was leaving the lecture theatre, a member of the audience whom I had not previously met and have not since, tugged at my sleeve and said, "You know, we would understand it much better if you called it 'Post-Existentialism'." Hope you do!

What is post-existentialism?

This book on post-existentialism describes work in progress at the Centre for Therapeutic Education, Roehampton University, UK (where we carry out research and train counsellors, psychotherapists, psychologists, and art and play therapists). We are all practitioners (psychological therapists) with a particular interest in the implications of continental philosophy for practice that I have termed "post-existential". As has been said, this development is in contrast to the rapid growth of cognitive behavioural therapy in what some would term our current "age of happiness" (Layard 2006a; Seligman 1995). CBT can be seen to include a way of not thinking which can be useful at times but catastrophic as the main approach to wellbeing (though similar criticisms can be applied to all therapies that start with theory). The post-existential takes as an important influence Heidegger's *Dasein* in exploring the "well" in terms of "being" (in the world with others), and is a particular mixture of some aspects of existentialism, phenomenology, psychoanalysis, and post-modernism.

"Post-existential" is taken to mean "after" Heidegger (1927 and—in a different way—after Husserl's phenomenology (1983), yet looking to retain what might be good from both existentialism together with aspects of subsequent developments such as post-modernism. At the very least, we might consider, as David Cooper suggests, that existentialism *"is worth revisiting at intervals for the help it may offer with themes of contemporary interest"* (Cooper 1990: vii).

So let's start by briefly going back to what might have been meant by "existentialism"—a name probably originating from Gabriel Marcel (Cooper 2003) and then taken up, at first very reluctantly, by other French philosophers such as Jean-Paul Sartre (1943) and Simone de Beauvoir (1972), though perhaps becoming particularly grounded in Martin Heidegger's work on existence, which he in turn developed from the work of Kierkegaard (1941, 1980) and Nietzsche (1883, 1888), and, in particular, with regard to phenomenology, Husserl (1983).

Whilst there appears to be no agreed definition, David Cooper provides a parody of what was taken as existence:

> ... a constant *striving*, a perpetual *choice*: it is marked by a radical *freedom*, and *responsibility*. And it is also prey to a sense of *Angst* which reveals that, for the most part, it is lived *inauthentically* and in *bad faith*. And because the character of the human life is never *given*, existence is *without foundation*; hence it is *abandoned* or *absurd* even.

> (Cooper 1990: 3–4)

However, how one responds to these existential concerns is vital. In a way, whilst there is no agreement as to what existentialism "is", for many in the 1950s and 1960s, the method of existentialism was phenomenology, which was particularly developed by Heidegger's teacher, Edmund Husserl, through the encouragement of Wilhelm Wundt, regarded by many as a founding father of psychology. Whilst Wilhelm Wundt was one of those who persuaded Husserl away from his more quantitative interests to develop Brentano's descriptive psychology (1995a) (whose audience included not only Husserl but aone Sigmund Freud), Wundt (1874) considered psychology to be partly a natural science and partly a social science. This fundamental definition of psychology, merging the political with the cultural/historical, is lost on most of psychology today, with devastating consequences for us all.

Hence, if we return to David Cooper's parody of existential terms, and if we attempt to study them experimentally, this is very different to a study that (at least first) looks at what emerges in terms of meanings. Thus, for Brentano, experimentalism is not appropriate (1995b), whereas current psychological practice has increasingly been dismissive of phenomenology. Husserl's hope for a pure phenomenology which we do not contaminate was not considered to be possible by the likes of Heidegger, Merleau-Ponty, or Sartre. Nevertheless, Heidegger managed to marry existentialism and phenomenology, and Merleau-Ponty developed a notion of meaning emerging in the between which became more dominant until Foucault (1974) and others questioned whether phenomenology was still relevant after the advent of structuralism and the developing influence of Saussure and structural linguistics. Later, Derrida (1990) importantly questioned if any system of thought, whether, for example, phenomenology, structuralism, or psychoanalysis, would always be blinded by its own definition. Yet would it not be possible to look at some questions regarding our being existentially—without this being about nostalgia (Oakley 1990) and an attempt to return to something that probably never existed (Borsch-Jacobsen 1991).

The versions of existentialism that appeared in the English-speaking world seemed to remove such issues of politics and psychoanalysis, unlike, for example, continental Europe, where Sartre would come to explore existentialism and Marxism, and Binswanger would speak of the existential analyst who "not only is in possession of existential-analytic and psychotherapeutic competence, but ... he must dare to risk committing his own existence in the struggle for the freedom of his partners" (Binswanger, in Friedman 1991: 426). Binswanger, of course, later said he had misunderstood Heidegger's notion of being, though he did say he felt it was a fruitful misunderstanding! Heidegger, in turn, considered Sartre's understanding of his (Heidegger's) work as rubbish! Heidegger did work with Medard Boss, who, some felt therefore, had the nearest possibility of looking at the implications of Heidegger's writings for existential practice. Interestingly, the so-called "British school" of existentialism adopted more of Boss's work (Cooper 2003), but attempted to drop Boss's interest in and strong influence from psychoanalysis. This is again in contrast to those who start with psychoanalysis and then consider the existential-phenomenological (Askay & Farquhar 2006). Importantly, neither are what is termed here the "post-existential".

We thus have the most popular currents of existential psychotherapy in the UK (as represented by Spinelli 2007; Van Deurzen 1997) and in North America (as represented by May 1996; Yalom 1980) as not requiring the possession of existential-analytic competence as essential and removing, in general, the political. The existential movement has a history of aristocratic and, indeed, sometimes what are seen as Fascist political tendencies. Yet, couldn't post-existentialism combine, for example, Foucauldian notions of power with existential concerns; and couldn't post-existential practice explore an unknown including an unconscious—it seems very different not to wish to start with psychoanalytic theories as opposed to allowing them to sometimes come to mind. Thus, one fundamental difference between the post-existentialist and, particularly, Anglo-Saxonized existentialism is the former's acknowledgement that inevitably we are all subject-to, so that the rejection of psychoanalytic dogma as a starting model does not mean, or indeed is a rationalization for, an attempt to be subject-to nothing.

There again, the relational school starts within psychoanalysis even with such offerings as *Beyond Postmodernism: New Dimensions in Clinical Theory and Practice*, edited by Frie & Orange (2009). Their book has a similarity in valuing post-modernism whilst considering that a relational post-modernism is unable to engage with such important aspects as experience and understanding (for an interesting review, see Snell 2009). Also, whilst at the same time questioning meta-narratives and the modern need for objectivity, empiricism, and reductionism. It is in order to show that this can all be done within psychoanalysis, albeit with a relational take.

The post-modern (Loewenthal & Snell 2003) may bring about the greatest change to what was regarded as existentialism in that we are seen as being, for example, subject-to language (Lacan), writing (Derrida), ethics (Levinas), and an unconscious (Freud). Thus, Sartre's "I am my choices" could be regarded as representing a very narcissistic age. In contrast, the post-existential person would be regarded as having some agency with an attempt towards a responsibility. For example, it might be that in growing up someone took a survival path, which may have been necessary then but may now be redundant and unhelpful to this person or others—perhaps he was therefore less able to take responsibility for who he was then, but has more, though not complete, agency as to where he finds himself now. Furthermore, whilst aspects of learning theory may be of help here, though more likely in the context of Polyani's tacit knowledge (1983), we might also be able to see constrictions in ourselves and how we constrict others—both politically, with various-sized notions of the letter "p"—as well as how our intentions are not always clear to us.

Foucault became interested in power and knowledge and the political status of psychiatry as science. With post-existentialism, we would now, in exploring our wellbeing, raise questions on power, knowledge, and the political nature of psychology as science. This would in some ways be similar to how Foucault and some existentialists questioned the political status of psychiatry as science, and at least a primacy would be given to first thinking of what is termed "mental illness" as dissimilar to a physical illness, but instead more to do with relations with others. Yet there would be vitally important distinctions: Foucault (1974) abandoned his early interest in phenomenology. But was this, as Hoeller (1986) points out, because he took Husserl's notion of transcendental phenomenology, which does not really allow for the historical and cultural? As further argued by Hoeller (1986), Heidegger with his *Dasein* as being in the historical/cultural world with others, enables phenomenology to be released from Husserl's attempts to show a pure subjectivity and thus "a universal doctrine of the structures of individual subjectivity and intersubjectivity" (Husserl 1977: 178–179). This opening up of phenomenology was further developed for psychotherapy by Binswanger, Boss, and Laing, and we term this "post-phenomenology" to distinguish it from Husserl's original transcendental phenomenology. Thus, if we could both be attentive to what emerges in the between of client and therapist and be aware of what is regarded culturally and historically as common sense, we could have an interest in how both our clients and those around them have brought and bring pressures on each other. This meeting, which could include the implications for the present of the client's history and the history of the culture, without being caught up in a potentially totalizing approach (in this case, for example, Foulcaudian genealogy), would be an example of post-phenomenology and might also be closer to what those such as Wilheim Wundt saw as psychology, though the post-existential should, it is suggested, always be beyond.

One exception to those existentialists mentioned above, and who may be regarded as leading to post-existentialism, is R. D. Laing (1969). He, as with existentialism, was more able to keep something open without defining it in a positivistic way, so that there is not the danger that can happen through taking away the mystery, of taking away the thing itself (Merleau-Ponty 1962). Laing, for example, suggested that whilst behaviour is important, what is really important is how one experiences behaviour (Laing 1967). Here again, Laing, and those influenced by him, are not being put forward as if their approach is the ideal, but that they are able to hold a space which is always only partially defined where something helpful for our thoughtfulness may at times emerge.

One result of all this concerns what we regard as psychology. For those such as Binswanger, who might be seen in some ways to be more in keeping with Wundt:

> When this *my*, or *our*, this *I* or *he* or *we* are bracketed out, the result is that psychology becomes "impersonal" and "objective" while losing, at the same time, the scientific character of a genuine psychologist and becoming, instead, natural science.... In place of a reciprocal, "personal" communication within a we-relationship, we find a one-sided, i.e., irreversible, relationship between doctor and patient and an even more impersonal relationship between researcher and the object of research. Experience, participation and confrontation between human beings in the present moment gives way to the "perfect tense" of theoretical investigation.
>
> (Binswanger, in Friedman 1991: 414)

Thus, unfortunately, "good" psychological research is currently determined by publication in quantitative, primarily American, journals, and relations between people are more for English departments where there is usually more chance of studying not only Freud and Lacan but Derrida, Foucault, et al. In the social sciences, there is an historical, cultural shift to behaviouralism, with desperate concerns for survival by some to quantify experience to show that it is evidence based. Yet, what is denied keeps re-emerging, and questions have again recently been raised as to whether psychology should really be the science of experience rather than the science of the mind (Ashworth 2004).

So post-existentialism can be seen, on the one hand, to be attempting to find a place between existentialism and post, post-modernism. Enabling us to take from the existential and the post-modern that which can be helpful to us in exploring our existence at the start of the twenty-first century. Another dimension of post-existentialism is to find a place between natural and social science, for starting with notions of existence is to imply starting with the human soul (Plato, in Cushman 2001) and the historical and cultural aspects of social (rather than starting with the natural) science. With this emerges the possibility of a political viewpoint that could engage with various notions of, for example, democracy, and the idea of an unconscious coming more from those such as Kierkegaard (1844, 1855) and Nietzsche (1883, 1888). Such possibilities open up returning psychology to its philosophical roots and, with it, important implications for those practices aimed at promoting wellbeing—including the way we train our students.

I have previously attempted to explore some of these dimensions: initially through how individuals and structures in society conspire to produce a form of alienating escape motivation (Loewenthal 2002). More recently, I have been interested in exploring, on the one hand, how post-modernism has emerged from phenomenology (Loewenthal & Snell 2003), and on the other, evaluating the usefulness of qualitative research for exploring relational aspects in therapy, with particular reference to the post-existential (Loewenthal 2007a, 2010).

I start in Chapter Two, "From existentialism (and post-modernism) to post-existentialism: from Buber to Levinas", to argue that face-to-face relationships potentially provide an essential educational basis for the good. Without such a relationship, for example in the education of psychological therapists, and in practices in general, there may be a diminished possibility for truth and justice, and a far greater possibility that violence will be done. In examining issues of the psychological therapies as a practice of ethics in terms of ideas of truth, justice, and responsibility, are there ethical post-existential considerations on which we can assist in an embodied way, so that we can help people not to do violence to others? Indeed, is it possible for us as psychological thera-pists not to interrupt our own and others' continuity, not to play roles in which we no longer recognize ourselves and whereby we betray not only our commitments but our own substance? Or is the notion of even an ethical basis a vain attempt to give false foundations to the psycho-logical therapies? An exploration of the above questions will be made, with particular reference to some implications of ethics as espoused by Emmanuel Levinas, who is argued here to be more post-existential than post-modern and is contrasted with the more modernist approach of Buber.

In Chapter Three, "Post-phenomenology and the between as unknown", with Julia Cayne, we argue that a way of approaching post-existential practice is illustrated through the idea that relation-ships occur in the between, which is largely unknown, except as sug-gested by Laing, through our experience. It is suggested that difficulty occurs, however, when we are not able to be grounded in our experi-ence, which could be seen as a form of ontological insecurity brought about by intolerance of unknowing. It is argued here that this intoler-ance can lead us to replace the possibility of our own experience with someone else's story of their experience which is presented to us as theory, whereby theory could then be seen as an obstruction of the between. Post-existentialism does not, however, discard theory, but requires the ability to: firstly, engage with our experience through the between, deferring the need to reach for theories; secondly, question whether the ideas that do occur to us are simply a return to theory as a familiar place needed in the face of our own anxiety or dread; and thirdly, remain open to where the return to such formulations becomes a way of reconstituting more of the same rather than permitting differ-ence. Such aspects are explored in terms of: the relational as a between that permits possibility (though, as discussed in Chapter Ten, creates a reification that can also take away from practice), for example through play. Though with a return to some existential phenomenological ideas which illustrate something of the dread of possibility as well as offer-ing an approach which may help us to sustain attention to experience in relationship and the post-modern. This can then be seen to raise ques-tions about the way knowing and language can create a binding that closes down rather than permitting the possibility of rupture which could move us elsewhere than intentionality. Here, the post-existential, with its post-phenomenology, provides an intersection between existential phenomenology (Laing, Heidegger, Merleau-Ponty), psychoanalytic (Winnicott), and post-modern thought (Derrida, Kristeva), where a between is permitted through a willingness to continually question in order to hold open rather than assimilate. A question then emerges about the kind of knowledge at play in post-phenomenological practice and how that might enable one to work as a psychological therapist. An epistemology of uncertainty is proposed.

Chapter Four, "On learning to work with someone with a label: some post-existential implications for practice, theory, and research", is written with Dennis Greenwood. Here we examine a clinical case study of psychotherapy that lasted for over three years and formed part of a research project exploring the possibility of psychotherapy with this client group. The practice example described here provided the opportunity to explore possible implications for both research and theory in relation to what is being described as post-existential. A phenomenological hermeneutic approach to case study is outlined, which allows the researcher the freedom to explore the theoretical implications for practice without being overwhelmed by the dogma of scientific method and its notions of truth or certainty. This chapter also explores aspects of the "subjective" limits of phenomenology and existentialism through Levinas' challenge to the concept of intentionality.

In Chapter Five, with Rhiannon Thomas, we provide a re-examination of the case of Lola Voss. The purpose of this chapter is to consider the possibility of a post-existential position regarding the representation of experience in language by first, within this context, contrasting existentialism with structural linguistics. Binswanger's "Case of Lola Voss" is re-examined, and an outline of existential and linguistic positions are given on the subjects of "reality" and "experience" and their relation to language. The question arises as to whether experience is to be found in what is said, or in the saying? A further question is then examined regarding whether it is perhaps self-deception that causes us to reach for pre-existing linguistic constructs to represent that which existed originally outside of linguistic categorization?

Chapter Six, "Laing and the treatment is the way we treat people", is written with Tom Cotton. It draws on ongoing research, initially conducted for a Masters in Psychotherapy (Cotton 2008), in which Laing's peers were interviewed both about their experiences of Laing and his work with the Kingsley Hall therapeutic community, and the possible relationship between psychotherapeutic treatment and the way we treat people as individuals. A further person interviewed is a contemporary resident of a therapeutic community, who reflected on his own experiences of treatment. The research was conducted in parallel with a film project, supported by a Wellcome Trust Arts Award, which explored Laing's work and the Kingsley Hall community in particular. The interview extracts featured here are with Paul Zeal, Haya Oakley, Steve Gans, Joe Berke, John Heaton, Jamie Moran, Gary Cairney, and the much missed, late Chris Mace. Their reflections are presented here within the context of the chapter's focus of interest and provide an opportunity to explore whether, in the current climate of evidence-based practice, materialistic demands on psychotherapy and the state endorsement of a medical model approach to psychotherapy, such as the Layard *Depression Report* (2006b) and the Health Professions Council's attempt to regulate the field, we are able to remain phenomenologically (or post-phenomenologically) open.

An exploration of "Post-existentialism, counselling psychology, and the diagnosis of schizophrenia" is provided with Patrick Larsson in Chapter Seven. This chapter explores some implications of post-existentialism for counselling psychology, with a particular focus on diagnostic categories. In particular, it is asked whether Cooper's (2009) assertion that we need to "welcome—and work with—the richness and vastness of clients beyond their diagnoses" (p. 122) is possible in practice? How do counselling psychologists retain such a "value base within a framework dominated by a medical model of distress" (Douglas 2010: 24), whilst making further inroads into the National Health Service (NHS) as practitioner psychologists? This chapter reviews the literature that pertains to the topic of counselling psychology and diagnostic categories, and critically examines the place of post-existentialism in relation to this issue. Research is also presented here that has been carried out by interviewing qualified counselling psychologists who have experience of working with individuals with a diagnosis of "schizophrenia". The results of this are arguably both encouraging and worrying. They are encouraging in that the counselling psychologists who were interviewed appear to have found a way of relating to the experience of the individual and taking the individual's experience into account in the therapeutic context to great effect. What is perhaps worrying is that there sometimes appears to be an almost subversive element to their work, whereby the "relational" stance they take to their clients needs be hidden and disguised using medical discourse. Even though this chapter will look at counselling psychology specifically, these issues may find resonance with psychological therapists in general. The case is further put that it is our duty as *psychological therapists* to challenge psychiatric categories and diagnoses. Indeed, it has been argued (Loewenthal 2008) that with post-existentialism, we should now be raising questions about the power, knowledge, and political nature of psychology.

Chapter Eight is written with Robert Snell, "A training in post-existentialism: placing Rogers and psychoanalysis". In the first part of this chapter, a case study approach is used that asks what are the important features of the therapeutic learning experience provided through an MSc/PsychD programme in Counselling and Psychotherapy in the United Kingdom, with the focus on the intended therapeutic learning experience. It is argued that much of the emerging dominant training model of today is unbalanced, with too great an emphasis on CBT and short-term cost-effectiveness, rather than on the provision of a sound understanding based on learning from lived experience. There is concern at the extent to which depths of thinking and feeling are brushed aside, and with this a focus on the relationship and understanding of people's experiences. The authors provide an analysis of this post-existential training, with particular reference to locating it historically in trends within European philosophy, the place of Rogers and psychoanalysis, and working post-existentially in groups. (All contributors to this book and students of the course have experienced Rogers as an introduction to phenomenology as well as having been in analytic psychotherapy). The chapter concludes by considering the appropriateness of Eurocentric approaches for other cultures.

In Chapter Nine, I explore research in the psychological therapies, in terms of changing notions of intersubjectivity. I suggest that a very different type of research could contribute to a way of exploring meaning, influenced by post-existentialism, which could open a challenge to the ideological assumptions behind our values, to the potential benefit of our individual and collective relations.

In Chapter Ten, "Towards a therapy without foundations", I return to the question of the paradox as to whether post-existentialism can facilitate a practice without foundations. In doing this, the preceding chapters are re-evaluated, with particular reference to the problems of reification.

This book represents work that has been carried out over a number of years but also, as ever, a moment in time. Various other papers could well have been chosen (see, for example, http://www.roehampton.ac.uk/researchcentres/rcte/index.html, November 2010). Hopefully, this book can play a small part in increasing the possibility that psychological therapies can start with practice, and all that entails.

CHAPTER TWO

From existentialism (and post-modernism) to post-existentialism: from Buber to Levinas

Del Loewenthal

Introduction

If one thinks that nature can only be researched by instruments, then does the measurement frame the material? I understand the Greek word *phusis* or *physis* to mean what comes out of itself, the natural, from its own origins. But *phusis* has become only the results of measurement, what comes out of an auditing process (see Loewenthal 2010): this is a major change, and was not the original meaning of the word. Force then becomes the critical word: force is used in an attempt to reveal the truth. Perhaps what doesn't come through in such notions of wellbeing is life itself with its wonderment including those aspects of which, as the French phenomenologist Merleau-Ponty suggested, may be defined by mystery? More generally, one may need to consider moving the parameters of science beyond the quantifiable to a different notion of the qualitative. This is not so much intellectual and rational but ethical, in a new dimension that is only starting to emerge (Loewenthal 2003). The science of quality might regard the ethical as arbiter; it is the wellbeing for one's fellow person. (However, advocating quality in this way to the current technological priests does sometimes make Galileo's job of advocating science to the Church seem rather easy.)

I wish to explore such questions as: what helps or hinders an exploration of the most effective expressions of our and other psychological therapists' (and their teachers') desire to help? Is it possible to have both justice and action? Are, for example, our theories mainly perpetuating unintentional violence? Has traditional thoughtfulness been replaced by theories with fields of knowledge, territories, and ownership of subject disciplines policed by economic licensing arrangements, which in turn attempt to control language and thought, appropriating difference sometimes in the name of difference? Alternatively, in examining issues of the psychological therapies as a practice of ethics in terms of ideas of truth, justice, and responsibility, are there ethical post-existential considerations from which we can assist in an embodied way so that we can help others not do violence to others? Indeed, is it possible for us as psychological therapists not to interrupt our own and others' continuity, not to play roles in which we no longer recognize ourselves and whereby we betray not only our commitments but our own substance?

In examining such questions, I wish to start by considering whether ethics is separate from practice. If ethics is defined, for example, as putting the other first (Levinas 1961), then should we all be striving towards this? An argument here is that ethics is not extraneous to transformative practice. To separate ethics from practice is perhaps fundamentally unethical? If this is the case, then this has profound implications for the development of practitioners whether the relational context is therapeutic, educational, or managerial.

An implication of ethics as a basis of practice is that there is an implied transformation where wellbeing for others comes before wellbeing for myself, including my apparent vested interest group. If I now take the terms "psychological therapist" and "client" to represent the relational in all the occupations I have mentioned so far, then an important question could be: "What does it mean for the person who is the psychological therapist to put the person who is the client first?" A corresponding question might be: "What does it mean for the client to appropriately put the psychological therapist first?" This form of post-existential human relations is very different to that used in our pervading managerialism of consumer relations, for we may, in putting the other first, have to consider ourselves to be responsible for the other's responsibility.

I think it is useful to explore what it means "to put the other first". It seems very different to giving one's life for others and hopefully helpful in clarifying consumerist confusion about the terms "client-centred" and "choice" which are currently being used in the UK and other European public services, where I, for example, have been working on an EU project on ethics and the relational as a basis for managing patient-centred care for older people (Loewenthal 2005). Can we all have wellbeing and the goods? How can we be involved in what we do for the good? (Loewenthal 2002). "Involvement" can mean being entangled, twisted, and confused, perhaps enabling us to not have to see the consequences of our actions through facing the face? Is it possible for us to also learn through our relationships and be moved by something other than the thought of hatred that seems too often to accompany the fundamentalism of a "Bin Laden" or a "Bush"? And can we be moved by something other than the increasingly domi-nant market ideology with, as has been suggested (Barber 2000), the attempted privatization of all things public and the commercialization of all things private affecting our relationships including what is meant by the notion of public service and how we attempt to educate.

I'd now like to explore the ethics of the relational, first by compar-ing aspects of the philosophies of Buber (who is taken to be existential) and Levinas (who I now consider to be post-existential and opposed to post-modern as he holds open the possibility of being "just in the moment" with another). I then wish to give an example of the values which, to quote the educationalist Michael Polanyi, if not taught and learned, then might be imparted and acquired through our relation-ships whether these be of the client and the psychological therapist, or indeed the learner and the teacher, the managed and the manager, or the researched and the researcher.

Why Levinas?

It has been suggested that

> In the twentieth century, continental philosophers developed a new type of foundation for ethics.... A relatively new line of thought made a distinctive relation to other people the central feature of ethics ... Martin Buber ... and Emmanuel Levinas are considered the most prominent members of this tradition.
>
> (Becker & Becker 1992a: 528–529)

Thus the inter-subjective, existential and post-existential theories of ethics of Buber and Levinas are the main focus here, as opposed to other notions of ethics which do not make a distinctive relation to other people the central feature. But why Levinas rather than Buber?

Again drawing on Becker and Becker (1992a: 528–529), Buber's (1922) two fundamental relations of "I-It" and "I-Thou" can be seen to exist between psychological therapist and client. In the "I-It" relation, the psychological therapist offers herself only partially, using the client as a means to some predefined end, grasping the client as a type and experiences her own self as a psychological therapist as a detached, isolated, separate subject. In being in an "I-Thou" relation, the psychological therapist offers herself wholly, participates with the other in an event that takes its own course, grasps the concrete particularity of the client, and emerges as a person in terms of reciprocity. For Buber, only in the "I-Thou" relation does the psychological therapist achieve genuine presence. "I-It" relations remain locked in the past. The "I" of the "I-Thou" is fundamentally different from the "I" of the "I-It". It is the relation that constitutes the selves of psychological therapist and client. Buber would, however, have acknowledged that, in practice, psychological therapist and client live in continuous dialectics between these two poles. Furthermore, the "I-Thou" relation does not really unite psychological therapist and client; instead, they achieve a reciprocity that acknowledges their distinctness.

Although, for Buber, the "I-Thou" relationship cannot become a goal, it is to be preferred. The person as psychological therapist should risk and offer himself fully and be genuinely addressed by the other, and therefore become genuine. A psychological therapist who did not experience the "I-Thou" would be greatly impoverished and so hence would be the client. An example of this is in the Henry James story "The Real Thing". This is where a commercially successful photographer earns his money selling photographs of what appear to be royalty, but are in fact photographs of actors (the constructed image, perhaps similar to the attempted construction of known competency-based outcomes in, for example, emotional learning). However, one day, some actual royalty, down on their luck, offer to pose for him. What happens is that soon there is a tension brought about in the taking of the photographs by a photographer telling "real" royalty how to look and the photographer re-engages the actors. The "royalty", after further unsuccessful employment as the photographer's domestics, are fired. Now would they have been better photographs if the photographer had photographed the tension with the real royalty (more "I-Thou" rather than "I-It")?

Buber is existential and modern, with the "I" in the centre, and this "I" is returned to, such that "Thou" is seen in relation to the "I", so that even a claim for distinctness is a difference in relation to the "I". Thus, the client is only seen as being different in comparison to something of the psychological therapist. There is always a return to the psychological therapist; perhaps if both attempt to be subjects and not really be subject to, the client cannot really be other.

Some implications of post-modernism for psychological therapeutic relationships

So far, this account might be seen as phenomenological, with both psychological therapist and client being changed by what emerges between them. But what of phenomenology in the contemporary world? What happened to Buber and phenomenology in the post-modern era? While the term "post-modernism" is often under suspicion (for example, Eagleton 1996) and is already being used historically, I have been involved in arguing that it can still have important implications on how relationships are examined (Loewenthal & Snell 2003). I am now arguing that Levinas is post-existential, in that though we are subject to, for Levinas (subject to putting the other first), the sharing of meanings can sometimes be possible. The relation of the psychological therapist to the client would define the ethical, but the other would remain wholly alien and inassimilable. The client's proximity is prior to the psychological therapist's "presence" and makes it possible; no totality (a whole that assimilates its parts) can integrate psychological therapist and client. The relation to the client is like a relation to infinity: perpetually beyond experience, making the organizing structures of experience possible. It precedes and conditions experience.

For Levinas, unlike Buber, the client's absolute transcendence prevents symmetry and reciprocity. From a Levinasian reading, the client becomes manifest through the face. It is the face of the client that both commands the psychological therapist not to harm, and solicits the psychological therapist's aid. For the psychological therapist to acknowledge the client's face is for the psychological therapist to have responsibility to the client and for the client. Thus the ethics of psychological therapeutic practices would not be about ethical codes, for to start with them would be unethical, but would concern primarily the relation to the other. Levinas challenges the ego-centric, narcissistic representation of the person by arguing that we are subject to putting the other first, with the consequence that we are responsible for the other's responsibility. Does this lead to a very different type of existentialism?

Emmanuel Levinas was born in Lithuania, in 1905, of Jewish parents. His family moved to the Ukraine, where he was during the Revolution of 1917, before he settled in France as a young man. He spent most of the rest of his life there, surviving a prisoner-of-war camp, and died in 1995. During 1928 to 1929, he was in Freiburg, where he attended the lectures of Husserl and encountered the writings of Husserl's student, Heidegger. Husserl, like Freud, was born in Czechoslovakia and both were to write seminal works appearing in 1900 (Freud on *The Interpretation of Dreams* and Husserl on *Cartesian Meditations*), both after having attended lectures on descriptive psychology by Brentano in Vienna. Husserl, thanks to the interventions of Wilhelm Wundt, and now recognized as a founding father of psychology, developed the notion of phenomenology. Levinas, in turn, is now credited with bringing phenomenology to France and greatly influencing Sartre, de Beauvoir, Merleau-Ponty, and such post-modern thinkers as Lyotard and Derrida. The development of phenomenology can be further considered as "post-phenomenology" (see Chapter Three and Loewenthal 2006), and its implications for such practices as psychological therapy, through such authors as Derrida and Roudinesco.

"To be or not to be?" is the wrong question

If we start with questions of wellbeing, what seems to happen is that we slip into questions where transformations have to revolve around my being, such that should we then ever look at another's being, we do so only by taking ourselves as the measure. Levinas argues that ethics (putting the other first) must always precede ontology (the study of being). Yet, for Hamlet, as for Heidegger and most of Western thought, the question has been, "to be, or not to be". Primacy is thereby given to the ontological, with perhaps devastating consequences. This has formed the unquestioned basis of many practices, with their emphasis on autonomy, egocentricity, and notions of a bounded, unitary self (Loewenthal 1996).

Levinas was very interested in Hamlet (Levinas 1985: 22); he challenged the ontological by suggesting that ethical questions must always come before those of being, and this, it will be argued, is a phenomenological, rather than a moral, necessity. For Levinas, as perhaps for Shakespeare, Hamlet is asking the wrong question, the result being that those he is closest to are killed off. This is because he puts himself first rather than the other first. By asking the question, "to be or not to be?", Hamlet shows himself to be concerned with himself before he is concerned with anyone else.

For Levinas, there was also a related important reading, in that by asking this question, it was as if Hamlet could be in charge of his own death. "Hamlet is precisely a lengthy testimony to this impossibility of assuming death" (Levinas 1989: 42). The tragedy of Hamlet is that he tries to stay on top of that which he cannot. Do most therapists, educationalists, managers, photographers, and so on, encourage a similar fate for themselves and their clients?

Greek versus Hebraic: autonomy versus heteronomy

It might be argued that it is not only photography that is more about pictorial rather than written representation (the "look" rather than the "book"), more caught up with the Greek rather than the Hebraic, rather like those management theories where all chief executives, even vice-chancellors, are encouraged to have visions rather than being locked away for mentioning them. Yet it is the notion of heteronomy that may be useful in order to consider whether Levinasian ethics might form the basis of wellbeing. Levinas points out that "every philosophy seeks truth. Sciences too can be defined by this search ..." (Levinas, in Peperzak 1992: 47). None of the professions mentioned are an exception in claiming that they seek the truth. Yet Western culture can be seen to contain two major philosophical traditions, the Greek and the Hebraic, each with its own underlying assumptions about the ways that truth, in terms of relationships, can be thought about and experienced. Furthermore, it is the Greek notion of autonomy that has more often than not assumed cultural dominance over the notion of heteronomy.

So we encourage the "me first" rather than the "other first"

I will first quote Levinas on heteronomy at length, before going through his text in more detail. The same will then be done for what he has to say on autonomy. Levinas describes the idea of truth in terms of heteronomy in the following way:

> Truth implies experience. In the truth, a thinker maintains a relationship with a reality distinct from him, other than him "absolutely other" ... for experience deserves its name only if it transports us beyond what constitutes our nature. Genuine experience must even lead us beyond the Nature that surrounds us, which is not jealous of the marvellous secrets it harbours and, in complicity with men, submits to their reason and inventions; in it, men also feel themselves to be at home. Truth would thus designate the outcome of a movement that leaves a world that is intimate and familiar, even if we have not yet explored it completely, and goes towards another region, towards a beyond. Philosophy would be concerned with the absolutely other; it would be heteronomy itself.... Truth, the daughter of experience, has very lofty pretentions; it opens upon the very dimension of the ideal. In this way, philosophy means metaphysics and metaphysics inquires about the divine.

> (Levinas, in Peperzak 1992: 47)

Levinas's notion of heteronomy raises questions regarding notions of truth. He seems to be saying that truth is not something outside experience (and yet, although this may seem contradictory, it is beyond our nature). But this does not mean that one's experiences are the yardstick for truth. We cannot claim to have "the truth" because it is our experience ("I've experienced it, so you can't take it away from me").

Experience is that which gets us in touch with what is other than that which we are. It is not "what we are", and it takes us beyond what we have been. So what we feel "at home" with may stop us genuinely experiencing. We can conceive of and experience our environment as something complicit with us and submissive to our preconceptions, but genuine experience in the Levinasian sense is a reaching towards a beyond, away from what familiarity surrounds us. Can it therefore be only in a relationship where the other is put first, in dwelling with the absolutely other, that truth is to be found? We will not arrive at truth if we see the beyond as something to be colonized and incorporated, which academics are often so good at. The truth will always be beyond.

This has enormous implications, including for ethics and the training of such practices as the psychological therapies, education, and management. We cannot appropriate truth to our experience: it is outside us. We have always, as psychological therapists, to be prepared to go beyond our "gut reactions". Only then do we have a chance, momentarily, to reach a truth with another. We tend, as Lyotard points out, to delude ourselves as to what is "truth" by forgetting that it is subject to our theories, to the place we are in, and the position we take up, which we can then start to think of as "natural", as our nature (Lyotard 1984). Truth becomes dependent on, for example, what school of psychological therapy we are in, and the danger is that this "truth" must be upheld as the particular theory shores up our position as psychological therapists and the universities and psychological therapy organizations that legitimize us. Shouldn't truth be beyond that? Yet we jealously guard our position, in a way that can lead to perversion and injustice.

Levinas perhaps helps us to raise crucial questions about ethics and vested interests. Our theoretical orientation, or club membership, can therefore never come before truth and justice. If one feels "at home", then may one be perpetrating violence? Truth is leaving wellbeing "at home". One cannot be "at home" with the truth; sometimes feeling things are "right" is wrong. For Levinas, if we are "at home", it is always about "me first", my place in the sun, in which case philosophy is needed to legitimize the corruption—to make us feel "at home".

In contrast to heteronomy, Levinas describes the Greek notion of autonomy as follows:

> But truth also means the free adherence to a proposition, the outcome of a free research. The freedom of the investigator, the thinker on whom no constraint weighs, is expressed in truth. What else is this freedom but the thinking being's refusal to be alienated in the adherence, the preserving of his nature, his identity, the feat of remaining the same despite the unknown lands into which thought seems to lead?
>
> (Levinas, in Peperzak 1992: 47–48)

Now we may all strive to be autonomous and in doing so not wish to consider that we reduce Others to the Same: to be only within our vision. If we do have doubts about autonomy, then we seek a philosophy, or school of therapy, to reassure us. In autonomy, one can be subject to nothing; it is as if we were the subject. A problem for psychological therapists is that autonomy is attractive and can be sold to our clients. Heteronomy is always in danger of being incorporated into the philosophy of autonomy. Thus certain notions of autonomy go unquestioned in our culture. However, it is not being suggested that autonomy should be dismissed, but that heteronomy should come first. For example, in education, the heteronomous learner might be considered more important than the autonomous learner. It is argued, therefore, that Hamlet, and most psychological therapeutic practices, have wrongly chosen autonomy over heteronomy, encompassing every Other in the Same. The other becomes a bit-player with, at best, a walk-on part on our stage. Thus, the client is a bit-player on the psychological therapist's stage (perhaps we, at best, train people to look good rather than be good).

The psychological therapies as ethical practices

For Levinas, "The face is exposed, menaced as if inviting us to an act of violence. At the same time, the face is what forbids us to kill" (Levinas 1985: 86). As psychological therapists, academics, and managers, what then are our values? I am assuming that we will always be subjective: our values determining how we hear and what we say. That is, in so far as we are able to say what our values are. So it is vital for our practice that we attempt to consider what we regard as essentially human: under what circumstances is the world an alive and meaningful place for us as people who are psychological therapists? Is it when we can assertively go after that which appears important to us (autonomy), or does it begin with putting the other first (heteronomy) in a way that recognizes the Otherness of the Other (their alterity)? In this way, our values and ethics are linked. Levinasian ethics are not therefore about my right to exist, it isn't even just about the Other's right to exist, but can be seen as my responsibility for the Other's responsibility to others.

Let us take Freud's three impossible professions: psychoanalysis, education, and management. Freud suggested the reasons why they are impossible is that one can be sure beforehand of achieving unsatisfying results. Yet surely, by inevitably being subject to that which we will never have full agency over, is to be educated for life rather than through the technical application of government-inspired competencies. This can produce unthoughtful psychologisms in the hope of autonomy, at best Oakeshott's (1991) "minds with no atmosphere". Being subject to, regardless of whether we see this as being: to an unconscious, to language or in the case of Levinas, to ethics, opens up the potential of being educated for not knowing, and above all, for wellbeing in terms of justice.

There are of course important criticisms of Levinas in terms of, for example, issues of gender and that he might unwittingly be caught up in a worldwide increasingly Christian conspiracy created by those who can't take the rawness of life and have instead come up with an aesthetic called "ethics" initially based on a confused story of Abraham telling half-truths to his son Isaac. However, if Levinasian ethics can be considered in terms of their implications, and not become a new technical mantra, then one implication is that if we put our concerns first, rather than the Other, then we are at best privileging a notion of wellbeing that is to do with giving a primacy to autonomy at the expense of others, and our society in general. Thus, a heteronomy that is putting the other first may be what is most appropriate in enabling wellbeing. Not only without such relational learning will our lives be impoverished, but if we hope therapeutic education can be primarily directly taught without some face-to-face, then this is more to do with the violence of late modernism with its associated apparent success in removing the radical in the development of these cultural practices (Loewenthal 2006; Lyotard 1984; Parker 1997). For, as Heaton (1993) argues, if we think practice can become subordinate to theory (including Levinasian theory) and the knowledge generated, with all the advantages for technicians to be trained, this can also take away from a thoughtfulness that can lead to wellbeing, whereby, through the relationship, individuals can, for example, also clarify their own and others' desire to help, thus ethics cannot be a basis for practice, though it can usefully have important implications.

Furthermore, therapeutic education without giving a primacy to actual practice will further move away from Plato's entreaty to see *therapeia* as the wisdom of regarding scientific and technical thinking as important but secondary to the resources of the human soul (Cushman 2001). Seen thus, the psychological therapies for one are in grave danger of losing their way (Loewenthal 2004). Perhaps if we are able to face the other as one human being meeting another, we will be more able, as Levinas suggests, to not do theoretical violence to this other. Wellbeing is not training people to appear to be concerned about the other person: is this really acknowledging the other? Instead of being primarily concerned with systems of power and knowledge, perhaps we should all be more concerned with justice on a case-by-case basis, for, as Levinas writes, real justice in wellbeing cannot be appropriated or territorialized, but requires us, from and through our relationships, to be just in the moment with another.

CHAPTER THREE

Post-phenomenology
and the between as unknown

Julia Cayne and Del Loewenthal

Introduction

This chapter is concerned, with what might be considered, a post-existential/post-phenomenological view of the relational. As such it takes a view of the relational as involving beings who are separate but neither isolated from each other or incorporating of each other, as in reducing the other to one's own world view. In other words, there is play in the relationship. A way of viewing the relational is that it occurs in the play between two people and it will be argued that what occurs in this between is largely unknown. There is, however, the problematic that as soon as we speak of the between, which represents a gap or disjuncture, the problematic of language tends to lead to defining and locating that which cannot be treated or defined as a "thing" and which can be known only through the phenomena that emerge. We are thus in the domain of temporal spatiality. Some ways in which we respond to the idea of the between are explored in order to highlight how the meeting between existential phenomenological, psychoanalytic, and post-modern ideas can inform post-existential practice (Loewenthal 2007a: 221–240).

The problematic of the between as unknown is traced here. Firstly, the between of relatedness includes a need for separateness in order

31

that play can occur. Laing (1967) could be seen as relating the problems of separateness and merger to ontological insecurity where the need to know the already known then takes precedence over experience in a relationship, whereas Winnicott (1971) posits the relational on transitional phenomena, although returning to existing theories of the unconscious as implicated through object relations. Secondly, the between of relating acts as a reminder of that which we dread which can lead to primacy being given to the known of an unknown, from various theoretical perspectives, so that we try to know being rather than allow the possibility of being surprised by being in a relationship. Thus, some ways of translating existential ideas are seen as problematic whilst the phenomenological thread is seen to provide a way of continually re-exploring experiences. Thirdly, through consideration of some postmodern ideas, the between can be seen to permit the unknown of an unknown, as that which resists symbolization but which may hold open possibility through the play of difference and language. Thus, a meeting between the existential/phenomenological, psychoanalytic, and post-modern is seen as enabling a continual questioning of the kinds of position we return to and take up whilst also realizing that too much unknowing can lead to chaos.

As a result of the preceding discussions, questions about the kind of knowledge at play in post-phenomenological practice and how that might enable one to work as a post-existential therapist have emerged. Thus, finally, there is consideration of the implications of a post-phenomenological approach, which by its nature cannot be predetermined and is thus not claimed as a modality, method, or treatment, but rather is seen as a method of critique within the context of practice and learning from practice. The post-phenomenological is considered to question ways in which theory can be used to close down possibility in practice and in learning about practice, whilst dread (for example, in relation to an unknown) is implicated in the problematic of closure of thought. Furthermore, postphenomenology can re-open the question of what kinds of epistemology are most appropriate for a practice discipline such as psychotherapy in which the post-phenomenological calls for the therapist to remain open to possibility and is thus required to tolerate uncertainty.

The relational as play between

In order to explore some implications of post-existentialism for practice, the therapeutic relationship is first explored through Laing's (1967) idea of the between and Winnicott's (1971) view of the transitional space. By juxtaposing these two views of the relational, some similarities and some differences will be highlighted.

The nature of the relational as involving separated but not isolated beings is concerned with the idea that separateness comes from a sense of ontological security. In other words, that no matter how much we doubt ourselves we still experience ourselves as real and alive (Laing 1965: 40). This essential experience of being alive and real accompanies a sense of being differentiated from the world and others. As a result of this security, there can be recognition that our own concept of things or experience of being is not the same as others, we do not therefore need to reduce the other to an object in our own world. Further, when our own worldview is shaken we have a sense of something secure to return to, such as our experience, rather than some else's (e.g., in the form of theory) although this may be useful at times too. Hence, security in our sense of our being and experience does not require a grasping at theories which could be viewed as seeking external stability for what is ontologically lacking.

Within the field of psychotherapy, it also seems that we speak of relationship as a thing and as though we know what we are speaking of, but in fact what seems to happen is that the relational becomes reduced to categories like "transference" or "working alliance". Such categories could be seen as an attempt to know what a relationship is in advance rather than awaiting our experience, which leaves open the possibility that we may not know what is occurring except through our experience (Laing 1967). Laing (1967: 12) further questioned the ways in which our own experiencing is negated, not least by theories which become re-placed between people so that what is actually experienced is lost and "*if our experience is destroyed we have lost our own selves*". Yet it seems paradoxical that the response to fear of losing our sense of our own being is to grasp at something, which facilitates precisely that.

One way of viewing the relational is that this between represents a gap that resists symbolization because it is not a thing and although may be described as too close or too separate cannot be measured. The lack of a stabilizing point makes us anxious in the existential sense, one difficulty being that gaps resonate with other gaps or absences, something recognized by Blanchot (1993) which lead us to return to that which provides the sense of security lacking in our own being. Phenomenology has provided a way of working as a psychotherapist in such a way that does not need an immediate return to theory in order to understand but rather requires us to continually attend to our experience. Such attention means neither dismissing the strange nor accepting the obvious and in a sense remaining open to an unknown rather than directing our thought to what is already known and can be explained or to the explanation itself. Rather, there needs to be a return to attempting a naïve description of experience. The phenomenological approach does not, however, exclude existing theories, which are seen as helpful as long as they are not used to replace our experience.

In this chapter, there will be return to various theories although these are not intended to provide fixed points so much as to begin opening other possibilities or versions of the stories told. Hence an example of a helpful and unhelpful way of attempting to speak of some of the issues related to the between is provided by Winnicott (1971), who may, in some ways, be seen as working phenomenologically (Chessick 1992).

The between of the relational was something that Winnicott (1971) conceived as the transitional space. His ideas are useful here because of the way the transitional space illustrates phenomena associated with unknowing which, if tolerated, can lead to creativity. He gave an example of the phenomenon emerging from a particular time and space as the "transitional object", which symbolizes an "intermediate area of experiencing". The transitional space is viewed as a phase of unknowing which opens up as the child makes a shift between what he calls the earlier concrete attachment relating and the symbolic attachment relating (Winnicott 1986). For Winnicott, these two kinds of relating involve the "concept of the subjective object turning into one which is objectively perceived" (1986: 133). In other words, there is a shift from what is subjectively perceived or created by the child towards the ability to take "externally perceived objects in and [set] them up as internal images" (Winnicott 1986: 133). The transitional object could be viewed as something to grasp at moments of uncertainty, and Winnicott (1986) also suggests that the transitional space exists in any situation where something unknown is going to happen, such as the curtain going up at the beginning of a play, and thus in many kinds of "betweens", for example: inner and outer reality, separateness and interrelatedness, and the concrete and symbolic. One could parallel this need for grasping with the therapist's need to grasp at theory too quickly in a relational experience.

There are two important aspects of these phenomena that Winnicott (1971, 1986) identifies: firstly, the transitional space is a place from which creativity emerges; and secondly, it is connected with loss. Thus, while there is a potential for something alive there is also a potential for anxiety and closure, the reminder of death equates with the death of thought and thinking for one's self. Can we tolerate the conflicting experiences of aliveness and death?

A useful example of such tolerance is linked to paradox which for Winnicott (1971) is concerned with the ability to create for oneself what was already there without initially realizing or having it pointed out that it was already there. The crucial response to paradox (e.g., aliveness and death) for the therapist is then to realize it is not there to be resolved, it has to be tolerated. The potential space as a paradoxical unknown exists but cannot exist, as space between one and the other, it invokes simultaneous joining and separation which leads to all kinds of phenomena associated with creativity. Paradox tends, however, to invoke anxiety and the grasping for an object as the other (the patient) or theory as an object (the therapist) could be seen as not being able to tolerate the anxiety.

The anxiety can be seen to emerge from awareness of such a space between or transitional space, which creates a shock, because of the reminder of loss resonating with earlier separations (Winnicott 1986). Further, Laplanche (1999) shows how the otherness of the other represents an unknown too. In light of these aspects of anunknown, it can be seen that loss operates in various directions through different dimensions namely: present and past, present and future and person-to-person. Whilst the possibility of creativeness is present, there is also a possibility for something deadening to occur at either end of the continuum of creativeness, which is seen as "space/time integration" (Winnicott 1971: 67). At one end of the spectrum is a tendency to remain out of touch with "the facts of life" seen as a problem in reality experiencing, while at the other end is an "estrangement from dreaming" (Winnicott 1971: 67).

Whilst the return to the above version of psychoanalysis is helpful in showing some phenomena that emerge through relationship as well as a link between past and present experiences, it could also be seen to create an artificial (or cause and effect) rift between them which pares away the relational from our being and also cannot allow for the future dimension (possibility, death). In other words, it can be seen that these ideas return for Winnicott to the existing theories of the unconscious as implicated through object relations which may lead to a rather two-dimensional (i.e., present relationship to past relationship/theory) way of thinking about experience. The therapist viewed as stand-in for mother or the return to theory closes down other possibilities in terms of the multi-dimensional/-directional nature of the experience of relationship. Some ideas about why we close down possibility will now be considered, and in the third section a further development considers the therapist not as a stand-in for parental figures but as other, as different. Thus, an implication of post-existentialism for practice can begin to be seen as commencing with our experience and permitting a return to theoretical concepts, although, as will also be illustrated, there is a need to remain open to possibility through, for example, deconstruction.

The dread of between

The existential and phenomenological strands of a post-existential approach offer helpful ideas about how we can wish to limit experience of gaps or betweens, the problem of always returning to theory as a form of comparison and how we might remain more open to our experience in relationship. One of the problems of the translation of existential ideas into psychotherapeutic practice is that existential phenomenological philosophers, such as Kierkegaard, Heidegger, and Merleau-Ponty, did not provide a system explaining the nature of being nor how to be in a relationship, but instead challenge us to remain open to new ways of being. They raise questions about the problematic of being where knowing theory replaces that which we dread both as our unknowing and the knowing that might emerge from the study of what it means to be human through our own experience.

In particular, it is useful to be reminded about what has been forgotten about Kiekegaard's version of existentialism and view of the gap or disjuncture. He points out that our dread of an unknown as infinite makes us grasp at finiteness or in other words we want to limit possibility (Kiekegaard 1944, in Friedman 1964). The philosopher Blanchot (1993) further argues, that spaces, gaps and disjunctures resonate with the final unknown of death and any experience of discontinuity or fragmentation sets up the chain of anxiety, the reminder of death followed by its refusal. In this refusal may also lie the repudiation of other possibilities. Thus an experience that resists symbolization, such as the between of relating, leads us to either fill the gap with something already known or to use Kierkegaard's word we become shut up. In a sense, we do not want to learn something new, from our experience, for ourselves, so learning becomes a repetition, if not of our own then of someone else's history. It is not, however, being proposed here that anything goes but neither is it being suggested that we should separate out aspects of being to treat or research. Instead we need to be alive and take note of what moves us, so rather than a return to theory in order to understand we need to be able to find our own ways of speaking through and of our experience, which is not to say that existing theory does not have something to offer as long as we are able to continually re examine it. For example, a way of re-reading psychoanalytic theories would be to view them as myths, which are stories that are never fixed in a single version, changing from age to age. In a sense, Freud recognized this through his reworking of myths such as Oedipus and in turn his stories could be re-read in similar vein.

Heidegger (1962) in particular, develops the argument that there is no justification for measuring human experience against pre existing structures such as theories or criteria, which do not exist in being having been separated from it. This kind of separation has resulted in the isolation of knowing from the contextualizing aspects of being and time which make for kinds of knowledge that are temporary, localized, and unique. When some aspect of human experience has been separated out for research, treatment, or indeed for understanding a relationship, it has become objectified and thus its humanity has been destroyed (e.g., past/present and id/ego/superego). The assumption is also made that it is now known in a once and for all kind of way. Heidegger (1971) however made a further shift between the study of being to the requirement to participate in the happening of being, for example through the poetic, which enables us to speak in previously unthought-of ways. It is argued here that a phenomenological approach can help us engage in relationship in ways that open up such possibilities and in the next section of this chapter what will be called post-existential/post-phenomenological thought is seen to develop these ideas even further.

In fact, much existential psychotherapeutic thought has not made the kind of shift described above and continues separating out human experience such as the givens or aspects of our relationship to the world and others (Mitweldt, Umweldt, etc.) in a similar way to psychoanalytic concepts. The attempt to make the unknown known then results in the temptation to finalize the meaning of such aspects of being as theory, thus believing we can know isolation, freedom, and so on, and forget to continually re-explore these human experiences and new ways, and forms they may take in a relationship. To put it another way, we need to be open to creating new meanings and rather than fix these meanings remember they are only that; meanings. For Merleau-Ponty (1962), meaning is relational and through the link between intentionality and intersubjectivity he critiques both *"extreme objectivism"* as in the Cartesian cogito and *"extreme subjectivism"* with the idea that the subject can be independent of or separate from the world. He argues that meaning emerges between differing worldviews; perhaps, in a sense, they lean on each other and spark against each other. About such meaning, he states:

> But it should not be set in a realm apart, transposed into absolute Spirit, or into a world in the realist sense. The phenomenal world is not pure being, but the sense which is revealed where paths of my various experiences intersect, and also where my own and other people's intersect and engage with each other like gears. It is thus inseparable from subjectivity and intersubjectivity, which find their unity when I either take up my past experiences in those of the present or other people's in my own. For the first time, the philosopher's thinking is sufficiently conscious not to anticipate itself and endow its own results with reified form in the world.
>
> (Merleau-Ponty 1962: xx)

The notion of the self as a starting point or as central may always be assumed, therefore, as the place of knowing and raises a question of whether the unknown can only ever be reached by jumping off from the stance of knowing or viewing the self as a pivotal entity. If the known is always seen as preceding the unknown, the return to self as a centrifugal force seems to result. For Merleau-Ponty, the discovery of unknown phenomena can be reached, not from their relation to the known but in the space between subjects. "Here there is nothing comparable to the solution of a problem, where we discover an unknown quantity through its relation with known ones" (Merleau-Ponty 1962: 178). He seems to be proposing that an unknown is not discovered, because it is not waiting to be found, it lies elsewhere, lies hitherto, or rather does not await us at a particular location. Possibility is thus seen as emerging through the between of intersubjective experiences which have the potential to call each other into question.

Phenomenology then provides a method for continually re-exploring human experience with the attempt to maintain the unstable, ambiguous, temporary, and contextual. Alongside existentialism, phenomenology opens up the importance of meaning as a way of understanding experience whilst recognizing itself as incomplete. The phenomenological attitude is one of reflection and is the opposite of the natural attitude which Husserl calls "unreflective consciousness" (Husserl 1929, in Kearney & Rainwater 1996: 17). Merleau-Ponty also argues that:

> Reflection is truly reflection only if it is not carried outside itself, only if it knows itself as reflection-on-an-unreflective-experience and consequently as a change in structure of our existence.
>
> (Merleau-Ponty 1962: 62).

However, this neither involves knowledge as reduced into being nor being reduced into knowledge and this means that the subject can never know being nor can being ever fully inform knowing. The best that we can manage is to seek examples through our experience whilst recognizing the dual problematic of the limitations of both the example which can never represent fully the experience and the ways our own perception may place self and the natural attitude at the centre in understanding the world and being (Merleau-Ponty 1962). One could say, therefore, that reflection on an experience needs always to recognize that something remains unknown, beyond our grasp and reflection, and is only reflective when it realizes this.

Early existential phenomenology, especially the thought of Kierkegaard (1944) and Heidegger (1962, 1971), appear to have anticipated something of contemporary Western approaches to knowing. Firstly, the problems they explicate anticipate the current tendency in practice and research, which seeks to measure everything so that the results can be used as a form of evidence for why various approaches to practice do or do not work. The kind of measurement that has dominance strips aspects of being from the experiential, relational context. Secondly, they await post-modern approaches which question the way fear of instability, related to the decentring of the subject, can lead us to seek to stabilize knowledge as truth rather than remaining open to local forms of knowledge that are contextual, meaning laden, incomplete, and unique truths. It is argued here that the confusion between meaning-making and theoretical knowing, as recognized through phenomenology, adds to these problems. Some post-modern ideas will now be considered as providing ways of helping us to give primacy to our experience in relationship, through difference. The phenomenological strand of post-existentialism is then seen to both inform and develop further, as post-phenomenology.

The between as possibility

Post-modern ideas, particularly those of Derrida (1978, 1990), are sometimes seen as being only critical and destructive because, for example, by closely reading the text, he highlights the way in which the main argument is also the place where the argument falters. However, to understand Derrida's position as purely destructive closes down the very thing he appears to attempt, which is that by revealing places of instability, he offers the opportunity to rethink ideas and thus opens up alternative possibilities. Further, such openings, as discussed earlier, are spaces or betweens where there is potential for aliveness and creativity as well as for deadness. His way of re-reading a text is seen as a way of developing what is termed here a post-phenomenological approach through the post-modern view of separation where the between re-emerges as a concern with difference and language. There is a danger in thinking we can master the between which is different to an attempt to destabilize the return to the known without assuming you know what's next. The relational between as the unknown of an unknown, which is not a thing, may resist symbolization and language; it may, however, have possibility.

In a sense, Derrida (1990) opens up a separation between knowing and unknowing by pointing out the way theoretical knowledge tends to both mark a place beyond knowing and simultaneously disguise the limit. It is suggested here that this applies to different forms of theorizing whether grand narratives, meta-narratives, or personal narratives, and Freud's (1976) idea about the dream knot provides a useful example. One way of viewing Freud's idea of the dream knot could be related to the way aspects of being, for example an unconscious, are separated out from being as discussed previously. Post-modernism, however, takes the critique further by illustrating how certain forms of knowing have a way of sustaining knowing in a circular fashion which by anticipating its own formulations continually re-constitutes them, thus hindering the opening for new ideas.

Freud was concerned with the *oomphalos*, which is the knot through we can never pass; it is the place that marks something beyond knowing, "the point of contact with the unknown" (1976: 186). The dream knot becomes the point in Freud's theory that represents something paradoxical within the whole Freudian metaphysics and is Derrida's (1990) focus for a critique of an unknown as purely waiting to be found as in the unconscious. Derrida (1998) highlights the knot, the *oomphalos*, Freud's own idea to show that there is always something that is beyond knowing, and indeed he points it out as the "unknowable". This seems to be something other than the unconscious and is spoken of, as the knot or tangle, in the text on dreams (Freud 1953). Furthermore, Freud's concept of resistance as a resistance to knowing, albeit of the returning repressed, indicates a resistance inherent in psychoanalysis, something that psychoanalysis does not want to know. Derrida (1990) points again to the problematic of language where the dream knot instead represents the way language cannot account for that which is absent or has no meaning. It seems, then, that the resistance to an unknown comes about not so much from the returning repressed as from the tangle caused by various known concepts, which cannot leave room for other possibilities or an unknown as unknowable. Thus, the resistance spoken of in psychoanalysis is a resistance to anunknown as unknowable on the part of psychoanalysis, which comes about at the juncture of various theoretical pathways. The knot as a meeting point for multiple pathways then also becomes a blind spot.

Furthermore, when the absent is made present, the unconscious made conscious or an unknown becomes known, the penalty is a presence incorporated into the binding of language, bound and knotted and then no longer able to function as subversive. Experience than becomes relegated to the category of the already known, whereas post-existentialism might challenge us to recognize that knowing is only temporary, incomplete, and relational as related to the context of the relationship within which the knowing emerged and the unknown remained submerged. Derrida offers the possibility that takes us beyond Winnicott's ideas about play. Derrida's notion of play arises through the play of difference, especially through language, rather than being posited on the unconscious and the return of the repressed.

The following two vignettes are provided by one of the author practitioners (Cayne). The first illustrates something of the above discussion about play and enables clarification of the difference between object relations, existential phenomenological, and post-phenomenological ways of working. Therapist and patient (who will be called Rachel) met for several years, struggling with the patient's seeming inability to tolerate the other. When she began to work with an autistic child, Rachel was struck by that child's inability to tolerate her presence and the change that came about when the child was suddenly able to take an object and begin to play with it herself. She stated that the child had acquired imaginative play which she said meant that the child could take a toy and create her own play. Not long after this, Rachel described designing and making a birthday cake of a cartoon character. Her husband, however, made his own suggestions about how she could have done it differently. They then had an argument. Rachel said she felt like she wanted to throw something at him, and the therapist said to her that she thought she had. For the first time, Rachel seemed to be able to take what had been said to her and play with it herself, commenting "oh, I thought that too, yes I did, I threw words".

In relation to Rachel, there was an experience of a frequent sense of confusion that seemed to arise from a lack of differentiation resulting in an inability to play. Firstly, there was no play as noun; elbow room, movement, no room to think. Secondly, play as verb; there was no playfulness, no play on words. The playing for time, however, meant that it took time to learn to think, which was just as well, in some respects, because perhaps Rachel needed time to get used to her own ideas and feelings and, in the existential sense, the therapist had to suffer (as in allow) confusion and not knowing what to say. Gradually, there was the realization of a need to work with whatever was on Rachel's mind without the need to speak of anything that might be judged as "deep" or "important", by some, but rather what mattered to Rachel. The post-existential, post-phenomenological way of working helps the therapist to stay with what matters to the patient, yet there are always other possibilities—for example, another would have been to explore the meaning of the particular cartoon character the patient created.

Post-existential phenomenological ideas thus mean recognizing both the helpfulness of ideas such as the unconscious, the dyadic view of relationship as in object relations, or even phenomenological description, whilst also being willing to move beyond to something other. In this shift, language becomes increasingly important, so whilst our work could be seen as enabling the construction of meaning, it could also be seen as requiring deconstruction. If one is able to wait, there are moments, often a kind of playful punning (like the throwing of something), that manages to speak the unspeakable. Derrida's (1978) ideas about "*différance*" as to defer as well as to differ help the therapist also to learn to wait without needing to explain so that unpredictable ways of viewing the world can emerge.

Through consideration of the second vignette the importance of language will be highlighted via some ideas from Lacan, moving to further consideration of why the realization that something always escapes our understanding is intolerable. For example, a patient announced, following a holiday break, that he was thinking about taking a break from therapy, citing a number of things that were happening to him in work and life as reasons. As he explored this idea, he began to speak of therapy as a prison, then a play on the word "break" occurred to the therapist, who responded by asking him if he thought he was trying to make a break for it. Here, the word "break" takes on a number of meanings, opening up the possibility for thought. One way of thinking is that the therapist's use of the word "break" interrupted the logical thought patterns (as a form of meta-narrative), opening space to think differently. Although the initial reaction may be one of confusion, there is often an associated curiosity that seems to enable the patient to think further. In this kind of moment, all kinds of meanings emerge, some known and some unknown. An example of multiple meanings and slippage between meanings becomes possible.

Another idea, however, is that this patient may have been saying something about himself and the prison of his own creation and by linking the idea of the break too explicitly to a meaning associated with the therapy and/or the therapist would miss this. Thus, the patient could be asking me to give him a break (this can be read in any number of ways too) in order to help him out of his usual ways of thinking, although leaving the meaning associated with the idea open allows all kinds of possibilities, some of which may emerge in some future context. Some ideas of Lacan are particularly helpful in understanding the relational as other than a literal relationship in association with language.

For Lacan, the subject is constituted by language and cannot therefore be separated from society or located as a central self or ego because of the inherent slippage of language and therefore meaning (Sarup 1993). Like Merleau-Ponty (1962), Lacan sees us as subject to language rather than possessors of it. Consequently, neither language nor notions of self can be viewed as immutable, and the unknown cannot therefore be located, for example, only as the unconscious. The way that an unknown breaks through is related to ideas about the signifier having precedence over the signified (Lacan 1977). This means that Lacan moves away from Saussure's view of language as a stable representation of human experience whereby a sign is composed of a stable relationship between signified and signifier (Kearney & Rainwater 1996). The signifying chain involves a continual interplay and slip between one signifier and the next, so that meaning is never final, further each signifier is a metaphor for another signifier. What was unconscious emerges as much through the slip as through language itself. In this sense, an unknown comes into play through difference, the difference between, and is invoked by the other via language. Hence the idea of an unconscious could then be argued to be an interpersonal phenomenon or group of phenomena. Also the therapist as speaking from the place of an unknown other, rather than only as stand-in for authority figures, becomes possible so that when the therapist interprets, they are not then experienced as speaking as some earlier figure (Lacan 1977). A post-phenomenological approach recognizes, therefore, that one of the problems with language is that it may be the wherewithal to opening up new meanings as well as the very means to keeping possibility closed down.

Kristeva's ideas about language are also helpful here, because she seems to recognize the way the symbolic can be both helpful and unhelpful. Her thinking around moments of transgression where something previously unspeakable can become symbolized (Sarup 1993) proposes another register, that of the semiotic, yet also suggesting ways in which the symbolic can be used to keep out anything unacceptable. The transgression as a breakdown occurs when the symbolic order can no longer sustain the zest of the ever present, but building semiotic pulsations, the symbolic can in effect no longer hold it together. The energy from the semiotic is usually directed psychosomatically, but in moments of rupture and revolution it can change the symbolic structures involving sound, movement, and sight as well as metonymy and metaphor (Kristeva 1974, in Moi 1986). What occurs in these processes mirrors the psychoanalytic functions of condensation and displacement where the signifier holds multiple layers of meaning or swerves across meanings, respectively (Bowie 1991). The kinds of transgression that can evoke these processes are connected to the poetic and loaded with energy, provoking the idea that "something" needs to be deciphered (Kristeva 1983, in Moi 1986). The moment of transgression is thus the moment when something unknown can break through, but it seems that the break through will not occur by attending to language as a literal representation which just reinforces the unifying structure of language. We need to work in ways that "make free with the language code" through the poetic (Kristeva 1975, in Moi 1986: 28). It is such transgressions that defeat the unifying processes of the transcendental ego. The poetic is therefore beyond intentionality.

The symbolic appears to represent something of a unifying order and a way of positioning oneself whereas the semiotic seems to represent something of the chaotic, undifferentiated, corporeal experiencing. Either can be unhelpful, leading to too much logic or too much chaos, respectively, and yet both are necessary. The continual process of interaction between the symbolic and semiotic sets up a series of binary oppositions which are inevitable but which also close out anything viewed as waste according to Grosz (1986). This waste is literal in terms of bodily waste but also represents what is socially unacceptable. It could be argued that the socially constructed need to deny such excess is also a way of closing down on the unknown as the unacceptable or what Kristeva (Grosz 1986) calls the abject, which both attracts and repels. In other words, it can be difficult in our culture generally, and in the world of psychotherapy specifically, to accept that there are things we do not know and whilst many theories are helpful because they were a part of some one's experience it is easily forgotten that they are the meanings, stories or myths told from a particular time. Like all stories, they are not the whole story, something always escapes and this form of waste can be difficult to endure. Thus remaining open to possibility is going to require a tolerance of what is called the abject, so in reference to the vignettes above, they are simply our meanings and associations and possibly an attempt to provide a meta-narrative in order to keep out the other.

Post-existentialism and a different epistemology

The preceding sections of this chapter have attempted to raise a question about the relational as a between that should not be reduced to theoretical conceptualizations which predict or generalize about the nature of a relationship. The nature of a between, as a gap or space, is considered here to resist formulation whilst simultaneously having the possibility of permitting the emergence of new meanings. The post-phenomenological thread of post-existentialism is seen to call into question the way theory can be used to reduce anxiety by filling this gap with knowing. The ability of practitioners to tolerate the anxiety or dread, evoked by the uncertainty of unknowing is considered to be crucial to working as a post-existential therapist. It is thus proposed that a different approach to knowing is required for those working as post-existential therapists. In this section, the meaning of epistemology is addressed before a consideration of what could constitute an epistemology that permits possibility. Unlike probability, with its concern with the predictability of the already known, possibility will be shown to be concerned with the unexpected, and what was previously unknown. However, one of the problems encountered at this point, by the authors, is that in setting out some ideas about an epistemology of possibility, they are caught in doing the very thing that post-phenomenology critiques. Thus positing, in advance, what an epistemology of possibility might be, leads to a risk that these ideas are then taken up in such a way as to become the technique for facilitating possibility. However these, like any ideas, are set within the context of this chapter at this time and may never be relevant to such a discussion again; they are the contextual, the ethical and the critical.

Epistemology is concerned with the beliefs that underpin knowledge and includes: the rational which seeks to provide logical arguments aimed at illustrating the truth of beliefs, the empirical which aims to provide demonstrable evidence to support beliefs and the pragmatic which is based on experiment through experience in a given situation (Jarvis 1999; Morton 2003). Theory thus consists of sets of beliefs and the ways in which we use knowledge can illustrate how we miss this point. As a supervisor once commented to a colleague, "theory is your forty feet of concrete", which seemed to mean that there is a certainty and safety that knowledge, as theory, provides. When one understands theory as a set of beliefs, however, it appears less stable than some might hope.

Epistemology is also concerned with how we decide whether a belief is true or false so that we can base decisions on more adequate knowledge. One of the problems with this deciding is that the methods used to collect evidence develop from, and thus tend to support, the kinds of knowledge they seek to legitimate. Hence, rationalism and empiricism attempt to develop methods in order to provide more logical or tangible ways of generating and testing beliefs (Morton 2003). It could be argued, however, that post-phenomenology utilizes phenomenological and post-modern methods to critique beliefs, within the context of practice, by revisiting experience and deconstructing the narratives, as both grand and personal theories, that have been constructed about those experiences. Whilst the logical, rational epistemologies have dominance, other kinds of epistemologies can also be identified. For example: a pragmatic epistemology is concerned with what works for the practitioner and knowledge is not generalized because it is more concerned with the local situation and individual learning (Jarvis 1999); the philosophy of Dewey (1960) proposed a provisional epistemology arguing for the importance of fallibility whereby the temporary and unstable aspects of knowing are just as important as the steady, more systematized aspects; an ethical epistemology might question the divorcing of knowledge from our responsibility to others (Jarvis 1999) and; an epistemology of deconstruction could be argued to be an approach that is especially concerned with a critique of knowing, being interested with noticing discrepancies between meaning and what is asserted as truth or knowing (Sarup 1993).

In light of the previous discussion, it can be seen that the certainty with which theory can be approached is problematic for post-existential practitioners. Thus, theory might more appropriately be utilized if it were not given primacy over any other aspect of human imagination, such as a poem or novel. Rather than being viewed as providing a reference point, to which we continually return, theory could be placed second to experience and meaning-making. Subsequently, it is argued here that there is less chance that we get tied up in the circularity of finding that which we already know, the certainty of which inhibits the possibility open to those who could be considered to work in the between. Epistemologies that are concerned with the contextual, the ethical, and the critical could be seen to be more likely to permit such possibility.

It has already been argued that the phenomenology of Merleau-Ponty and its concern with intersubjectivity, as the meeting between differing experiences, which have the potential to call each other into question, is where possibility might emerge (Merleau-Ponty 1962, 1964). The meaning of possibility here is also taken from an existential perspective where the between is seen as so shocking that we seek innumerable ways to avoid or fill the void which evokes dread. Thus, the paradox here is that post-existential or post-phenomenological thought could also be a way to avoid or fill a void. To be *"educated by dread"*, however, is for Kierkegaard (1944) the way to be always open to the world:

> When such a person, therefore, goes out from the school of possibility, and knows more thoroughly than a child knows the alphabet

> that he can demand of life absolutely nothing, and that terror,
> perdition,, annihilation, dwell next door to every man, and he has
> learned the profitable lesson that every dread which alarms [aeng-
> ste] may the next instant become a fact, he will then interpret reality
> differently, he will extol reality, and even when it rests upon him
> heavily he will remember that after all it is far, far lighter than the
> possibility was.

> (Kierkegaard 1944, in Friedman 1964: 371)

Thus, ultimately it is only when we can face that which we fear most
that we can truly learn and learn to speak from our experience, but first
we must allow possibility which, "corresponds precisely to the future"
(Kierkegaard 1944). A state of uncertainty or unknowing is demanded.

For Laing, the possibility of experience, such as occurs in the between
of the relational, has precedence over theory (Laing 1967). He appears
to call for an ability to tolerate "the zone of the no-thing" in order for
new ways of thinking to be allowed, created even, so that as therapists
we become able to hear the other rather than our theories (Laing 1967).
His ideas perhaps point to the way psychotherapeutic theories have
not generally been concerned with shared experience tending to either
cause confusion about what is theory and what experience, as in the
case of the unconscious, or splitting aspects of our humanity apart. An
example of this would be the way behaviour and experience can be separated by focusing on only one or the other, whereas Laing suggested
that practice as a psychotherapist needs to be based on noticing how
behaviour and experience interact. Furthermore, he sees experience as
being too often denied, and yet how else are we to permit the really
crucial moments in practice which are for Laing (1967: 34) "unpredictable, unique, unforgettable, always unrepeatable and often inde-
scribable"? Thus, it is argued here that practice as mediated through
post-existentialism, post-phenomenology invokes tolerance of doubt
and uncertainty in order to permit possibility.

In considering these ideas about possibility, the unique and
contextual aspects of psychotherapeutic praxis are evident. Whilst
Lacan provided a large body of theoretical work, he also appears to
have understood the importance of context and his notion of textual
knowledge is helpful because he highlights the way learning in practice as well as from practice needs conditions that are specific to the

situation being considered (Felman 1987). Thus, learning about practice can be seen to require a different kind of approach that is concerned with the possibility for something new to emerge. As Lacan proposed to his students, this means not bringing everything back to the known by trying to understand, which gets in the way of something new and different, thus one is required to cease attempting to understand (Fink 1996). According to Lacan, learning is not, therefore, about the acquisition of ready-made knowledge but concerned with the conditions that enable "textual knowledge", which is situation-specific, to be created anew (Felman 1987). Post-existential practitioners could then be seen as requiring the condition that makes possible thinking about experience, without attempting to understand or theorize, so that something new (new meanings) can emerge. In line with phenomenology, the criteria for what needs to be learned through practice cannot be pre-empted, but will be local, unique, contemporaneous. Some of the issues related to the problematic of learning about theory rather than from experience, which throws us into the unknown, have been discussed previously by the authors (Cayne & Loewenthal 2007).

One way to view practice relates to the work of Emmanuel Levinas and his concern that ethics should be given primacy. For Levinas (1997), the ethical involves acceptance based on unknowing rather than because we think we have come to know some one. Thus, being with another involves relating without pre conceptions rather than knowing through a pre-ordained set of rules and practices that could become a self-serving cycle. The implication here is that either there is no such thing as a typical, ordinary, or predictable experience because it all depends on context, or on the contrary, the unique is the ordinary. In this sense, those practising as post-existential psychotherapists could be seen as always facing the unknown. Levinas is concerned with the nature of an ethical relationship where the need for understanding hinders acceptance of the otherness of the other: "*The labour of thought wins out over the otherness of things and men*" (Levinas 1984, in Hand 1989: 78). One of the problems with putting thinking or knowing first is that these activities actually hinder acceptance of the other and tend to lead to the incorporation of the other's experience as theory. In the act of assimilation, the other as different becomes lost and the text (theory) becomes stripped from its context (experience), which is part of the problem trainees have in actually understanding concepts such as transference. The ethical can now be seen as connected to possibility in the sense that permitting our unknowing in a situation can allow the space between, rather than maintaining closure that keeps thought restricted to well-worn pathways.

Another aspect of an epistemology of possibility that is being proposed here is the important role that critique has for anyone claiming to work in the between. Here again, the use of "the" between invokes the problematic of being located in this way through language. The previous discussion highlighted the way Derrida (1990, 1978) opens up the space between knowing and unknowing and shows how knowing can become a way to hide our unknowing. The binary opposition knowing/unknowing provides a useful example of his metaphysics of presence which highlights how binary oppositions can show what is concealed through what is revealed, including the effect of concealing from ourselves that we don't know. As the other in this binary system, an unknown is always subverted by the known, and categories of knowing never explicitly permit either what is unknown or the unknowing. What is also then avoided is how the unknown might subvert and destabilize the known. Derrida's (1978) form of deconstruction also attempts to show how power is at play so that the authority of the dominant element, which holds power over the other, can be revealed. The splitting of one element of the binary from the other also sustains closure, preventing the play of difference and ensuring that critique of that which is dominant is resisted. The scientific, rational, and empirical, which are concerned with concrete evidence and the way it legitimizes this particular view of the world, are caught in this epistemological power structure. Any form of categorization, even based on contextual, ethical, and critical epistemologies, can be caught taking up the same position.

Conclusions

This chapter has attempted to address the relational as a space between, which is essentially unknown, in order to illustrate the interplay between existential phenomenological, psychoanalytic, and post-modern ideas, thus proposing a way of approaching post-existential psychotherapeutic practice. The between as a temporal-spatial occurrence cannot be reduced to an object but can be experienced through the play between, which requires the ability to tolerate various unknowns. The reaching for theoretical explanation rather than tolerating the confusion of our experience is seen to lead to knowing as a replay of someone else's known rather then knowing from our own experience. Some aspects of Winnicott's ideas are seen as related to the phenomenological requirement for description and tolerance of experience. His ideas are helpful in understanding something of the relational through the idea of the transitional space, especially the between as resonating with loss (Winnicott 1971). These ideas are also seen to parallel the therapist's need for a symbolic object, represented by theoretical explanation. Where this theory becomes less helpful is that it limits the relational to an object relation that closes down as yet unknown possibilities.

It has also been proposed that that some existential ideas are worth revisiting. For example: firstly, Kierkegaard highlights our need to limit possibilities in the face of dread which can take the form of limiting both our experience and learning from it, for ourselves and; secondly, Heidegger argues against theories or criteria which have been separated from being and have lost their connection from context and time. Existential psychotherapeutic thought has at times reduced existentialism to that which it originally attempted to critique by reducing being to categories such as givens. It has been argued here, however, that phenomenology is an approach that requires us to continually re explore experience, as involving relational phenomena, because of its unstable, ambiguous, temporary, and contextual nature.

Phenomenology is important as a starting point for engaging in experience of a relationship because it requires a delay in the kind of theorizing that can itself obstruct relating. If, however, relationship is seen as a between that is largely unknown, the anxiety provoked by unknowing can in turn create a sense of instability or ontological insecurity that can impel us to return to the already known of theory. Whilst such stabilizing points may have a place, they will also limit possibilities, especially if we are unwilling to continually question them. Intersubjectivity is seen as having the possibility of taking us beyond our own worldview, beyond the intentional, so that we are opened to wonder. Thus, phenomenology provides a starting point, and psychoanalytic theories some ways of helping us symbolize experience, whereas the post-modern offers ways of preventing such theories from becoming too fixed. The meeting between these ideas leads to what has been called here a post-phenomenological approach.

Some aspects of our experience always resist knowing, and we can prefer to remain blind to the way any knowing is incomplete as well as the fact that some aspects of experience resist knowing and remain unknowable. The blinding is created by the very thing that we think helps us see, in the sense of understanding; our theories become the focus of the place beyond which we cannot go and this point is often the main crux of an argument. While Lacan sees the slip and slide of language as opening possibility especially through the unknown other, Kristeva shows how the interplay between the symbolic and the semiotic both prevent too much chaos and yet permit movement or play.

For a therapy influenced by post-existentialism, the decisions we make about various betweens: patient/therapist, inside/outside, the story/the telling (the saying and the said) cannot be taught and learned mechanistically. The therapist represents an unknown, but neither as a knower or unknower; "I don't know" is also too certain. We are talking about something else, something that isn't, something that language destroys; in a sense, we represent the gap, a spatio-temporal rift. We cannot, however, learn about this, because it is not a thing, and anyway, as Gans (2006) says, "calculation kills desire and effaces the otherness of the other". We have to learn to tolerate what he calls "the between of indecidability". But can we bear the uncertainty of the unknown in order to play imaginatively with our patients; and perhaps each other?

The idea of the between also raises a question about the kinds of knowledge that enable a post-existential, post-phenomenological practice that tolerates the uncertainty of possibility. The relational is seen to call into question both therapist and patient, and therapists need to keep questioning, therefore, their theoretical assumptions and their relationship with knowledge. When theory is understood as a set of beliefs arising from human imagination, we become less certain and, it could be argued, more able to play and allow new meanings to emerge. There is then less likelihood of reducing the other's experience to the already known and there is the possibility of creating knowledge anew in each unique encounter.

CHAPTER FOUR

On learning to work with someone with a label: some post-existential implications for practice, theory, and research

Dennis Greenwood and Del Loewenthal

Introduction

This chapter examines a clinical case study of psychotherapy with a person diagnosed with dementia which lasted for over three years and formed part of a research project exploring the possibility of psychotherapy with this client group. The practice example described here provided the opportunity to explore possible implications for both research and theory in relation to what is being described as the post-existential. A phenomenological hermeneutic approach to case study is outlined, which allows the researcher the freedom to explore the theoretical implications for practice without being overwhelmed by the dogma of scientific method and notions of truth or certainty. This chapter explores the "subjective" limits of phenomenology and existentialism by looking at the work of Buber and the "I-Thou" relationship and considering the challenge made by the continental philosopher Emmanuel Levinas to the whole concept of "intentionality".

An assumption is made in this chapter, and throughout this book, that there is an association between the terms "counselling", "psychotherapy", and "psychoanalysis". As Bond (2000: 24) suggests, "it is not possible to make a generally accepted distinction between counselling and psychotherapy" and "when used in their widest sense, they encompass each other". The generic terms of "psychological therapist" and "psychological therapy" are used here and they refer to counselling and psychotherapy (which is taken to include psychoanalysis).

Background to the case study

The research explored in this chapter formed part of a study (Greenwood 2003) looking at the "possibility of psychotherapy with a person diagnosed with dementia". This study was aimed at examining whether therapy was possible with this client group—or did the symptoms associated with dementia, particularly those that impaired cognitive functioning, exclude a person from having psychological therapy? It was assumed that researching the issue of "possibility" was not dependent on the extent of the sample examined, since one successful clinical example would be sufficient to identify that psychotherapy was possible with this client group. Furthermore, it was considered that a longitudinal case study would be an appropriate choice of method to explore this research question.

At the outset of this study, one of the authors of this chapter (Greenwood) began by working as a therapist with Kay, the subject of the case study presented in this chapter, and this fact exerted an influence on the research design. The phenomenological-hermeneutic method used to present the findings of the research emerged as a consequence of considering the ethical and methodological issues associated with integrating clinical material into an appropriate form of research.

The subject of the case study was given the pseudonym of Kay, for purposes of confidentiality, and she was an eighty-five-year-old woman who had been resident in a nursing home for about four to five years. She had moved into the home to be with her husband, who suffered from severe dementia, as the nursing home specialized in this type of care. At the time Kay entered the nursing home, she was not in need of this type of care herself but had wanted to stay with her husband. Kay did not want to be separated from her husband, so she shared a room with him at the nursing home. A few months before the beginning of the therapy, Kay's husband died.

After her husband died, not only was she faced with this loss but also the dilemma of where she was going to live. Although she had not really been in need of care when she was admitted, the staff of the nursing home and Kay's relatives thought that she had physically and mentally deteriorated in the interim period, and she had been diagnosed as being in the early stages of dementia. Kay still had a house that she could have returned to, but her son and daughter did not think that Kay would cope living on her own. The nursing home staff suggested to Kay that she might benefit from speaking to someone about her concerns and, as a consequence of this, the therapy began. The nursing home was one of two owned by the therapist, who worked in a nursing management capacity in the other home, but was not actively employed in the home where Kay was resident.

Ethical issues

Research into practice raises a range of ethical issues, and McLeod (1994: 172) states the following:

> Research carried out by practitioners on their own client's raises a distinct set of ethical dilemmas. These issues have received little attention in the literature, probably because most discussion of research ethics has focused on large-scale studies ... The main ethical problem in this type of research arises from potential conflict between the therapeutic and researcher roles taken up by the practitioner.

McLeod (1994: 172) suggests that therapists have a duty of care in a relationship with a client, which can conflict with the role of researcher where the requirements are "to collect data and make a contribution to knowledge and understanding". The duty of care might be seen to begin with the issue of confidentiality. Bond (2000: 150) maintains that confidentiality in psychological therapy is "fundamental".

Gravey and Braun (1997) would appear to concur with Freud (1911) by suggesting that there are significant benefits for psychological therapists in reporting on case material. Reporting case material would also be seen as part of practice supervision and would be regarded by many psychological therapists as an essential part of offering therapy (Gilbert & Evans 2000). Bond (2000: 191) provides a possible resolution to the issue of confidentiality and the need to explore client material by stating, "The legal and ethical emphasis is on protecting personally identifiable information. Therefore it is best practice to anonymize cases for discussion in counselling-supervision."

So the reporting of clinical material is an established psychological therapeutic and academic procedure where the ethical priority is the maintenance of patient privacy and anonymity. The implication of Bond's (2000) assertion, which was adopted, is that by ensuring the anonymity of the subject being discussed the link with this person is being assumed as non-existent, and subsequently the ethical requirements for permission are removed.

A method for practitioner research

A re-evaluation of Freud's approach to research was carried out from a phenomenological-hermeneutic perspective giving rise to a method that stressed the importance of descriptive data rather than any preoccupation with the pursuit of definitive truth.

The inherent assumptions that form the basis of scientific method can be questioned by logic, according to Russell (1978), who restates the argument presented by Hume that just because something has been seen to occur any number of times does not mean that it will happen again in the future. This is a leap too far for logic and the best that can be attained is a high probability that something will happen again because it has always been observed that way; probability, according to Russell (1978), is not fact. So the very possibility of generating definitive "truth" can be questioned according to this rationale.

Crotty (1998: 30) describes the work of Werner Heisenberg, who spoke of the "uncertainty principle", arguing that observation by ordinary human senses does not permit the scrutiny of the subatomic structure of objects in the world around us. This has the potential effect "of turning laws of physics into relative statements and to some degree into subjective perceptions rather than an expression of objective certainty". This critique of the positivists' position identifies the impossibility of ever "knowing" what is independent of consciousness when the only way to know this is through consciousness, a theme developed with reference to the work of Husserl.

Therefore, there is an important challenge to the scientific assumption that truth and fact are a constituent part of objects that exist in the external world and that scientific method is a legitimate approach to discovering them. The deductive method is dependent on a person to produce synthetic judgements of what exists in an object in the external world; the word "synthetic" comes from the Greek words "*synthetikos*" and "*syntithenai*" meaning, "composition, component" and "to put together". Inherent in this meaning of synthetic is a sense of being produced and not naturally existing, judgements that come from people and are thrust on to objects that exist in the external world. The phenomenological ideas of Husserl (Moran 2000) emerge from this challenge to science by arguing that the world exists independent of a person's perception, and that knowledge and truth are constructions generated from human experience.

According to Moran (2000), Husserl was interested in examining the act of perception or thinking in relation to the external world, claiming that the link between a person and an object is the essence of phenomenology. The assimilation of what a person has seen into a form of presentation is what Husserl (Moran 2000) describes as the concept of intentionality. The intentional is concerned with the move from the way an experience feels to the interpretative picture constructed by that person. Hence, the focus in phenomenology moves away from the detailed scrutiny of an object in the external world to the examination of the observer's view of that object. Moran (2000) suggests that Husserl, who was influenced by Descartes (1637), believed that the contents of conscious perception should be taken as a given, regardless of whether they come from a direct relationship with an external object or as part of a person's imagination. Moran (2000: 142–143) states:

> Husserl believed all knowledge, all science, all rationality depended on conscious acts, acts which cannot be properly understood from within the natural outlook at all. Consciousness should not be viewed naturalistically as part of the world at all, since consciousness is precisely the reason why there was a world there for us in the first place.

Husserl's phenomenology (Moran 2000) aims to establish a method, based on the concept of reduction, to investigate conscious thought as the primary source of a "real" picture of the external world. Rather than being an overlooked part of a naturalistic theory, consciousness is given elite status in the science of subjectivity. As Moran (2000: 133) states:

> Husserl designated phenomenology as a "pure" science, by which he means, following Kant, one stripped of all empirical content, one which provides essential knowledge of the invariant structures at work in all knowing, perceiving, imagining, and so on, irrespective of what goes on in the actual world, irrespective of the existence of the world.

Hence, objects in the external world are given epistemological primacy in a traditional view of science, whereas Husserl believed that the focus of all knowledge in the world around us was based on a person's conscious reflection. According to this phenomenological argument truth, knowledge and fact are thrust onto the external world as a human construction, and as a consequence, it is consciousness that needs to become the focus of scientific scrutiny.

Heidegger (1927) challenged the sovereign position given to intentionality by Husserl, arguing that a person's way of thinking must be influenced by their experience. Husserl had positioned consciousness in a far too detached and autonomous place for Heidegger. As stated earlier, Husserl's (Caputo 1987: 54) position was inspired by Cartesian ontology. This suggests the possibility of being able to separate reflective consciousness from actual experience, thereby creating "the self-neutralizing capacity of the *Being* of consciousness, of the possibility of pure reflection, that is to say, of 'transcendental consciousness'". In contrast, Heidegger's theory of *Dasein* (Caputo 1987) attempts to provide an explanation of how a person's position within the existing culture of the external world influences the way they experience and think about the external world, which is their intentionality. *Dasein* describes the very process of being, the ontology of a person who exists in the external world and is subject to it. Heidegger (Caputo 1987) claimed that you cannot perceive the world around you without having been influenced by the experience of existing in it, and been subject to the way it has been seen previously and continues to be seen by the other subjects already in the world. Heidegger (1927) appeared to create a space for epistemology that engages the ontological with the reality of living in the world, rather than identifying the internal (Husserl) or the external (science) as the basis for knowledge and truth.

Heidegger (Caputo 1987) fundamentally challenged the "transcendental" assumptions that Husserl associated with phenomenology, particularly the dissociation between consciousness and the world of experience. Heidegger's subject, a person, is not potentially reflectively detached from the world around them, but rather their conscious perception of the world emerges from the rigours of living and the relationships they have with the people around them. Heidegger's (1927) view of a person living in the world, the concept of *Dasein*, is not a static process, but rather a dynamic process that changes over time.

Crotty (1998: 98) illustrates Heidegger's ideas in the form of a hermeneutic circle as shown in Figure 1 below:

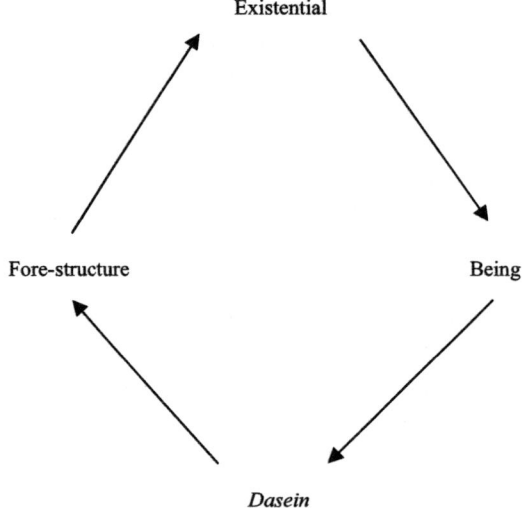

Figure 1. Heidegger's hermeneutic circle.

The process begins with an innate concept of being (fore-structure), an acknowledgement that a person exists and lives in a world full of objects and other people. A person living in the world (fore-structure) is subject to the experience of the institutional and cultural influences (existential) that exist in the world at any particular moment in time, and they will exert an influence on that person's experience. The opportunity of the individual experience of living (being) in this moment in time emerges from a combination of fore-structure and the existential. Heidegger felt that this existential experience of living in the world had the potential to directly influence and change the "being" of a person, how they think and feel, and he described this in the concept of *Dasein*. The meanings that emerge as a consequence of remaining open to the creativity and experience of *Dasein* will potentially influence the fore-structure of experience, and so a dynamic and cyclical process is conceived.

There are fundamental epistemological implications of Heidegger's concept of *Dasein*, with the claim that a person's perception is directly affected by the influence of living in the world and being subject to experience. The epistemological leap from science to the phenomenology of Husserl involved accepting that meaning and truth were not inherent qualities of objects in the external world, but rather products of the consciousness of a person. Heidegger's concept of *Dasein*, although developed as part of an exploration of ontology, implies that the conscious thought of a person is directly influenced by the experience of living in the world. Perception is subject to the culture that exists at that moment in time.

The resulting case study method was used in this research, which sought to reveal multiple meanings by a process of searching and then re-searching the therapist's account of the therapy, and was also strongly influenced by Bleicher's (1980) work on the phenomenology of Heidegger and Gadamer. There are four stages to this phenomenological-hermeneutic case study method (Greenwood & Loewenthal 2005), but it should be noted both that the number of stages depends on the amount of "re-searching" for meanings that takes place and that there is no limit to this part of the process.

Stage 1

Begin with the therapy that forms the basis of the observation.

Stage 2

A therapist makes a written account of what took place in a session soon after the meeting (preferably directly afterwards).

Stage 3

These early reflections are subject to the considerable influence of the therapist's pre-understandings, perhaps in terms of their cultural background and gender that are inherent in any account of human observation. The therapist's supervisor can exert a potential influence on this stage by being involved in a process of reflection on the data from the sessions. At this stage, the initial data will have been subject to a re-interpretation, so allowing for additional meanings to emerge out from the influence of the pre-understandings.

Stage 4

The researcher will subject this therapeutic account to further scrutiny when writing up these findings in the form of a report providing a further opportunity for meanings to emerge and the possibilities to be explored.

The case study described in this chapter emerged as a consequence of following the stages outlined above and inevitably represents the final stage of the method. In order to write an overview of this case, it was necessary to go through the various stages of the method so that the themes or meanings associated with the relationship could emerge. In what is described below, one of the authors (Greenwood) is both the researcher and therapist.

The beginning of therapy

The meetings began with a session that was something of an introduction. Kay appeared very pleased by our agreement to meet weekly. The therapist asked her about the expectations she had for our meetings. Kay spoke a great deal about her husband and how she was admitted to the nursing home with him, and that he had subsequently died. She then went on to describe how she met her husband and how he had introduced himself to her at a dance. He was very persistent with his interest in her and when she told him that she was engaged, he said to her:

> *... that can easily be broken!*

Kay was beaming with pride as she recited this experience. This meeting with the therapist was also an introduction, so it suggested a potential comparison. Kay appeared to want to try and tell me as much as she could about herself, and she went on to speak about an illness that she had suffered as a child:

> "*I had double pneumonia and pleurisy.*"

The doctor informed Kay's mother that the illness was serious but that Kay would be better off being nursed at home. According to Kay, he had straw laid outside the house so that the carts going by would not disturb her sleep. She proudly described how her mother had given up her bed for Kay and had sat by her bedside, sleeping in the chair. Kay described how she remained frail and did not eat well for some time. She had lost a lot of weight, and her eldest brother used to say that if she walked over a drain she would be in danger of falling down between the grate.

Kay spoke about her father and how he had always been there offering practical support and advice, and how her husband was similarly understanding. If she ever had a marital argument, it was her husband who took the initiative to "make-up". She gave the strong impression that her husband was very loving and that it was a good marriage.

The sessions following this first lively meeting were mainly focused on re-telling the same account. There was very little variation, and it was told in a way that made it seem clear that Kay was not aware that she had been repeating something that she had told before. The therapist was confronted with his own diminishing marginal interest in the account as the weeks went on; it became increasingly difficult to really listen to what Kay was saying to him, which could have been a form of resistance on his part associated with counter-transference issues that are considered later in this chapter. However, it became evident to him, following clinical supervision, that certain contextual issues (such as the label of dementia and the setting) imposed upon his reaction to Kay's repetition of her experiences, and these are explored in the following section.

Contextual issues

The therapeutic relationship with Kay was subject to the fact that she had been labelled as having the early stages of dementia, and this appeared to exert a significant influence on how the therapist heard what she was saying during the sessions they had together. They met at a nursing home that cared for people with dementia, and as the therapist walked in to meet Kay each week he would often be confronted by other residents who would stop him for an apparently indecipherable conversation. On occasions, other residents, who were obviously disorientated, would try and enter the room where the therapist was working with Kay, even though there was a sign outside the door requesting for people not to enter.

The diagnosis of dementia was also brought into the sessions with Kay by her routine references about day-to-day life in the nursing home, which inevitably included accounts of her interaction with patients who were confused and disorientated. The interpretation of these accounts was influenced by the fact that the therapist is also a registered nurse who has worked with people with dementia for many years and consequently have developed many pre-understandings associated with the diagnosis of dementia. The therapist found it difficult to listen to Kay when she repeated the same account on numerous occasions, finding himself more preoccupied with the thought that this was behaviour associated with someone suffering from dementia, rather than listening to what was being said.

The therapist found it difficult to listen attentively and reflect on the repetition without associating this with the fact that Kay had been labelled with an illness associated with short-term memory loss and consequently a possible susceptibility to repeating herself in this way. In the early stages of the meetings with Kay, The therapist experienced feelings similar to those represented in a film staring Bill Murray called *Groundhog Day*, in which the main character is caught in an apparently never-ending circle of repetition. Early on in this endless repeating, the character in the film appears to enjoy the advantages of knowing what was going to happen next, but he soon finds this overwhelming and becomes bored and detached. The work with Kay was subject to continuous repetition; the stories she told were recounted by her as if they were being told for the first time, however they would very often be a repetition from the previous session. The therapist did not make any attempt to inform Kay that she had already told him this particular story before, or work with the idea that there may be something to interpret in relation to the repetition; rather, the repetition was immediately associated with the symptoms of dementia.

Working with someone who had been labelled as "cognitively impaired" appeared to bring about a way of listening that was more about coping with this endless repetition rather than being in a relationship that was about really listening to the other. The repetition had apparently become embroiled with a pre-understanding of what to expect from a person with dementia (Greenwood & Loewenthal 1998; Greenwood et al., 2001) and the therapist appeared stuck with an inability to move beyond this, to challenge and explore the underlying content of what was being said. The label of dementia, associated as it is with recognizable symptoms, had been placed on Kay, making it very difficult to see her as a person separate from the diagnostic associations.

The difficulty of the diagnosis was discussed in supervision, and the need to listen to the differences in the repeated accounts was highlighted as a way of maintaining a focus on what Kay was saying, but this proved very difficult to do in the early stages of the work together.

A further example of how the therapist was strongly influenced by pre-understandings associated with the diagnosis of dementia also emerged in supervision. Right from the start of the work with Kay, he had, without really being able to recognize the potential significance, introduced a routine of telephoning the nursing home to remind Kay that he was coming that morning.

When discussing the circumstances around a session that Kay had missed, it emerged that due to apparent time constraints the therapist had not telephoned the nursing home to remind Kay of their meeting, and he was oblivious to the potential implications associated with this. When reflecting on this issue in supervision, it was apparent that the routine of telephoning Kay had emerged out of the pre-understandings the therapist had about the diagnosis of dementia; an apparent assumption that she would never remember unless reminded just before the arranged time. In supervision, it became apparent that this routine never gave Kay the chance to remember or forget the session and inhibited the possibility of exploring issues associated with the boundary of time in the therapy. It appeared that the diagnosis of dementia was exerting a significant influence on the therapist, and it became easier to recognize how my own motives had played a big part in sabotaging this particular session.

Ferenczi (1900: 9) suggests that an early assumption about a patient can influence the way they are heard and seen, "we perceive everything in terms of the diagnosis which we had previously established". Laing (1990: 33), writing about working with people suffering from schizophrenia, highlights the difference between looking at a patient in terms of a diagnosis, in contrast to seeing them "simply as a human being". More generally, Loewenthal (2002) writes about the possibility of the person who is "the healthcare worker" meeting the person who is "the patient". The experience of working with Kay demonstrated how at times it was difficult to see the "person" because of the diagnosis, which made it difficult to experience anything other than a "person with dementia" even though the intention had been otherwise.

The contextual issues imposed on the relationship, influencing the way things were being heard and perceived, and this raised the issue of whether the therapy could move beyond the pre-understandings associated with the diagnosis of dementia. Buber (1922) differentiates between two types of relationships: an "I-It" and an "I-Thou"; the latter is based on the intimacy of a real meeting and contact with something other than oneself; it is concerned with how we become aware of the world that is "other" than the thoughts that pervade our minds. Buber's "I-Thou" described a quality of openness and reciprocity to another person or object, and he illustrates its potential by focusing on a relationship between an "I" and an inanimate object—a tree. The "I-It" relationship, according to Buber (1970), was concerned with the more routine relationships that fill a person's life, when there is no opportunity or interest in moving beyond the superficial in relating to another person or something other than oneself. The thoughts that "I" have about another person can dictate how "I" see that person; it is the thoughts and perceptions of the "I" that identify and create the "It" in Buber's conception of the "I-It" relation and the absence of an openness to see the other as anything other than this. The strength of the contextual issues and the pre-understandings associated with the therapist's previous experience of working with people with dementia made it difficult to move beyond what Buber describes as the "I-It" relation and to see Kay as something "other" than the understanding he had created of her in his mind.

Young (1994: 62) makes a link between Buber's "I-It" and "I-Thou" (without specifically referring to Buber) and the psychoanalytic use of transference and counter-transference by suggesting that, "In a phenomenological description you are no longer an 'it' but a 'thou' as a therapist." Young (1994: 62) suggests that counter-transference is concerned with reflecting on the projections that emanate from the patient and considering how these resonate with the therapist's own experience and further claims that "counter transference is the progressive closing of the spatial gap between the therapist and the patient". According to Young (1994), working with transference and counter-transference in the therapeutic relationship opens up the possibility of moving beyond the "I-It" and towards the "thou", by creating an openness or reflective process in relation to what is taking place between the "I" and the "thou". The following section considers how an exploration of the relationship with Kay in terms of previous experience, reflecting on transference and counter-transference, appeared to allow the "person" to emerge. The movement towards the "I-Thou" appeared to allow a potential disassociation with the diagnosis of dementia within this relationship. This reflection on transference and counter-transference in relation to Kay coincided with the therapist's own exploration of psychoanalytic theory and provided the basis for reconsidering what was taking place when they met each week.

From "I-It" to "I-Thou"

The subsequent meetings appeared to be opening up an opportunity to relate to Kay and go beyond the pre-understandings associated with the term "dementia". The following section shows how jokes about sexuality and other experiences suggested a transferential parallel between our relationship and that of her husband and father. Symington (1986: 31) describes transference as a "process whereby the analyst is sucked into the patient's outer personality structure", and this appeared to be nothing to do with a diagnosis of dementia. Our relationship appeared to identify the strong need for Kay to have companionship and not to be alone, and illustrated the place that her husband and father had left in her life. There were also counter-transferential issues, which Symington (1986) describes as the analyst incorporating the patient in his/her "outer personality structure", that had the potential to provoke the therapist to a personally motivated response linked with issues relating to his mother.

The consideration of transference and counter-transference developed from the therapist's experience of Kay's use of sexual innuendo, which was evident very early in the relationship, as the following quote from his notes might suggest:

> K mentioned things about, wanting her husband ... my wife being potentially upset with her because we were meeting—sexual innuendo. A sense that she is recognizing the absence of a relationship in her life with a man since her husband died and the sexual implication of that.

There were repeated jokes about the way that their meetings might appear to others, and it began to emerge that she might be positioning him in a place associated with other relationships in her life. Kay would often compare me with her husband and father; in the same session, she said "you're just like my husband, you talk and act just like him", and later "you're like my father".

The positioning of the therapist in relation to her husband was emphasized more clearly in the following example taken from the case notes:

> K touched my knee quite a few times towards the end of the session.... She made some jokes about us having an affair. Then she stood up to go. She came so close I thought she was going to kiss me. When I opened the door ... the "engaged" sign on the door ... came between us and just at eye level. She said "yes that's good we are engaged, don't tell your wife".

It appeared that her sexuality was strongly associated with her desire not to be alone and that her husband had met this need for her. The experience of a life-threatening illness as a child, to which Kay referred on frequent occasions, appeared to create an anxiety about being alone. She had been required to spend a considerable amount of time on her own through both the intense period of her illness and into her rehabilitation.

This experience of transference provoked counter-transferential feeling for the therapist associated with my mother. The acknowledgement of these thoughts in him appeared to be associated with the recognition of a relationship that was other than the preconceived thoughts associated with the "I-It" and seemed to be a clear movement beyond the contextual issues mentioned previously and towards the "I-Thou". Young (1994: 62) explores the interaction of transference and counter-transference while asserting its association with the "I-Thou", and states:

> ... I enter you. You withdraw. Or I may contain my distress. I push through your defences. We become one and then separate but feel love, hatred or ambivalence or frequent oscillations among these at many levels: a relationship.

A problem with using terms like "transference" and "counter-transference" is that they are linked with a theoretical construction and provide the opportunity to re-label using different terms but producing the same effect. This relationship could be described as an example of transference and counter-transference, which might just be an alternative to the diagnosis of dementia. The relationship between Kay and the therapist was acknowledging the "response" that Levinas (1981, 1984) assumes as part of being with "an-other". Moran (2000: 337) offers the following interpretation of Levinas:

His main point is that the "other" is not another me, nor is it something defined by its relationship with me, but rather something or someone completely other and unique. The other is incommensurate with me. Moreover, the other, as that which calls me, calls for a response from me ... .

At this point, Levinas (1967) is going beyond the "I-Thou" that Buber describes, since Buber relies on the "I" to discover the "Thou", and Levinas is identifying a point where the "other" person is noticed as separate from the "I". As "I", the therapist, sat with K experiencing the feelings that have been described in this case example, "I" am acknowledging that those feelings were caused by someone other than me. Levinas felt that this phenomenon was hugely important, calling it the "non-intentional" (Greenwood 2008), in identifying the limitations of subjectivity and the importance of a real relationship with another person. Buber's "I-Thou" was too dependent, according to Levinas (1967), on the subjectivity of the "I", and in the case being presented here, too dependent on the therapist's account of what happened. The experience that is presented here provided the basis for recognizing the existence of a relationship between two "I's", and that Buber's "I-Thou", and phenomenology in general, was too egocentric, too dependent on the conscious account of the "I".

The feelings that the therapist appeared to provoke in Kay and how he responded to her, which might be described as transference and counter-transference in psychoanalytic terms, could be seen as examples of the call being made to respond to the "other" referred to above. Perhaps the meetings were engaged in trying to explore an understanding and recognition of this response. The experience of being in a relationship where contact with another person brings about a particular response or set of feelings provides the opportunity to acknowledge the other person in their "other-than-me-ness" to be able to induce this reaction. This would not just be about what was being seen in the other person that related to oneself, but to go further and recognize the person that has provoked this response as someone separate and also capable of being provoked themselves.

The fact that this therapeutic relationship had entered into the speculation and exploration of our responses to each other suggested that it had become more than just an insular interpretation of how a person with dementia might behave in a therapy setting. The issue of whether the work of Levinas did appropriately illustrate what was being experienced in the work with Kay is not particularly significant, as this will always be dependent on the particular orientation of the therapist. However, what does appear important is the fact that it potentially illustrates how this relationship moved beyond the issues associated with the diagnosis of dementia.

An incident occurred that both reconfirmed the contextual issues that were influencing the therapy but also illustrated the raw humanity of this therapeutic relationship. During the week between sessions, Kay had apparently became unsettled and agitated, culminating in her walking out of the nursing home late one evening, a fact not immediately noticed by the staff. The therapist was contacted to assist in the search for Kay, when her absence had been discovered, as part of his other responsibilities within the organization. This caused him considerable consternation at the time, as he felt that his position as therapist would be compromised by getting involved in a search for her—however, it was clear that her immediate safety was the priority. After a few hours' search, Kay was found by the police, and "the therapist" brought her back to the nursing home. Once the search was over, the therapist felt he needed to take advice on how to proceed with the therapy, recognizing the importance of continuing the therapy while acknowledging that any future sessions were subject to this shared experience was a significant learning experience for him as a therapist.

It appeared that the diagnosis of dementia had received a powerful confirmation in their relationship by involving them both in this emergency situation. However, searching and finding Kay on this cold rain-swept evening and then taking her back to the nursing home highlighted how important it was to recognize that therapy frames a meeting between two people who have very separate lives and experiences.

K's physical health began to deteriorate, and she appeared to become very frail. The therapist tried not to get too involved in matters relating to her physical care and avoided conversations with other staff that related to this. However, it was difficult not to notice that care staff were having to do more for her, and that she was becoming dependent on them for personal care. This period of ill health imposed a long interruption on their meetings, and during this time there were periods when it appeared that she might not recover. However, Kay did recover and they started meeting again.

The therapist had always seen Kay early in the morning but had changed the time because her increased physical dependency made her reliant on staff, and this meant that she was not ready to see himat the original time. So they met later in the morning. Kay would be sitting in the lounge when he entered the home, and she would wait there until she saw the therapist and then follow him down to the room where they met.

Kay was missing quite a few sessions due to her health, and these would be cancelled on the day of the session in person, "I don't think I can talk today, maybe next week". The frequency of these missed sessions increased. I The therapist explored this in supervision, and as a consequence decided to suggest that they stop meeting but allow her the possibility of meeting in the future.

In the following few weeks, she told the therapist how by meeting him at this time she would lose her seat in the lounge. This became an issue for her to such an extent that she could not speak of anything else. This appeared to be associated with a need to find her place—and that was not with the therapist, , it was sitting with the others in the lounge where she appeared to feel secure. They had one final session together when it agreed that it appeared to be the right time to break off from meeting weekly. It was also agreed that Kay could see the therapist again if she wanted to at some time in the future. The session and the agreement to meet on a weekly basis ended at this point.

Conclusions

The early stages of this therapeutic relationship identified a difficulty in seeing Kay as "a person" because she appeared to be seen more as "a person with dementia". As a consequence of recognizing the way a diagnosis was influencing the therapy, it appeared possible to consider other aspects of the therapeutic relationship, and reflecting on the transference in the relationship appeared to be an important part of seeing beyond the label of dementia.

This form of "post-existential" research has potential implications for both the training of therapists practising with people who have been labelled with a diagnosis and for researchers who are looking for a method for practitioner research.

This particular case highlighted how the pre-understandings associated with a diagnosis can be imposed on the therapy, not only by the therapist through his/her training but also the setting. The setting in the case of Kay, in a nursing home caring for people with dementia, reinforced the assumptions made by the therapist and by Kay, not only about dementia but also issues associated with sexuality and the elderly.

In terms of research, this case study provided the opportunity to highlight the value and importance of a descriptive account as a form of practitioner research. Traditional research methods have positioned descriptive methods in a subsidiary position in relation to experimental methods. However, this chapter provides an example of a phenomenological-hermeneutic method unashamedly emphasizing the importance of vivid description as a means of generating meanings in relation to practice without the need to focus on generating truth.

This case provides an opportunity influenced by post-existentialism to explore an experience of therapy and to speculate on the meanings that emerged from the process of reflecting through the stages outlined, which represent a form of practitioner research. The method outlined in this chapter describes a process of re-searching and looking beyond the initial meaning, and in the case of Kay, it concerned looking beyond her diagnosis, as this provided a closed explanation of the experience in terms of symptoms associated with an illness. The "I-Thou" relationship provided a basis for looking at the therapeutic relationship in a more intimate way, going beyond the diagnosis of dementia. However, the "I-Thou" is dependent on the "I" to meet the "Thou" and consequently has the potential to overwhelm the possibility of really meeting a separate person who is other than the person seen by the "I". Levinas (Greenwood 2008) developed the concept of the "non-intentional", taken from Husserl, which acknowledges the possibility of meeting another person separate and prior to being overwhelmed by the pre-concepts of the "I". By looking beyond the diagnosis, beyond the therapist's preconceptions, there was an opportunity to explore the possibilities that were associated with Kay as a person.

CHAPTER FIVE

Language, experience, and representation: a re-examination of the case of Lola Voss

Rhiannon Thomas and Del Loewenthal

Introduction

"The Case of Lola Voss" is one of Binswanger's papers on schizophrenia in which he considered a young woman whom he encountered during his work in the Bellevue sanatorium. Lola was of a German/Spanish/South American heritage and appears to have also spoken English and French. The relevance of this is in her moving between German/Spanish/English in her creation of her own language meaning system. However, what seems to be missed, in a case in which "language" features so prominently, is what Lola might be saying. What is intended by "saying", in this context, is a reference to her language system, in that it is assumed to still be a form of communication—or at the least to carry significant meaning—rather than whether this is also a retreat from the world. The position taken by Binswanger, in his construction of an existential analysis is that Lola's "superstition", as he sees it, is evidence of her experiencing the "hostile crowding of the world" (Binswanger 1963: 340); a world from which she is in "flight" and in doing so, her "existence" has surrendered itself in so large a measure that it remains totally closed to itself. This concept is consistent with the existentialist

73

position that an "essential function of language is communication, meaningful exchange between persons" (Macquarrie 1972: 106).

Macquarrie goes on, however, to state that within this existentialist conception of language, "there could be no existence ... apart from language" (Macquarrie 1972: 106). This indicates a greater ambiguity than in the position taken by, for example, Merleau-Ponty, for whom the possibility of experience external to, or even preceding, language exists. For Binswanger, writing in the case of Lola Voss, the importance of language is at the same time recognized and yet somehow difficult to reconcile with the concept of language as a product of the individual in communication with the world. Without this being-in-the-world through language, can Lola exist?

This concept is surely linked to the existentialist position that the "essential function of language is communication, meaningful exchange between persons ... (and) there could be no existence ... apart from language ... language is what externalises thought and makes it accessible to the other person" (Macquarrie 1972: 106). From this position alone, it would indeed appear that Lola is becoming unreachable, that her relation with the world needs to be addressed, with a more conventional use of language a sign of such a recovery.

A re-examination of the case of Lola Voss

Within much of existentialist thought, "language does not create the existence of the world. It is, rather, a manifestation of our prior world disclosure that takes place through an implicit, bodily attunement to one's surroundings. Our prelinguistic experience of the world is always inherent to our use and understanding of language" (Frie 2003: 147). In other words, within this construct, the individual is free to represent, through language, his own experience that is structured subjectively, albeit in constant meaningful relation to the world. This is evident in, for example, Merleau-Ponty's concept of lived experience, wherein the body "is our expression in the world, the visible form of our intentions" (Merleau-Ponty 1962: 5), the concept of intentionality fundamental to this.

In this sense, our bodily expressions are not subject to language; the processes of bodily experience both pre-exist and co-exist with language. Whilst it is acknowledged within existentialism that "experience is not easily described and always exceeds our attempts to define it in words or concepts" (Frie 2003: 1) the central assumption is that experience external to language, can exist, whilst thought, cannot. "The Existentialist rejects the image of language as a straitjacket on the thinking that goes inside it" (Cooper 1990: 162) but at the same time, thought is "no 'internal' thing and does not exist independently of the world and of words" (Merleau-Ponty 1962: 183). However, what appears absent from this concept, is the possibility articulated by such as Lacan and theories of structural linguistics that it is "language which constitutes us as a subject" (Sarup 1993: 6)—in the case of Lola Voss, of course, it is both language as a universal concept and languages in a "tribalist" (Cooper 1990: 162) sense.

Whilst at one end of the continuum are those such as Sartre and Laing, for whom "experience resists definition" and for whom "our efforts to convey the particular features of our experience are imperfect because experience is impossible to convey in words" (Frie 2003: 188), at the other is Heidegger after the *Kehre* who "provocatively claims" that "there is no thing when the word is lacking", or that "language speaks" and "thus is the master of man" (Lafont 2002: 185). Occupying what appears to be a similar position to this post-*Kehre* Heidegger is Wittgenstein, for whom the social and interpersonal reality that people experience and live in and through is primarily constructed by language. Wittgenstein's argument in many ways mirrors that of Vygotsky, who states that the subject—and thus, one would assume, what is taken to be the experience of the subject—"is shaped by the tools and instruments that he comes to use" (Vygotsky 1962: vii). However, the structuralist position of Saussure essentially rejects the possibility of unique, individual experience on account of the fact that the experience is structured exclusively by the pre-existent language—in essence, discounting the notion of the linguistically creative influence of pre-, or non-linguistic experience. With this in mind, "experience" becomes a different concept.

These are apparently very different positions, and this raises significant issues in terms of whether primacy is given to the experience itself, or the manner and specifics of its representation in order to understand how that experience has been structured. The question emerges as to whether an alternate, perhaps post-existential, position can be found which seems to allow for the potential both that the subject's experience is structured by language and the subject's language structured by experience in a manner in which neither possibility is discounted by the other. What is argued here is that existentialist and structuralist or linguistically idealistic positions are not necessarily as distant as they at first appear, and that in, for example, Binswanger's "Case of Lola Voss", a form of resolution could found between on the one hand, the existentially defined concept of experience, and, on the other, the formative and "first class importance" (Macquarrie 1972: 148) of language that is fundamentally of help to the patient in question. In relation to Lola, therefore, it could be helpful to consider both the existentialist positions on experience of, for example, Merleau-Ponty and Laing, and at the same time, linguistic theories of Saussure and Wittgenstein.

It could be argued that what Lola was attempting, at least in part, was a resolution between her three languages—and what those languages themselves represented. It is worth noting that her mother was Spanish, her father German, and thus English—in this context—was perhaps a relatively neutral language (at least in the context of familial relations). In some ways, what is attempted in this chapter could be seen as a similar effort to reconcile different languages and find a different meaning that emerges; the languages of existentialism and structural linguistics cut and pasted together in a manner reminiscent of Lola's creation of her own meaning system and translated into something that manages to hold open both possibilities.

The case of Lola Voss

To paraphrase Binswanger, Lola was a wilful, spoilt young woman in her mid-twenties who was indulged as a child and rarely denied anything. She fell in love with a young Spanish student doctor who was unable to marry her in the immediate future, and disappointed in love, Lola's behaviour became more erratic than it had been previously—although there had been concerns for a number of years. Her family had her entered into a sanatorium where she met Binswanger—the "second physician" to see her. Importantly, no information is given as to how often they met and over what period of time, and whilst she appears—at least from his perspective—to have opened up to him, we are given no details of their relationship or any therapy that took place. Instead, what we have are circumstances and Lola's deterioration, which is viewed somewhat from a distance, both metaphorically and literally, as Lola is, after a time, released from Bellevue and thus the rest of Binswanger's information is gained through written correspondence. What is absent is any real sense of Lola's experience and any real sense of the between. Arguably, what does not exist in this case is what emerges in the *"Mitwelt"* of Binswanger and Lola Voss—instead, her case is presented in something of a one-sided way and then interpreted by Binswanger, an interpretation in which Lola becomes more and more absent. He describes her as "with an animated facial expression, but somewhat stiff in her gestures" and with a "manner ... vivacious and open, but ... speech ... laboured and foreign" (Binswanger 1957: 269).

It seems relevant that her speech should be described as such, an implication being that her speech was "foreign" in terms of her difficulty with it, her lack of ease in the use of language. (It is assumed that they conversed in German, although this is not stated as such.) Lola was able to describe to Binswanger the main focus of her illness, which centred initially around hunchbacks, an umbrella, a rubber-tipped cane, a nurse at the sanatorium ("that one"), and clothes, although what is evident during her communication with Binswanger is the expansion of this to include almost every aspect of her life. Her construction of her own language/warning system is described by Binswanger and includes separation of syllables of English, Spanish, or German words (e.g., *"Gomo"*, *"Cuarto"*, *"Schirm"*) and their realignment into new "meaning" phrases "no go", "no care", and so on. Lola does not distinguish between the languages and puts them together with what appears to be a disregard for the traditional usage of the words, their usual combination, and understood meaning references. Her construction of the new phrases seems to be random—for example, from the word *"mano"* (for hand), she takes the *"no"* but ignores the *"ma"*, with no discussion in the case for why this should be so. (Note: it is deliberate at this point to avoid the use of terms such as "signifier" and "signified" in order to begin with a position that does not incorporate linguistic theories.)

A question that arises is what might emerge if we consider instead Lola's language as evidence of attempts to continue to engage with the world rather than of surrender and retreat from it. One possibility is that in an effort to speak of her experience, she needed to go outside of her pre-existing linguistic categorizations of the worlds. It could be seen that in the construction of a new language, a hybrid of three of her languages, the syllables connected together in a way that revealed a different meaning, Lola was stating that her existing use of language did not adequately fit with her experience.

Binswanger's basic assumption is that Lola is in flight from the world, evidenced by her construction of this personal language system. And yet, in her construction of "no go", "no care", and so on, Lola is arguably not constructing a "closed system" (Frie 2003) but something that is understandable to everyone—she is still communicating in what is essentially a traditional form and is speaking of alternate experiences of heightened and reduced anxiety. However, what she is also perhaps expressing is a sense that the word "umbrella" ("*Schirm*") does not just indicate the object but, upon investigation, is found to have a second meaning, related to the word "*si*" in Spanish. Apart from the definiteness with which she fixes upon this "other meaning", what Lola has done is surely what we are all doing on a daily basis—looking for hidden meaning within the words and gestures of others in order to decipher what is "really" intended, and doing so by the displacement of feeling onto other persons, objects, or, in Lola's case, words. In a state of intense anxiety, this tendency is often heightened, for many people to the extent where they are mistrustful of accepted meanings and look instead for clues that are not immediately apparent. From this perspective, Lola is perhaps being driven by a search for "true" meaning, the search of someone who finds it difficult to trust herself and those around her. It is perhaps relevant at this point to mention, of course, that Lola's family did not tell her that she was going to the sanatorium when they brought her to Bellevue. They instead told her she was going on a visit of some kind.

In making this statement, however, what may be happening here, in essence, is exactly what Lola does, finding two disparate pieces of information and selecting from them before putting them together to find other meaning. Is it difficult for Binswanger to accept what Lola is doing because, in many ways, the process she is following is akin to the analytic process of interpretation? Except, of course, in her case, it is madness!

Bodily experience

Although Lola continued to reside within language, to Binswanger, her own personal, closed language was used to isolate her from the world, from society. Yet she still, arguably, continued to "experience" outside of language and society and through what Binswanger saw as a bodily experience of her surroundings. However, the perceived reality of this bodily experience is not explored in any detail in such a way that could have opened something up for her.

Lola is disturbed by a number of—initially at least—specific incidents that themselves merit investigation. We are told of the umbrella-hunchback incident and yet are missing any real detail, any description. What was the umbrella like? What was the hunchback like? When did she first experience fear in relation to hunchbacks? What were the circumstances beyond the fact that her father bought/ gave her the umbrella just as she caught sight of the hunchback? Lola appears to mistranslate in a search for meaning—but one question that arises is, the meaning of what?

Arguably, the possibility of the importance of physical, bodily sensation is something to explore. Lola feels in danger, from what is never really explored beyond an existentialist abstraction. Binswanger assumes primarily the "meaning" of her clothes anxiety from an anthropological perspective, but the narrowness of this is arguably not connected to Lola's actual bodily experience—what is it like to wear the clothes? What do they feel like against her skin? What is the sensation in particular of new clothes? Binswanger focuses on the representation to the world signified by the clothes, not on the physical sensation of wearing them. New clothes, in particular, or any clothes in fact, impact upon the individual's sensory experiences; sight (colour), touch (texture), smell (fabric), and so on. According to Frie:

> to reduce pre-linguistic or non-verbal experience to that which can be verbally articulated is to neglect a crucial fact—the non-verbal realm exists precisely because there is a dimension of human experience that cannot be adequately represented in language.
>
> (Frie 2003: 148)

With Lola Voss, rather than seeing her language use as a symptom of a disconnection with the world, perhaps it is possible to see instead her frustration with the inadequacy of existent language to express her experiences. Not least within this is the sound of the words, the physical reality or sensation of them, the choice of "*no*" over "*ma*" could perhaps make sense in these terms.

At the same time, if we take a Laingian approach, everything we believe is rooted in our unique experience and yet, due to the suffering it engenders, in the representation of it we adopt false truths, distinct from the ones we actually experience. Lola's creative use of language, her sculpting of new meanings from the words of objects she saw around her, fits with this concept. From this perspective, Lola is perhaps expressing the difficulty she has in bearing her experience and is creating something that enables her to detach from it, make (non)sense of it, in order to cope with it. By refusing to enter into this world with her, Binswanger arguably compounds her distress, her disconnection from the world, and her "madness". He is, in essence, inflexible—he asks that she communicate with him on his terms—the standard by which he is judging her connectedness with the world—but does not enter into her language in order to investigate the possibility of the experience that is motivating it.

Reality, experience, and language

Central to this is the concept of "reality" and where—and if—"reality" is taken to exist. If "reality" cannot exist, then neither can experience, for experience is surely rooted in our concept of personal reality. For existentialism, "truth" or "reality" is personally constructed: "These things are not lying ready made for our inspection; they have to be appropriated through personal endeavour" (MacQuarrie 1972: 140). From this position, in language "man expresses himself; but he is himself the self-transcending being, the one who already knows in himself the mystery of existing". For Heidegger—before the *Kehre*—"the locus of language is not in the proposition but in the reality itself" (MacQuarrie 1972: 147).

At the same time, if the post-modern concept of the deconstructed, or "shattered" subject (Heartfield 2002), subordinate to language (Barthes 1984: 145), is considered in relation to this, the question becomes not only "how can I describe my experience?", but "how is it possible that I can experience, in order that I describe it?". To Lacan, if "I" am experiencing, "I" am already in the externalized field of the other, a field of language and culture determined by those who came before me. "I is another" (Lacan 1977: 23; Sartre 1937: 97). The rejection of the notion of the transcendental or constituent subject, "seems to eliminate a basic presupposition" of traditional psychology (Løvlie 1992: 120) which places at its centre the "fiction" of the "unified monolithic, reified, essentialized subject (ultimately) capable of fully conscious, fully rational action" (Lather, in Kvale 1992: 103). To embrace this concept is to be distanced from the humanistic possibility of maturity and self-actualization and the idea of human life as one where a "pre-existent goal is (either) triumphantly reached or tragically" unattainable (Rorty 1989: 29).

What is left in place of the Kierkegaardian concept of the authentic subject is a subject which cannot be but relative and de-centred (Sarup 1993: 24), only coming into play through the principle of difference. From this perspective, the self, or "I", that is perceived is itself a linguistic construct—as is, from this perspective, one would assume, experience itself. The whole notion of "experience" is itself not just constructed linguistically but is a linguistic construct.

On the other hand, if we dispense with the transcendental subject, so also disappears the possibility of expressing anything other than the "deceit of the symbolic" (Butler, in Wright 2000: 41). What is again relevant in the case of Lola Voss, albeit from an altered position, is her reformation of linguistic relations. To Binswanger, this is evidence of her development of her faith in the "omnipotence of words" (Binswanger 1963: 263), something with which he sees it necessary to do battle.

For Binswanger, Lola's wellbeing was dependent on her return to meaningful speech and concomitant relatedness to others (Frie 2003: 147). However, in so doing, Binswanger—perhaps inadvertently—underlines the linguistic nature of our existence, something of particular relevance for Lola Voss. A question that comes to mind is what language meant to Lola: Spanish, the language of her mother; German, the language of her father; English, representing something else. She appears—perhaps quite rightly—to be confused by it all.

From a Lacanian perspective, Lola could be argued to be attempting to re-acquire "the ability to symbolise experience through words (in order to be) able to use this to replace experience with words as a form of repression" (Kemp 2006: 3). Her inability to do this, her difficulty in deciphering the "true" meaning of the words and objects around her, puts her in a place where she is rebelling against the fact that signifiers point only to other signifiers and insisting instead that she has discovered the true relation between the sign and it's signified. In effect, however, she is—from this perspective—left in the trauma of the real. She could be seen to be discovering the difficult indirect relation between word and meaning, signifier and signified, and beginning to live in a world where this relation can be reformed, taken to mean something else. This becomes just too difficult for her, and instead "*Schirm*" becomes "*si*", becomes a yes in response to internal questioning. From this, linguistic perspective, it could be argued that Lola has recognized, through the inherent instability of language, the instability of the world—perhaps connected to her growing up in a household of multiple languages. What means one thing to her (German) father, means another to her (Spanish) mother. The meaning of words is unstable, in sound, origin, and implication. It seems that in order for Lola to tolerate the possibility of multiple meaning, the therapist must also, including the possibility that her language system is not wrong, but bears the same relation to "reality" as do other phantasies.

In his discussion of Cézanne's apples, Lacan gives the signifier the power both to kill and create. This arguably has parallels with Lola's umbrella—given to her by her father—in particular given that she determines her own meaning from it, thus effectively killing the actual with her signifier instead assuming a super-natural power. In re-examining this case of Lola Voss, there seems to be much that goes undiscussed in relation to the potential phallic symbols of the man's cane and the umbrella given to her by her father.

Existentialism versus structuralism?
Lola's experience/wordplay as metaphor

From an existentialist perspective, "in language, man expresses himself but he is himself the self-transcending being, the one who already knows in himself the mystery of existing" (Macquarrie 1972: 149–150). For Heidegger, the "Word gives being to the thing" (Silverman 2000: 56), whereas for Lacan, the word "murders the thing" (Silverman 2000: 56). From a structuralist position, until there is language, thought and experience are essentially amorphous and cannot, therefore, exist in the way that we understand them once they are given structure by language. One potential way out of this apparent opposition is the concept of metaphor. Where Lacan and Heidegger converge is in the understanding that for Lacan, creation and murder are two sides of the same process. A possibility is that the concept of metaphor allows for both the possibility of the bodily experience, and at the same time, linguistic signifiers which refer to other linguistic signifiers.

Specifically in the case of Lola Voss, her creation of new language meanings could be seen as metaphor, referring both to her experience and to meaning that is specifically linguistic in origin. In assuming, instead of a rigid, superstitious, and unhelpful language game, a poetic creation of word/meaning relatedness, it becomes possible to hold on to language and experience simultaneously.

The distinction which some linguists might draw between Lola's use of the word *"Schirm"* to create the *"si"* in answer to her internal questioning, is the difference between "live" and "dead" metaphor (Haack 1994: 7), a difference brought about by the relative degree of conventionalization which that metaphor has undergone. A "dead" metaphor would most likely be what Zijderweld would term cliché, whereas a "live" metaphor is one which "almost always feels discordant at first" (Indurkhya 1984: 95). One example which always springs to mind is Dylan Thomas's description in "The Hunchback in the Park" of "the wild boys as innocent as strawberries". Following this argument, a live or "novel" metaphor, goes beyond noticing existing similarities, to creating them (Indurkhya 1994: 95). This is similar to the position of Carmack & Glucksberg (1984) who argue that "metaphors do not use associations between concepts, they are used to create them" (Carmack & Glucksberg 1984: 445). In other words, a "live" or "novel" metaphor could create conceptual links which a "dead" or "clichéd" one does not. From this position, the question becomes whether it could be possible to use language, structured as metaphor, to create satisfying associations between an unsymbolized experience and a verbal signifier.

> One possible way forward could be in Indurkhya's distinction between ontology on the one hand, and the structure of the world on the other, the argument being that it is possible for the experiential world to be both created and mind-independent at once.
>
> (Indurkhya 1984: 106)

> It is similarity-creating metaphors that provide us a means to break the shackles of our language and culture and give us an ability to ungroup and regroup environments into different meaningful patterns.
>
> (Indurkhya 1984: 145)

This could be seen as compatible with the idea of using language—in its social sense—to describe something of our experience but is something which those such as Black dismiss as an "implausible contention" (Black 1993: 35). He states that "to view some metaphors as ontologically creative falls short of claiming that they are creative" (Black 1993: 35). Instead, what is posited is that the hearer or reader is given "a new vision or a new insight" by the ways in which a metaphor user "can bring into prominence known features ... which he thinks deserve special attention" (Khatchadourian, in Black 1993: 36).

To an art historian such as Ernst Gombrich, what Lacanians would consider language speaking the subject is discussed in terms of "making and matching" (Gombrich 1960) or "schema and correction". The concept is similar, the idea that the forms we use, either visual—which could also be termed linguistic in the sense of a visual vocabulary—or spoken, pre-exist us, and indeed structure our perception. However, it is possible to see a difference in terms of the possibility for Gombrich of adapting our pre-existing schema to better suit our purpose, or our unique vision and desire to create. Seen within this context, what Lola was doing was arguably a creative act, keeping alive the possibility of a connection with the world.

Gombrich (1960) insists that when we, for example, are making a snowman, the question is not "shall we represent a man who is smoking?", but "shall we give him a pipe?". He states that "it is only afterward that we may introduce the idea of reference, of the snowman's representing somebody ... we can discover a likeness .... But always ... making will come before matching, creation before reference" (Gombrich 1960: 85). What this suggests is that the first part of the representational act is, in fact, spontaneous, but that in order to make sense of it, we relate it to something which is pre-existent of its creation. In relation to Lola Voss, this opens something up that is beyond either a purely existential or structural linguistic base and seems to reconcile the two—the possibility that both language and experience can be simultaneously the "clothing" and the "body" (Merleau-Ponty 1962: 182–183), at times either limiting or allowing for something creative and expressive.

Conclusion

What appears to have taken place in the "Case of Lola Voss" is that those around Lola, Binswanger included, dismissed her creative use of language as evidence of her illness, rather than attempting to engage with it. Language was seen in this context almost entirely as an act that communicates speaker and hearer, and thus by failing to use language in a conventional sense, Lola was deemed to be in flight from the world. At the same time, it could be argued that those around her compounded this by refusing to open up communication with her. The fact was that it made sense to her, it helped her make sense of her world and her experience of it, and in actuality, as we have seen, was perhaps not such a perversion of traditional language structure or usage as it first appeared. As stated by Cooper (1990), "in order for a 'sedimented' system of communication to have become established, people must once have expressed themselves more idiosyncratically" (Cooper 1990: 162).

Whilst Binswanger's existential analysis took note of Lola's difficulty in being-in-the world, her superstitions, her anxiety and its displacement, what was missed by holding this position alone was the possibility that in this case, to approach from a perspective incorporating concepts from structural linguistics may have allowed a reconciliation of language and experience in which neither is exclusively dominant. For Lola, the confusion of her Spanish-German-English world arguably mirrored that which connected to her mother, father, and perhaps to her fiancé. To state that her linguistic confusion was entirely something with, for example, an Oedipal base—her linguistic struggles a product of her relationships with her mother and father—is perhaps missing the actuality of Lola's experience of the languages themselves. However, at the same time, the reverse is also the case.

Perhaps in this idea we are moving towards something that could be termed "post-existential" (Loewenthal 2007a). A belief in the innate creativity of the individual and his or her own personal experience—making always precedes matching—but an acknowledgement that representation is bound by a pre-existent vocabulary within which the individual struggles to communicate his or her own experience—making is incomplete without matching. In addition, a bearing in mind simultaneously of existentialism and perhaps of phenomenological description and of certain concepts of structural linguistics. The outcome of this, in the case of Lola Voss, is an analysis that is dynamic and potentially facilitating—allowing for the possibility of an emergent relationship which considers multiple possibilities and acknowledges the complex and often elliptical relations between questions of language and experience.

CHAPTER SIX

Laing and the treatment is the way we treat people

Tom Cotton and Del Loewenthal

Introduction

In many ways, when exploring a relationship between treatment and the way we treat people as individuals, we might be seen as exploring the grey area between psychotherapeutic treatment epistemologies and, what might be considered, the ontology of psychotherapeutic treatment. In other words, the gap between the theory of treatment and the being or doing of treatment—the gap between ideals and actuality. It could be seen as a slippery liminal space, which should (and does) challenge even our most basic assumptions about theory and the knowledge structures on which we base them. This space can provide an opportunity for valuable exploration, reflection, and learning, and yet, all too often, the uncertainty that arises here is met by the attempt to shut this space down, or simply ignore it and retreat behind entrenched psychological therapistized positions. Might a post-existential perspective help us to remain open to what emerges in this space, or might it be just another way of attempting to shut it down? In this sense, we might hold in mind the chapter's title not only in reference to "clinical treatment", but also to the treatment of the research participants and their experiences as well.

This chapter explores the experiences of a group of research participants, including Laing's peers, which we wish to consider when exploring this liminal space, particularly in regard to treatment and how the way we treat one another as individuals might impact on that treatment. In the current mental health mainstream, Laing's work now tends to be "regarded more as a 'typical' sixties extravagance than an important contribution to our understanding of serious distress" (Smail 2007: 14). Whatever one's view of that perception (and we acknowledge that it would take up at least an entire book to unpack it), Laing's psychoanalytic-existential-phenomenological perspective might be considered an important path towards a post-existential framework.

As a young psychiatrist in the 1950s, Laing developed a stance against what he saw as the uncritical psychiatric and psychoanalytic orthodoxies of the time. Expected to administer insulin comas and bear witness to psychosurgery, Laing became increasingly "anxious to discover how these miserable, frightened, and deeply confused people experienced the world, and how they would respond given half the chance to communicate freely" (Burston 1996: 33). When left alone to communicate as they chose, free of the therapist's need to interrogate, know, diagnose, and treat, Laing discovered meaningful disclosure, and this was to become a hallmark of his approach (ibid.). Indeed, this attitude became key to the nascent existential-phenomenological approach to psychotherapy, which was, in part, "a protest against dehumanization in psychology" (Wertz 2005: 167).

In many ways, it was the medical-diagnostic and subsequent prescriptive-intervention approach to treatment model—what we might now call the medical model—that Laing sought to challenge. In particular, it was the psychiatric Kraepelinian paradigm of schizophrenia which was deemed to derive from a clear organic nosology (and, indeed, still is by many) of which Laing was critical. By contrast, it is argued that Laing posited that schizophrenia might be seen as an expression of the interpersonal double binds and knots—key concepts derived in part from the work of anthropologist Gregory Bateson (1958) and the economist Thomas Schelling (1960)—and embodied by a person labelled "schizophrenic". Furthermore, Laing deemed that this label had been meted out by familial and wider cultural agencies. In this light, he saw traditional psychiatric treatment as a perpetuation of the double bind, now played out by the opposing roles of doctor and patient. The doctor looks for a set of signifiers indicating illness and finds them by virtue of the fact that a "patient role" signifies an ill person, particularly when he or she refuses to accept the doctor's definition of this illness. The definitions that these roles, or embodied stories, automatically prescribe has immense power. Szasz goes as far as to characterize this struggle for definition, in the way we use words like "mental illness" to impose our realities on one another, as "the struggle for life itself" (Szasz 1973: 24–25).

In 1965, Laing co-founded the mental health charity the Philadelphia Association (PA), which aimed to challenge accepted ways of understanding and treating mental and emotional suffering. The first of several PA therapeutic communities, founded by key members of the charity, the psychiatrists David Cooper and Aaron Esterson, and psychiatric social worker Sid Briskin, Kingsley Hall was regarded as an "experiment in living" which could operationalize Laing's maxim of the treatment being the way we treat people. Here, people who had received a diagnosis of schizophrenia lived without boundaries alongside psychotherapists, supposedly in the absence of doctor or patient roles. While Kingsley Hall was not the first therapeutic community in the UK, it has come to be regarded as one of the most controversial. The temporal context of the community—it opened its doors in 1965 and closed them again in 1970—goes some way to indicating the countercultural ideology that existed within, which in turn sheds some light on the subsequent mainstream psychiatric reaction to Laing and his colleagues. Their work, including Kingsley Hall, opened up myriad questions about ethics, power, and certainty in treatment—not all of them intentional. Arguably, however, rather than stemming the drive towards a more mechanized, standardized approach to treatment in the intervening years, these questions merely provided the ammunition needed to bring it about.

Today, we operate increasingly in a cultural *mise en scène* where our attachment to the certainty that late modernity promises has engendered a mindset which often sees uncritical theory as the "scientific" rule, rather than the exception. This climate has proven to be fertile ground for the "colonization of the psychological and social by the biological" (Read, Mosher & Bentall 2004: 4) and has ensured, for example, that over the last forty years, fewer than one per cent of the 33,648 studies that researched schizophrenia examined the impact of parental care on those who had received the diagnosis (Read, Goodman, Morrison, Ross & Aderhold 2004). This is despite the growing body of research that relates childhood trauma to the diagnosis (Bracken 2002; Romme 2009;); highlights the systemic flaws in genetic research into its biology (Boyle 2002; Joseph 2003; Schwartz & Susser 2006); raises questions about the impartiality of pharmaceutical drug trials (Pilgrim 1990); and the inconsistencies in evidence supporting the chemical imbalance theory in regard to the origin of mental illnesses as a whole (Kirsch 2009).

Yet, despite these inconsistencies, the psychotherapeutic medical model—which shares with the biological model an "insistence on the correct explanation of a disorder and adoption of the concomitant therapeutic action" (Wampold 2001: 11)—has enjoyed a burgeoning hegemony. Psychotherapeutic hegemony is nothing new, of course. In a letter to Freud, Bleuler likened psychoanalysis' core ideology to a religious creed where "the principle 'all or nothing' is necessary for religious sects and for political parties" (Bleuler, in Bentall 2004). As such, psychoanalysis was the dominant creed for much of the twentieth century, and no doubt, our attachment to theory creeds will ensure many more to come.

As the state increasingly encourages a medical-model psychotherapeutic monoculture (Layard 2006a, b; Health Practitioners Council), are we able to ask difficult, yet important, questions about the "medical-model-friendly" forms of therapy, such as CBT, which endorse some of the medical model's assumptions? Can these modes of therapy be seen as a way of not thinking about something? While not thinking about something (the cause of deeper troubling mechanisms, for instance) might be useful at times, "it is potentially catastrophic as a principal approach to well-being" (Loewenthal 2008). What then might we not be thinking about? One obvious answer might be: all that's beyond a reductionist "present-at-hand" Cartesian view of the world that the medical model endorses. For within this view, "the perspective necessary for seeing the world ontologically is lost; and the subsequent interpretation of the world as made of substances is inevitable" (Gilvin 1989: 66). Because this narrow materialistic view finds it difficult to quantify the complex relationships between culture, power, the unconscious, language, and the myriad other agencies that human experience is subject to, they are consigned to the "non-scientific" ghetto in mental health, where they can be safely disregarded. The problem is, in attempting to disassociate from these fundamental aspects of human experience, we simultaneously disassociate from the fundamental intersubjectivity that wellbeing is bound up in.

True reflection presents me to myself not as idle and inaccessible subjectivity, but as identical with my presence in the world and to others, as I am now realizing it: I am all that I see, I am an inter-subjective field, not despite my body and historical situation, but, on the contrary, by being this body and this situation, and through them, all the rest.

(Merleau-Ponty, in Friedman 1991: 201)

With Merleau-Ponty's words in mind, with what framework might we think about the nexus of intersubjectivity between client and therapist? An existential framework might be one starting point. However, with existentialism's modernist emphasis on "I"-centricity, the notion of the Other has the capacity to become lost in the "I" of the observer. Post-modern discourses, on the other hand, might offer a way of decon-structing modernist orthodoxies (Loewenthal & Snell 2003), but they often share a weakness with these orthodoxies in regard to objectivity in relation to knowledge, as well as a "conceptual flaccidity and gen-erously inconclusive nature" (Smail 2007: 12). It has been suggested elsewhere in this book that a space between existentialism and post-modernism, where Heideggarian *Dasein*, Foucauldian notions of power, Lacanian notions of language, Freudian notions of the unconscious, and Levinasian notions of the Other, for example, might provide a locus to explore issues of "well-being, raise questions on power, knowledge and the political nature of psychology and science" (Loewenthal 2008: 318). It is through this lens that we might view what now follows.

Perhaps Laing's greatest achievement was his claim that the contents of the psychoses were meaningful and intelligible (Bentall 2005: 227), providing that one could look past the obstacle of the investigating "I" and retain an open space where the historical, temporal, and cul-tural contexts of the Other's *Dasein* could be explored. In challenging the mental health orthodoxies of the 1960s, Laing and his colleagues attempted to keep this space open "without defining it in a positivis-tic way" (Loewenthal 2008: 31), and Kingsley Hall represented a treat-ment setting where this attitude might be put into practice. The muddy grey areas, between theoretical idealism and the reality of practice in Kingsley Hall's "experiment in living", therefore, are fertile ground for our focus of enquiry. As we shall see, the experiences of those involved in this open space were neither conclusive, nor entirely positive.

What follows are extracts from Cotton (2008), research that asked: "What relationship, if any, is there between the way we treat people and 'The Treatment' in Psychotherapy?" The research was carried out with Moustakas's (1990) Heuristic method, whereby, by immersing themselves in the research subject and participants' interview data, the researcher encourages a spirit of self-discovery in which aspects of indwelling tacit knowledge might illuminate the research process. The interviews for this research study were semi-structured around the research question and were videotaped for use in a parallel documentary film project about Laing's work, in which all participants had agreed to appear under their actual names. The interview participants were colleagues and/or peers of Laing, with the exception of Gary Cairney, who at the time the interviews were conducted was a resident in Arbours therapeutic community. Gary's experiences of treatment add a valuable context to the experiences of people who were (and most still are) psychotherapeutic practitioners.

Once the interviews had been gathered and transcribed, the data were subjected to six Heuristic (Loewenthal 2007b; Moustakas 1990) steps to arrive at a thematic depiction of the participants' lived experience. These steps begin with Immersion, where the researcher goes back to the data time and again, and Incubation, where the researcher then retreats from the immersion phase, encouraging tacit knowledge to emerge. Returning to the data with new insight, the researcher then begins to reduce the data of each participant into an Individual Depiction, which they feel accurately represents the participant's lived experience in relation to the research question. After further phases of Immersion and Incubation, the researcher gathers each individual depiction into a Composite Depiction that represents the common themes experienced by the group. Extracts of the Composite Depiction from Cotton (2008) now follow, and are clustered around the following five main themes.

1. "Good" treatment involves respecting the Other as an individual.

   This first theme was further divided into two sub-themes:
   a) People are not closed units,
   b) The relationship between darkness and deeper understanding.

2. "Bad" treatment is a consequence of ignoring the Other's individuality.

3. Kingsley Hall attempted to be a model of "good" treatment.
4. Where Kingsley Hall failed to be a model of "good" treatment.
5. Some consequences of "good" treatment lacking clear structures.

In the Heuristic method (Moustakas 1990), Individual Depictions usually precede a broader Composite Depiction in which themes are collated. For issues of space, this phase has been left out here. Additionally, Cotton (2008) used anonymous participant names in accord with the Heuristic method, whereas in this chapter, the actual names have been referred to with full consent of the participants.

1) "Good" treatment involves respecting the Other as an individual

This theme expressed what participants believed was an ideal of "good" treatment at the time of Kingsley Hall. This ideal remained undiminished for participants in relation to the contemporary mental health context (the exception being Gary Cairney, who, as in subsequent thematic groupings, comments on the latter alone).

Chris Mace, Chair of the Psychotherapy Faculty, The Royal College of Psychiatrists, felt that the predominant aspect of "good" treatment was framed by recognizing that:

> "At one level, it's an invitation to be very careful about the impact of everything that the therapist does in their presentation, how they appear, how they behave, on the basis that everything has an impact which may be helpful, may be not helpful."

John Heaton, psychotherapist, particularly interested in the writings of Wittgenstein and an influential early member of Laing's Philadelphia Association, felt more specifically that "good" treatment should stem from the therapist's attempt to enter into a dialogue with the patient's experienced world:

> "If I'm hearing voices, it's far better—instead of telling me I've got schizophrenia and then giving me the drug—to talk to me about what do the voices say, what do they mean, you know: what's it all about, these voices that keep telling me to do this or that? You know, to enter into a dialogue with me and my voices, if you like."

Joe Berke, originally a psychiatrist from New York, was a resident in Kingsley Hall and is the co-founder of the Arbours therapeutic community. Joe offered a contemporary anecdote which described how a patient's behaviour seemed to make no sense when viewed with the expectation of making logical sense. This behaviour, Joe considered, made sense when he attempted to connect with the patient's experienced world instead:

> "There was someone who came here recently who upset one of the therapists by suggesting "could I sniff your underarm?" And then she said, "Can I get into your bed?" Now this is taken to be a kind of, breaking boundaries and inappropriate behaviour. But what the person was really saying—and she was scared—was "can I sniff out the scene here? Can I sniff you out, to see that you're not harmful to me, not threatening to me? Can I lie in your bed, that is, can I be nice, warm, and comfortable, because I think you are?" And if you translate it, into an interpersonal statement, then it makes sense."

Steve Gans, a psychotherapist, came as a philosophy lecturer from the USA, and was involved in developing the Philadelphia Association's Portland Road community. Steve felt that in having the world as they have experienced it heard by a therapist, a patient might be able to hear themselves, perhaps for the first time:

> "I can, sort of, go back to my own therapy. Analysis. And, I felt heard there actually for the first time. … I was able to compare that with what had gone before, so that I can now characterize it. And I would say that people were relating to me from their idea that they had of me and they didn't really see me …"

The significance of feeling heard was voiced clearly from a patient's perspective by Gary Cairney, who believes he was unable to get treatment via the UK's National Health Service because his borderline personality disorder diagnosis was of lower priority to psychiatric services than, for example, schizophrenia. Moreover, Gary felt that this diagnostic rigidity ultimately had a negative impact on a patient's sense of self and identity:

> "You can get into a cycle of negative, or bad acting out, self-destructive behaviours if you get involved with the NHS. Whereas here … [a therapeutic

*community] ... you're seen as more than just a diagnosis. In fact here, they
don't want to talk about your diagnosis, they're not interested, they want
to see you as a person. ... I think there is a common truth to all human
beings, in that when you are treated like a person and when you are treated
like a three-dimensional entity, then it has to have some kind of effect on
how you view yourself and how you are then going to interact with the
rest of the world."*

Rather than focusing on symptoms to be cured via the attempt to accurately frame a diagnosis, Jamie Moran, Principal Lecturer in Psychology at Roehampton University, who participated in one of E. Graham Howe's training groups with Laing in the early 1960s, felt that the therapeutic setting was a healing place where the client's damage could be explored in the relationship itself:

*"People cannot be healed by going off alone, in that sense, because they
have to bring into ..[the therapeutic].. relationship, the harm that was
done, the tangles, the knots, and deal with that within the relationship.
And that's part of what's healing, to be able to embrace the dark side, but
in a new way."*

This emphasis on the destructive potential of relationships introduced two important sub-themes.

a) People are not closed units

In attempting to have a dialogue with the patient's experienced world, participants felt that the therapist must appreciate, what they saw as, the wider context of mental illness—principally, its interpersonal character, whether as an expression of a relationship between two people, members of a family, social groups, or different cultures.

Haya Oakley was involved in setting up the Philadelphia Association's Archway community, and was for many years the PA's chair. Here, she describes her experience of working in a Philadelphia Association community house and an exchange with a Greek Cypriot shop owner who had regular encounters with a particular patient:

*"He said, 'we get this young man coming in here—he sometimes frightens
the customers, but we're not afraid of him—he grabs something, but we
know that somebody will come later and pay for it'. So there's a culture*

where they weren't frightened. Because they weren't frightened, they didn't try to chase him away, they were very relaxed about it. No crisis occurred around it. You know, you can imagine very easily a slightly different cultural context where there would be a major crisis and the police would be called ..."

By extension of this, the therapist is also a member of wider society and therefore, the therapeutic relationship was seen by participants as a crucible for these wider social relationships, as Chris Mace explained:

"The original, Laingian position was that psychiatrists, psychotherapists are agents of society, and the operant "we" is a much bigger "we", so that what you find in the therapy room is some sort of microcosm of something that is being played out in all sorts of similar ways in society."

b) The relationship between darkness and deeper understanding

Participants spoke of a deeper relationship between darkness and joy, which they felt underpinned the interpersonal context of mental illness. The tension between these two opposites seemed to be expressed internally on an individual level (and therefore influencing the interpersonal), as well as existing—crudely speaking—as opposites in separate people in relationships with each other (as the above anecdote about the Greek Cypriot shopkeeper perhaps illustrates). Joe Berke stated:

"Psychotherapy is an attempt to bring some degree of joy into one's life. And you can't have joy without insight, and awareness, and understanding. So it's an attempt to exchange darkness for light, blackness with understanding. Most people find it very difficult. They don't want to understand what goes on in them, or between them and others."

Attempting to split off this darkness was also seen as a denial of true selfhood. On a social level, in investing the power to remove our individual and collective darkness to mental health practitioners, Jamie Moran felt the consequence might be:

"that person has authority, because they say, 'yes, I do know how to fix it. I know how to give you a pill, I know how to give you a religious panacea, I know how to give you political panacea. Do as I say and you will be happy again.' So that's one of the bases for authority. For authoritarianism."

2) "Bad" treatment is a consequence of ignoring the Other's individuality

This second main theme embodied several varying sub-themes that were clustered around the view that failing to enter into some kind of dialogue with the patient's experienced world had a detrimental and sometimes dehumanizing effect. These sub-themes ranged from the difficulty of attempting to observe humans from a scientific perspective, to the unwittingly damaging effects of a medical model of treatment. Like the first theme, this belief applied both to treatment at the time of Kingsley Hall, and to treatment in a contemporary setting, as Steve Gans considered:

> "It means Dia-gnosis in Greek, which means a knowing through, a seeing through, but then it gets perverted from its original Greek into a very diminished sense of that and it becomes a kind of categorization, or objectification process—so the DMS-IV (the fourth edition of the Psychiatric diagnostic manual of mental illnesses) is a very good example of people's attempt to then generalize qualities or characters which they then read back over or lay on a person, saying then this person 'presents' these symptoms and therefore can be diagnosable as, you know, this "disorder ..."

Haya Oakley acknowledged how this diagnostic hermeneutic circle could be used to defend against the therapists' own fear and feelings of helplessness:

> "We're afraid of empty-handed-ness, we're afraid of the despair that some of this creates in us. . . . so it's easy to think of the person suffering from 'a condition' rather than to get to know X and face his despair. . . ."

In some cases, the therapist's need to distance themselves from this fear/despair was seen to potentially damage a patient with an insecure sense of self, who might well embrace the therapist's proffered diagnostic-identity-as-defence, in the absence of any secure alternative, as Gary Cairney found:

> "We all have a relationship with our diagnosis. I have—because ironically, when it comes to these kinds of patients (Borderline Personality Disorder), they don't have much of a sense of self. So once a sense of self is projected onto you—in my case, it was that I was a borderline patient to be feared,

not to be trusted—then that can be quite glamorous and so it gets quite difficult, knowing whether you're the person that you think you are, or the person that they think you are. ... I've seen a lot of people embracing their diagnosis, embracing their pain, seeing themselves in a very one-dimensional way."

Once the diagnosis has been prescribed, Gary Cairney felt that two things may happen. Firstly, it becomes harder for the therapist to see the person beyond the diagnosis. This person and their unique life experiences may, of course, then be at variance with their diagnostic identity, leading to a potential further loss of actual identity:

"Once you've got the diagnosis, you are everything to do with that diagnosis. I've certainly had a lot of things written about me that just aren't true, and they've only made sense once I've read the diagnostic manual ... [DSM-IV]... I'm like 'ah –that's where they're getting this about me, because it tells them in the book. If they see these symptoms, they must therefore assume all these things about me.' And it's not scientifically based."

Secondly, the diagnosis can serve as a mask to obscure complex mechanisms in the patient–therapist relationship. Certain aspects of these mechanisms can feed back into the diagnostic picture and be read as further evidence of the patient's correct diagnosis, as Gary explained:

"... there's a hell of a lot of projection going on in both directions and, you know, it can become a self-fulfilling prophecy if people are saying you're X, Y and Z, sooner or later, you are going to feel that way, especially if you've not got a fully-formed. ... Ego, or superego, kind of, structure."

Some participants, such as Steve Gans, felt that problems with the diagnostic framework were in fact only symptomatic of a broader problem with the scientific perspective:

"From that basis of the bias of science we go to the fact that psychiatrists are really psychopharmacologists, so then that goes hand in hand with the drug industry and the insurance industry and so that's a huge political and economic support that this kind of lends. ... It's very hard then to see through that lens, meaning ... not just be caught in the way you can only

look through the lens, but actually see through the illusion that the lens is actually creating."

This sentiment reflected a largely anti-psychiatric drug stance within the group, as Joe Berke outlined:

[Largactil] *"... was originally developed to induce hypothermia, to put people on ice. They call tranquillizers chemical straight jackets ... to shut them up. 'We don't wanna hear what they have to say; they're too disturbing. They might tell us something about ourselves. They might be mirrors of ourselves.' The treatment is, I think for the most part, is about shutting people up, it's a sadistic attack on people."*

As Gary Cairney described, another perspective was that drugs were a convenient form of containment where there weren't the resources to deal with people's problems individually.

[In hospital] ... *"if you started screaming, or getting upset, someone would come along and say 'what's wrong, what's happening?' And, they look through the window at you and check that you're ok every half an hour/every hour, depending on what symptoms you're exhibiting. But, my experience was that it was just a holding pen. Nothing therapeutically valuable was happening ... if you act out, nine times out of ten, they want to solve it by giving you a pill. So, for example, if I was having a panic attack, they'd give me a Valium. If I couldn't get to sleep, they would give me a sleeping pill. If it got quite serious, they would hold me down, give me Hyperperidol and knock me out."*

Despite the critical stance, some participants felt there was a place for psychiatric drugs. However, in attempting to develop improved drugs for patients who may be taking anti-psychotic medication, Chris Mace acknowledged that:

"I think there is certainly a ..[medical].. bias in the field of treatment research for quite obvious reasons, that where the interest is in finding ways of helping people who are already diagnosed as having schizophrenia to feel less distressed. ... You know, there's an automatic motor fuelling new research of that kind in a way that the people who are interested in developing new psychological treatments don't enjoy."

While several participants felt that the days of anti-psychotic drugs with deeply unpleasant side effects were over, this view was not shared by the one participant, Gary Cairney, who had been prescribed them more recently:

> "I've been on anti-psychotic medication and it's—what it does to you is, um—it's very powerful stuff. It stops you feeling like you, and I was on a tiny amount. ... I thought, 'what on earth does it feel like to be on fourteen milligrams of this stuff?!' So one day, I said, 'well, there's an easy way to find out' and I took five milligrams, which was kind of like a third of the way there. And it was just the most horrible experience for forty-eight hours. The way that I wrote about it in my diary was that I felt evil. It felt that my soul had been taken from me. ... It might deal with the symptoms of the schizophrenia, or the voices, or whatever, but if it robs them of what it is to be human, then that's a question that needs to be explored. And I don't think it is explored enough in the world of psychiatry."

3) Kingsley Hall attempted to be a model of "good" treatment

Having given some consideration to what they felt was an ideal of "good" treatment and what constituted "bad" treatment, participants talked about how at its inception, Kingsley Hall represented the attempt to put these ideals into practice. Prominent themes in this third thematic group were the social context in which Kingsley Hall evolved, both its aims and the hopes people invested in it. As Jamie Moran stated:

> "It always never makes any sense in understanding someone, to ignore what they're fighting against. I mean, many ideas and movements really make no sense unless you know what they're replying to. ... I think, in a way, what was being opposed in those days ... [the 1960s] ... has, in some senses, only got worse today. And that is a kind of way of living which is superficial. It's a kind of a way of living where people build bubbles around themselves and they have a superficial notion of happiness, fulfilment, ambition. It's something that's heavily locked into the capitalist system. It's something that's heavily locked into what I would call 'the abuse of rationality', 'the abuse of reason' to police the surface, and to use reason in such a way that you actually—you know, all the so-called empirical methods of science can be used in this way, that you never look at anything any deeper or more fundamental in life. And the areas in which these deeps

intrude include madness, neurosis, but of course, includes other things as well. It includes mystical experience, or all kinds of things, once you start seeing them, they're there. But this superficial way of living is designed to block all this out and to keep the human defended from depths, and to keep them 'happy' on a very shallow level."

One strong sub-theme expressed how participants experienced the psychiatric profession at the time of Kingsley Hall as being informed by wider society's fear of madness. As John Heaton stated:

"It sounds crazy now but this is absolutely true, that in the fifties and forties, it was often thought to not be a good thing to talk to them (people who had received a schizophrenia diagnosis) very much because you'd just be drawn into a crazy talk, so to speak. You know, it's crazy talk and therefore best not to get involved with. ... There was maybe a fear about it and psychiatrists were just reproducing lay persons' fear of madness."

Paul Zeal became a resident in Kingsley Hall in 1966. After two years living and working there, he began a psychotherapy training and was later involved in setting up the Philadelphia Association's Archway community, along with Haya Oakley. Paul reflected on how during his tenure at Kingsley Hall, families were seen as being a core part of the destructive aspect of society that labelled people as mad:

"What we felt was that the family as an institution was destructive and that society was made of families, therefore society was destructive and that the people who were most destroyed psychically were those who were deemed to be most mad. So if one could hear what they were saying then one might find some sanity."

Kingsley Hall therefore was felt to be a sanctuary, an important place where people could remove themselves from these social agencies and the methods of treatment that claimed to represent them. In this respect, Joe Berke considered Kingsley Hall as an alternative society:

"Kingsley Hall was part of the sixties ... in that context, Kingsley Hall ... [was an] ... alternative place to be if you suffered. And more than that, it was a place to be where suffering could be seen not as something negative but something positive. If you were psychotic, you weren't crazy, you were

going through a trip, and one just had to help you go through this. And so forth. So that was the context for it. The creation of an alternative society. And indeed, at Kingsley Hall, we were creating a revolution."

Kingsley Hall's attitude to treatment was engendered by a sense of wanting to explore a space where people could experience each other beyond what was seen as repressive social structures in society as Paul Zeal explained:

"It was about finding enjoyment in adversity. It was about being intellectually rigorous about what one can see about what was going on. It was about studying and learning from what one saw as going on. It was about allowing a voice for very distressed states of being."

4) Where Kingsley Hall failed to be a model of "good" treatment

In this thematic group, participants described how the utopian ideals embodied in Kingsley Hall could not meet the reality of living in a supposedly leaderless group, where some very disturbed behaviour was acted out—not all of it by the "non-patient" patients. Power structures were inevitably engaged with, but made more destructive by the need to disguise them because they contradicted the community's polemic.

Before October 1966, when it was made illegal, LSD was an established psychopharmacological treatment and was used in Kingsley Hall to induce neo-psychotic states of consciousness which both "non-patients" and "non-therapists" could work through therapeutically—an attempt to fast-track psychical growth. John Heaton described how the reality of LSD use failed to live up to these Utopian aspirations:

"I think many people would say it's … [LSD] … a rather dangerous tool. … Like a lot of these things, it helped people only for a few weeks and then you found, or I found, after a month or two you were rather back to the mundane sort of things that people have to work through."

Haya Oakley described how the egalitarian ideal that LSD would facilitate a shared psychotic experience between "non-patients" and "non-therapists" was similarly debunked:

"To be schizophrenic is not like being on acid, it's not the same. Yes, you can induce a state of paranoid psychosis under the influence of drugs, but then you recover from that."

Moreover, when the ideal that residents, regardless of the degree of their illness, could become well solely on the basis of being freed from the pathological tangles of society and treated as individuals, began to appear to be another Utopian myth, there was a sense of disillusionment, as John Heaton described:

"There was a great excitement that Kingsley Hall would lead to liberation, and if you didn't treat people like psychiatrists treat people, we would all become well and fine. And certainly, there was that sort of myth around. Of course people got disillusioned because it just wasn't true. Some people who at Kingsley Hall I know ... it did them a lot of good, but there were some people who went into mental hospitals."

This revealed a deeper problem with the ideal. Kingsley Hall had a clear discourse in terms of what "good" treatment should incorporate. However, its ideological stance in regard to the rejection of prescriptive notions of diagnosis and delivery of treatment prevented it from being clear about how this "good" treatment should actually be carried out, as Chris Mace outlined:

"... there is something about what could be described as a total approach to treatment. ... That's consistent with an idea that somehow the cumulative effects of the treatment that someone has received, whether it's through society or their families, all other aspects of their personal experience somehow needs to not only stop, but in critical ways, changed. ... That's not quite the same as a related question as to how far the treatment that is then actually provided in situ in the real community is going to do that. It can be intended to do that, but does it?"

Participants such as Steve Gans felt that Kingsley Hall consequentially suffered the inevitable fate of all Utopias:

"There's a great tradition of Utopias and there are great problematics with Utopias. The fact was that it ... [Kingsley Hall] ... was Utopian, and it

had flaws. One of the first Utopias was supposedly the Platonic one: the Republic, and of course, it had huge flaws. This was because it was hugely autocratic."

One of the few Kingsley Hall treatment tenets, the removal of hierarchies, became one of its biggest flaws. The Kingsley Hall "non-hierarchy" was not only unworkable, it created a vacuum that was filled by a covert hierarchy which became all the more confusing when residents had to deny its existence, as Paul Zeal explained:

"It was an early adventure in running a therapeutic community. But, it was polemically outside of that discourse. No staff, no patients, no rules, except the ones arrived at together. But of course, life is made of making rules and transgressing them, and pressing them upon others. And all of that went on."

Jamie Moran stated:

"I don't personally like hierarchy, I don't like it anywhere, I don't like it in churches, I don't like it in politics, I really do not accept it. But I am aware that .... What can happen in an un-hierarchic situation is actually, far from some kind of equal place for everyone being found, simply the biggest ego comes to the fore and it actually becomes the law of the jungle."

While most participants expressed their admiration for Laing the theoretician and healer, for Joe Berke, Laing the person was often seen as the biggest ego on the block.

"I was a naïve, idealistic young man. I thought he ... [Laing] ... was the cat's meow. Everything he did was fantastic. Later on, in retrospect, I realized he liked to play with people. He was a mind-fucker of the first order in other words. He could enter into people, and exchange with people positively or negatively. He was like the mythological trickster. He was a healer and a destroyer. And when he was bored, he'd become a destroyer. When he'd had enough of you, he'd become a destroyer."

Where this unacknowledged hierarchy was rationalized away, or flatly denied, the community demonstrated perfectly the very kind of double binds, knots, and layers of mystification that Laing had recognized in society at large in the first place, as Joe explained:

> "I didn't realize that for my first years I was there. And I didn't understand why I felt so terrible at times in the milieu when everybody was trying to get a piece of him [Laing], and everybody was trying to get close to him, and so forth."

For some participants, such as Chris Mace, this led to a difficult question. Despite all the ideals, who was Kingsley Hall really for? "Non-therapists" or "non-patients"?

> "I think there are many questions about Kingsley Hall, in terms of how it worked, and who the beneficiaries were ... It seemed very quickly to attract importance as a social experiment. So there are a lot of potential gains, even before you come to issues of celebrity and fame and power."

5) Some consequences of "good" treatment lacking clear structures

This thematic grouping consists of issues that participants felt arose as a consequence of the first four thematic groupings. Most people felt that Kingsley Hall as it was in the 1960s would not be possible today. While this didn't manifest in a strong feeling of regret in itself, there was a strong regret that today's society, and today's mental health system in particular, has become over-regulated. This was partially seen as a consequence of the wider social trend of pathologizing existential life issues. Participants feared that the net result of this trend would be ever-increasing restrictions imposed on what they perceived as the more liberal end of the mental health treatment spectrum—psychotherapy.

Above all, participants felt that the lack of partitioning between "abnormal" and "normal" in Kingsley Hall would be considered bad practice today. John Heaton explained:

> "A Kingsley Hall place would be impossible now. If you tried to do that sort of thing, you would be sent to prison probably, or certainly thrown off the medical register .... Kingsley Hall was a place where, as Ronnie said, there was no treatment. You had some, shall we say, relatively normal,

if one can use that word, and a few very crazy people, all mixed together,
a sort of hodge-podge. It would be thought now as very … it just wouldn't
be allowed. It would be just out of the question."

Haya Oakley described her frustration when trying to set up a new therapeutic community, the ethos of which seemed lost on the local authority she was negotiating with.

"I mean, the number of times we tried to set up a house in Oxford. The
number of meetings …. I mean, trying to explain to institutionally
minded people that the whole idea was to encourage communal living and
a communal kitchen that was part and parcel of, you know, the therapeutic
environment. No, they wanted you to be able to lock your door, have your
own sink in the corner of your—so on and so on."

Another sub-theme was the feeling that one legacy left by the more liberal end of the psychotherapy spectrum has been a disengagement from mental health treatment politics, thereby excluding itself from the debate about diagnostic systems, as Haya Oakley explained:

"There's been a sort of recoiling from you know, the notion of a diagnosis
in its "good" intention—and not just good intention, its good usage."

Further, Haya found the consequences of retreating from issues of regulation were seen as opening the way for regulatory needs to be prioritized over patients' needs.

"… we are already being forced into boxes that we do not fit into, you
know. Of having to create psychiatric diagnosis. Having to dispense treat-
ment plans, you know, having to inform our psychoanalytic patients in
advance what they are to expect in analysis, instead of it being what it is,
which is a mystery to all, and so on. Having people who work with the
mentally ill, (be) more worried about their responsibility to the safety of
the public, than the wellbeing of their patients, you know, sort of security
measures become—I mean, it's like politics at large."

Lack of public engagement was seen as extending into the psychotherapeutic community's lack of engagement with political aspects of mental health issues. This seemed to find particular expression in the 2006

Bill (Department of Health 2006) to reform the 1983 Mental Health Act, which proposes enforced treatment in some cases where patients are deemed to be a threat to others, or to themselves.

A final sub-theme was the desire for more vigorous and open debate on what constitutes mental illness, as Gary Cairney described:

> "We're on the verge of a big, big, big revolution—and now it sounds like I'm barking mad—but er, they're going to find, there's going to be big discoveries and both with talking cures, existential stuff and also with pharmaceutical interventions …. 'Cos ironically at this moment in time, even the psychological therapists, they don't know very much about whether it's nature, nurture, you know, they can't answer very simple questions. And that's not me criticizing them, it's just the fact that they don't know the answer.'"

Discussion

What emerged from the analysis of the participants' interviews is the feeling that therapists need to adhere to diagnostic categories, and therefore treat patients as a collection of symptoms, rather than as individuals, had an essentially dehumanizing effect. This in turn was felt to have a negative effect on the patients' psychological wellbeing. This is borne out from a patient's perspective by Gary Cairney, since for him, diagnosis also seemed to serve the function of closing down a space where difficult questions might be asked about the relative roles of client and therapist, and how this affected his treatment. His experiences also illustrate how an uncritical system of treatment has the potential to compound suffering, rather than alleviate it. It also speaks of how, in focusing on the symptom, treatment places an emphasis on symptom management, rather than exploring and alleviating the forces that might create the symptom.

It is interesting that psychoanalysis—as capable as any other system of diagnosis of trapping itself in a hermeneutic circle—was not seen to be part of this diagnostic problem. Perhaps this is to be expected from a cohort who, broadly speaking, have practised at one time or another with a psychoanalytic perspective.

In many ways, Kingsley Hall may have suffered from the vacuum left behind after this diagnostic problem (psychoanalytic, psychiatric, or otherwise) had been, in appearance at least, dismantled. The aspiration to have no system meant that it seemed as though Kingsley Hall lost itself in the profound confusion of adhering to an unacknowledged system whose existence had to be denied to keep the "non-system" system intact. It sounds like a classic "Laingian Knot" (Laing 1970), and it might well be. If nothing else, in attempting to purge the treatment setting of the hierarchies, double binds, knots, and layers of mystification that he found in wider society, and succeeding in unwittingly acting them out in Kingsley Hall, Laing seemed to have inadvertently proved his theory.

Yet mental health treatment doesn't exist within a Utopian bubble. Institutions that deliver treatment, receive funding, and sustain careers are subject to myriad economic, political, and cultural forces. They need to be seen to be delivering something. Out of these needs arises the desire to deliver reliable systems. Tellingly perhaps, how "good" treatment should be delivered was therefore often defined by participants in terms of what it should not be: i.e., "bad" treatment. Despite Laing's contribution in claiming that "the psychoses are intelligible" (Bentall 2005: 227), was his failure to create a credible alternative system of treatment the most important factor in laying his legacy so open to attack (ibid: 239)?

Perhaps the central question here might be less about the style of treatment system we operate, and more a question about systems that are resistant to critique? Despite Laing's attempt to keep open a space for reflection, he could be as resistant to criticism as the orthodoxies he was challenging. Being—to use current cultural values—"reflective and transparent" about the way we treat each other as individuals and how that affects treatment is often counter-intuitive in the real world, not least because revealing how we might be doing something wrong conflicts with the vested interest of needing to prove how we are doing things right. The same problem faces mainstream institutions and counter-culture iconoclasts alike, and Laing's projection of Utopian ideals into the "open space" was no different from the ideologies projected by the former. But with Laing consigned to the lunatic fringe by mainstream health, in the current drive towards psychotherapeutic monoculture, perhaps nowhere is the issue of system critique more difficult than in the current politics of evidence-based research. If we're being critical of what's not working, we run the risk of losing authority, influence, and funding. It is understandable, then, that these all too human vested interests lead to theories becoming orthodoxies, which, in turn, "are about power, not truth" (Smail 2007: 13).

Whether it is the current preoccupation with the medical model's promise of certainty, or the hegemony enjoyed by biological psychiatry in the first half of the twentieth century (and arguably once again in recent times, thanks in part to genetic and neurobiological research), mental health has long been susceptible to orthodoxies, as Bleuler's above letter to Freud (Bleuler, in Bentall 2004) illustrates. However, perhaps more now than ever, based on these ideologies, we live in an age when "idioms of the psychological and the psychiatric replace Christianity and humanism as the ways of making sense of self" (Porter 2002: 218). Where these idioms verge on what Hayek terms the "scientistic"—as distinct from scientific in claiming to know the most appropriate way of investigating its subject before considering what the subject is (Hayek 1979: 24)—then these idioms risk sliding into the very kind of subjectivity that science seems to find so problematic. Whichever the case, there is a point where "rationality" to the exclusion of all else becomes the exact irrational "faith" that these idioms may have unwittingly usurped.

Crucially, this faith seems to play directly into what appears to be a persistent muddling between the study of mechanism and the pursuit of cause. "Drunk on the extraordinary power" of new technologies (Rose 2005: 4), the neurogenetic industry can present reams of data to show the biological mechanisms of psychopathology, and somehow make the leap that this demonstrates cause. This is rather like pointing a high-powered satellite at the UK's M5 motorway and observing the flow of traffic in order to analyse a phenomenon called "rush-hour". The trouble is, no matter how much the technology is refined, without actually asking the drivers why they get in their cars in the first place, one can only ever end the research journey in a hermeneutic cul-de-sac. This leads to the assumption that the observed traffic mechanism (or neurological activity), and the cause of "rush-hour" are one and the same. This conveniently negates the argument that "meaning is not in the brain, but only in the interaction between the living human being and its natural social environment" (Fuchs 2005: 208), and perhaps reveals the fear that the problem is not "in the individual, but in the social and psychic order" instead (Rose 2005: 6).

Hoarding all our eggs in this research basket creates a powerful bias towards mechanistic, biological assumptions of mental illness, and therefore fuels a disposition towards the rigid attachment to symptom and diagnosis. It is perhaps understandable that in this era of late modernism, we should be tempted to assume that there is a technological answer for all the problems we face; yet the attempt to divorce these problems from their social contexts, and isolate them in the individual "pathology" of the Other, has a worrying ring of marching jackboots to it.

Implications for theory in practice

Does the "phenomenological research" contained in this chapter present a different kind of basket in which to place eggs, or is it merely the same basket with a different weave? With this in mind, the following attempts to relate the above research to practice.

The Kingsley Hall community may have demonstrated that whether one works with a system of diagnostic labels, or a "non-system" of "non-labels", when this system (or "non-system") ceases to regard the Other's experience with phenomenological openness, then this experience becomes co-opted into the ongoing maintenance of the system's (or "non-system's) epistemological support structures, and the Otherness of the individual becomes invariably lost. Jacqui Dillon, Chair of the Hearing Voices Network, England, a service-user-led nationwide support network for voice hearers, offers an illustration of this paradigm. Hospitalized in her mid-twenties during a traumatic breakdown in which she was assailed by threatening voices and hallucinations, she tried to explain to her consultant psychiatrist that she felt she understood what was happening to her. When she suggested that the voices were replaying the sexual abuse she had suffered as a child, she was told that not only was she describing a symptom of her "schizophrenia", but that dozens of other patients had described similar "delusions".

> What I was experiencing was never considered to be a natural and human response to things that had happened in my life. The fact that I listened to my voices was evidence of my illness, and wanting to keep them in order to understand more about myself was seen as me being resistant to treatment.
>
> (Dillon, in Romme 2009: 190)

Laing would no doubt have been vitriolic about the injustice of this double bind, and might well have remarked how the rigid adherence to a diagnostic label and subsequent treatment pathway resulted in treatment that mirrored the abuse. But had Laing presided over a mainstream system of mental health treatment—instead of playing the role of its iconoclastic scourge—would he really have fared better? This is not an entirely idle question, considering the difficulties he seemed to experience when attempting to live up to his own polemic in the day-to-day reality of Kingsley Hall.

Thanks in no small part to pressure from service-user-led organizations, such as the Hearing Voices Network, there has been a recent gravitation from symptom management to recovery in the treatment model for psychosis. Yet the question remains (as in all areas of psychological distress), how this new "recovery model" (Ramon, Healy & Renouf 2007) should be delivered. In relation to the wider question of mental health treatment, Barlow suggests that "to ensure psychology's seat at the health care table, psychologists would do well to clearly distinguish treatments that are targeted at certain well-defined pathologies by calling them "psychological treatments" at which point only psychologists would possess "the in-depth training in cognitive and behavioural sciences and their application (5+ years) to put them in a unique position to develop these treatments" (Barlow 2005: 734). Such naked tribalism masks the fact that despite all of the prolific medical model-aligned psychotherapeutic outcome research, there is very little evidence to show that it provides any more "useful framework for conceptualizing psychotherapy" or specific psychotherapeutic interventions than any of the other modes of psychotherapy (Wampold 2001: 204). Worse, this "Slavish adherence to a theoretical model and maniacal promotion of a single theoretical approach are utterly in opposition to science" (Wampold 2001: 217).

With the rise of the neuro-genetic research industry, which often begins its investigation—and reaches its conclusion—from within the framework of diagnostic assumptions, the need for philosophical scepticism is greater than ever before. In this respect, in their eagerness to sit at the same "empirically validated, scientific" table as the neuro-genetic research industry, medical-model-aligned orientations of psychotherapy risk driving around in circles in the same hermeneutic cul-de-sac.

Let us not be under any illusions, however, that the research contained in this chapter doesn't fall into the exact same hermeneutic cul-de-sac. In attempting to arrive at Composite Depictions of the research participants' experience, how much of their meaning has been reduced, compressed, and ultimately transformed one way or another by the "interpretation" of the researcher? In this sense, is it really possible to psychologize phenomenology into "phenomenological research", or does the project become yet another "methodolatry" (McLeod 2001: 100)—or worse, a methodolatry in denial? Put another way, while from a phenomenological perspective, we may seek to ask the drivers on the allegorical M5 motorway mentioned above what compels them to get in their cars in the first place, are we able to hear what they say before we rush to create yet another totalizing conclusion about what it was we thought they meant?

Is it possible to exit this cul-de-sac? David Smail suggests that one approach might be an inversion of the medical model approach to research. Rather than developing theories that we attempt to validate through practice, we would do better to adapt our theories to what we encounter clinically—rather like the true spirit of science (as opposed to scientism) challenges us to do in the first place. Thereby, the clinical observation that: "we are not in control of our conduct; therapeutic change is not demonstrable", could be answered by: "Need to identify the causes of conduct beyond personal agency. These are likely to be biological as well as social." Likewise, when we find: "The causes of our conduct are frequently mysterious, and rationally unalterable", we need to respond with the theoretical flexibility to recognize that: "Rationalist explanations are insufficient; need to account for the disjunction between conduct and the accounts we give of it" (Smail 2007: 23–25).

Thomas & Bracken note that despite all the "assumptions, priorities, meanings and values" employed in "psychiatric technologies … a great deal of their success is determined by the relationships in which they play a role" (Thomas & Bracken 2005: 168). Gelso & Carter (1994) found this relationship to have a pivotal role in treatment, yet also found that it was the most under-researched aspect of treatment. Wampold found that the "common factors" between modalities, embodied in this relationship, were really responsible for "psychotherapeutic benefits rather than the ingredients specific to the particular theories" (Wampold 2001: 23). He suggests as a way of moving beyond the "research design bias" of the medical model (Wampold 2001: 214), psychotherapy might benefit from adopting a "contextual model", which "emphasizes a holistic common factors approach" and, "provides an alternative metatheory for psychotherapy" (Wampold 2001: 30).

Might then a post-existential framework open a space where we can think about these intersubjective issues of culture, power, language, and experience from a critical point of view, while attempting to retain our focus on the "face of the Other" (Levinas 1989: 82), who entreats us to ethical responsibility, rather than the self-interested concerns of the "I"? In so doing, can we resist the temptation to weave what we find in this open space into yet another totalizing theory? And what about a place for post-existentialist research? Can phenomenological research enable this "open space", or do research methods, such as the method of Heuristic research, as in this chapter, do a similar injustice to the Other?

Conclusion

In questioning possible relationships between psychotherapeutic treatment and the way we treat one another as individuals, we are engaging with one of the oldest debates in history: how should we organize society and, based on that, how should we treat one another? The reason it is one of the oldest questions is because it also happens to be one of the most difficult questions for any non-totalitarian society to address. By turn, it is also one of the most difficult questions to ask when applied to society's relationship with the type of behaviour we consider "in need of treatment". Should human psychological suffering be separated off into pathological disorders contained within the individual, or should it be treated as an extension of the existential, intersubjective problems that are inherent in the experience of being human? Either way, those who offer psychotherapeutic treatment need to ask rigorous questions of themselves. Is our mental health system analogous with a progressive society where the possibility of relationships between treatment and the way we treat people is able to be critically examined, or is it analogous with a closed society in which self-examination is seen as a threat? If the latter is true, then as Szasz warns, we invest our mental health care systems with the power to employ "an array of therapeutic prohibitions and prescriptions of truly Orwellian proportions" (Szasz 1988: 191–192). In this sense, using David Smail's inversion of the medical model's approach to research as an analogue, rather than asking how we should treat one another based on our organization of society; perhaps we might ask instead how we should organize our society based on how we should treat one another.

In terms of being able to engage in forms of psychotherapy within the burgeoning structures of state regulation that truly put the Other's experience first, we find ourselves trapped in a Catch-22. Prescriptive treatment structures advocated by, for example, the medical model have the potential to dehumanize patients, downplay the importance of relationship, and discourage thinking about the myriad factors that feed into human experience; yet without engaging to one degree or another with this discourse, psychotherapy may increasingly find itself unable to provide any kind of treatment at all.

Many of these problems go to the heart of the interpersonal dynamics of the therapeutic encounter itself and seem to ask: "as we move from God to Science to the person … is the person the new God and which person is it: the researcher or the researched?" (Loewenthal 2007b: 223). If so, we would do well to remember that "the category of 'I' is philosophically meaningless without its complimentary category of 'you'" (Laing, Phillipson & Lee 1969: 3). In the same way that Laing attempted to open himself to the *Dasein* of the individual's psychosis by exploring the ever-problematic intersubjective weave between "I" and "you", might a post-existential stance help us remain open to the *Dasein* of the liminal space between what we consider to be treatment and how we treat people as individuals? If so, then the Levinasian entreaty to put the "you" before—not just in complement to—"I", might well be central.

CHAPTER SEVEN

Post-existentialism, counselling psychology, and the diagnosis of schizophrenia

Patrick Larsson and Del Loewenthal

Introduction

This chapter will explore some implications of post-existentialism for counselling psychology with a particular focus on diagnostic categories. Issue will be taken with Cooper's (2009) argument that the question of diagnoses in counselling psychology has been extensively debated in the literature. Even though Cooper's assertion that we need to "welcome—and work with—the richness and vastness of clients beyond their diagnoses" (p. 122) is one which should be encouraged by counselling psychologists—is this possible in practice?

There is the question of how counselling psychologists retains its "value base within a framework dominated by a medical model of distress" (Douglas 2010: 24) whilst making further inroads into the National Health Service (NHS) as practitioner psychologists. This chapter reviews the literature that pertains to the topic of counselling psychology and diagnostic categories, and critically examines the place of post-existentialism in relation to this issue.

The chapter also presents research carried out by interviewing qualified counselling psychologists who have experience of working with individuals with a diagnosis of "schizophrenia". The results of this are arguably both encouraging and worrying. They are encouraging in that the individuals who were interviewed appear to have found a way of relating to the experience of the individual and using this relationship in their therapeutic work to great effect. What is perhaps worrying is that there sometimes appears to be an almost subversive element to their work, whereby the "relational" stance they take to their clients needs be hidden and disguised using medical discourse. Even though this chapter will look at counselling psychology specifically, these issues may find resonance with psychological therapists in general. As such it is our duty as psychological therapists to challenge psychiatric categories and diagnoses even though this may lead to forms of psychological therapist conflict (Golsworthy, 2004). Loewenthal (2008) argues that with post-existentialism we should now be raising questions about the power, knowledge, and political nature of psychology.

Brief history

Throughout the 1800s, psychology emerged as a distinct discipline of its own. During this time, psychologists adopted the scientific and philosophical foundations of the time into practice, as mental illness was treated with a variety of approaches believed to have specific efficacious effects. The treatment of the 'mentally ill' began in the institutions, and it was not until Freud advocated what became known as talking therapy in the form of psychoanalysis that care administered in hospitals and other institutions shifted to home-based treatment (Cohen, 1993).

Decades later, behaviourism would follow psychoanalysis as the next treatment for psychological disorders, based on the reductionist, deterministic theories of Watson, Skinner, and their contemporaries (Wampold 2001a). By the 1950s, the influence of dynamic, humanistic, and other theories led many psychotherapists to abandon what was known as the medical model ideology and seek new, psychosocial understandings of mental problems. The medical model argues that mental disorders exist *a priori* and through empirical research their respective aetiologies can be identified and ascribed pharmacological interventions (Cosgrove 2005). Rogers was one of the founders of what was to become the humanistic movement, which opposed the ideas of psychoanalysis and behaviourism by emphasizing optimal functioning as opposed to pathology and a conceptualization of the person as an individual "self" (McLeod 2003).

Counselling psychology emerged as a distinct profession in the 1990s, and in 1994 was officially recognized by the British Psychological Society (BPS) as having a unique identity and philosophy of practice (Corrie & Callahan 2000). As defined by the British Psychological Society's Division of Counselling Psychology Psychological Therapist Practice Guidelines (2006), counselling psychology emphasizes a "value base grounded in the primacy of the counselling or psychotherapeutic relationship", and within this suggests that we are "not to assume the automatic superiority of any one way of experiencing, feeling, valuing and knowing" and will "challenge the views of people who pathologize on the basis of such aspects as sexual orientation, disability, class origin or racial identity and religious and spiritual views". Counselling psychology differed from psychotherapy (Jacobs 2000) and counselling (Dryden, Mearns & Thorne 2000) by accreditation route and psychological therapist practice being grounded in the scientist-practitioner model (Lane & Corrie 2006), as well as by placing an emphasis on psychology as the knowledge base of the discipline (Barkham 1990).

The uniqueness of counselling psychology has as its core a "respect for the personal, subjective experience of the client over and above notions of diagnosis, assessment and treatment, as well as the pursuit of innovative, phenomenological methods for understanding human experience" (Lane & Corrie 2006: 17). Grounded in a philosophy of non-pathologizing, or a reluctance to use labels to describe client difficulties, and a respect for the uniqueness of each individual and their self-actualizing tendencies, counselling psychology became a part of the "third force" which aimed to challenge the prevailing orthodoxies of psychoanalysis and behaviourism (Rizq 2008). Because of this, counselling psychology has been described as being relational in nature as it places the therapeutic relationship at its core over therapeutic technique (e.g., O'Brien 2010).

With this philosophical position came an inherent objection to the medical model of psychology and the use of the American Psychiatric Association's (APA) Diagnostic and Statistical Manual of Mental Disorders (APA 2000), hereafter DSM, as a means of pathologizing clients' distress. Counselling psychology sought to distinguish itself from clinical psychology and other better-established psychological therapist domains within psychology in order to legitimize itself as a unique domain of knowledge and practice (Pugh & Coyle 2000). Other contentious issues (James & Bellamy 2010) augmenting counselling psychology's psychological therapist positioning include the debate on evidence-based practice (Milton 2003), the use of psychometric testing for assessment and the measurement of psychological problems (Kanellakis 2003), and the use of diagnostic categories to describe client difficulties (Strawbridge & James 2001; Turner-Young 2003).

In many of these debates, counselling psychology has attempted to construct a position on these issues that is distinctive to itself. However, this has raised some difficult questions for counselling psychology as it faces the reality of working in psychological therapist settings that are dominated by the medical model. As Bury & Strauss (2006) asked: how, if at all, can the use of diagnostic labels in practice be reconciled with counselling psychology's humanistic value base? How should counselling psychology position itself, as a profession, in relation to matters such as diagnosis, psychological testing and standardized approaches to "treatment" delivery (Lane & Corrie 2006)? Woolfe (1996) argued that the scientist-practitioner model was essential to the formation of the discipline: "Counselling psychology, therefore, can be seen as located in a pivotal position between narrow scientism on the one hand and a failure to take sufficient account of a scientific method on the other" (p. 11). As Corrie & Callahan (2000) argued, if counselling psychology is to further develop within the NHS, it must embrace the ideology of "evidence-based" practice and conform to the role of the scientist-practitioner model.

However, some argue that the scientist-practitioner model cannot capture the essence of the therapeutic relationship that is integral to the work of counselling psychologists, and the model is in danger of driving counselling psychology towards the "scientism" it aimed to challenge in the first place (Carter 2002). With the NHS increasingly becoming a common source of employment for counselling psychologists (Bor & du Plessis 1997), where psychiatric classification is the dominant language for discussing and thinking about an individual's difficulties (Golsworthy 2004), counselling psychologists might find themselves in a position where they will have to adopt a medical discourse. Hage (2003) argues that the process of counselling psychologists moving away from focusing on issues of health and adaptation and moving towards aetiology and pathology has already begun. This process contributes to what has been called the "great psychotherapy debate" (Wampold 2001b) raging between the medical model and the contextual model, whereby the contextual model would aim to promote the demedicalization of psychology while at the same time develop a suitable alternative (Pérez-Álvarez & García-Montes 2007). As Golsworthy (2004) argued, this is an ongoing and timely debate within the profession of counselling psychology at a moment when psychological understanding and methods are beginning to have greater political recognition, and that a move towards the medical model could threaten the very attributes that make counselling psychology distinctive (Lane & Corrie 2006).

Golsworthy (2004) argued that counselling psychology is situated within a clash of culture with regard to the medical model; on the one hand, the Division of Counselling Psychology Psychological Therapist Practice Guidelines (2006) argues that counselling psychologists should not pathologize or discriminate in terms of behaviour while at the same time engage in the language of the DSM, which assumes a set of normative behaviour. He argues that it is the counselling psychologist's job to empower rather than to control, and in order to do this,

> ... we need to take our educative role seriously: our clients have the right to be informed about powerful systems that affect the way their distress is conceptualized and the relationship of this to drug (and other) treatments. We can assist our clients in understanding the implications for them of diagnosis, allowing them to make decisions about their care from a position of knowledge.
>
> (p. 27)

As Rizq (2007) pointed out, this debate might seem to belong to one of the tired old dualisms that dominate the landscape of psychological theory; however, in the context of the philosophy of counselling psychology, these questions are essential, for as Kinderman (2009) argued: "The future of counselling psychology relies on what perception is dominant" (p. 20).

The medical model debate and diagnostic categories

The medical model has a perceived history dating back to antiquity, but it was not until the Renaissance when mental illness was seen in a different light, and individuals such as Pinel in the 1700s based their theories of organic mental disorders on the renewed interest in the human sciences while paralleled by a reliance on naturalistic explanations of human behaviour (Kyziridis 2005). This laid the foundations for a set of fundamental assumptions regarding the nature of mental disorders, including: that they were naturally occurring categories; that they were inherited categories with a predictable deteriorating course; and that the symptoms of mental illness were caused by diseases of the brain and the nervous system (Pilgrim 2007).

During this time of reason, society sought to rid itself of the "unreasonable", giving rise to the asylums which would house them and the psychological therapists who sought to "cure" them: psychiatry was the direct product of this act (Bracken & Thomas 2001). The framework for the organization of mental disorders was developed particularly by Kraepelin in the late 1800s, who contributed the most to the foundation of the modern concept of "schizophrenia", then known as *dementia praecox* and later given its current name by Bleuler (Adityanjee, Aderibigbe, Theodoridis, & Vieweg, 1999; Andreasen 1997). Kraepelin's organization of mental distress supported the idea that that distress can be legitimately and accurately categorized (Boyle 1999), thus laying the foundations for diagnosis and the eventual development of the DSM (Cooper 2004), also known as a neo-Kraepelinian approach (Double 1990). The modern assumptions of the medical model of mental distress have been outlined by Scheff (1999), including: causes of mental illness are largely biological; types of mental illness can be classified using the DSM; and mental illness can be treated safely and effectively with psychoactive drugs. The manualized approach to mental distress through the DSM also resulted in the legitimization of a profession whose sole responsibility lay in diagnosing and treating individuals considered mentally ill; psychiatrists became the custodians of the medical model and continued to conceptualize distress using medical terminology, thus treating mental disorders like they would any other physical disease or illness, through drugs, surgery, and other forms of physical and organic interventions (Laungani 2002).

The medicalization of distress and the use of diagnostic labels placed the source of distress firmly within the individual; this may foreclose consideration of the social context and interpersonal relations as sources of unhappiness or dysfunction (Hare-Mustin & Marecek 2001). As a result of the medical model, psychological theory has proposed a neat division of mental states: the neurotic (normal anxiety) and the psychotic (madness); this allows psychological therapists to differentiate between the "worried well" and the "insane", and it is this division that determines the type of treatment received, with the neurotic receiving counselling and psychotherapy, and the psychotic receiving drug treatment, electro-convulsive therapy, and hospitalization (Marshall 2004). However, the medical model's problem focus, which places the problem within the individual, and the failure to include more recursive causality, is inconsistent with counselling psychology's identity and values (Eriksen & Kress 2006).

The use of a medical model of mental distress has encouraged the development of diagnostic categories, with the most prevalent diagnostic manuals used being the DSM and the World Health Organization's International Statistical Classification of Diseases and Related Health Problems Mental Disorders chapter (WHO 1994), hereafter ICD. The DSM and the ICD have been seen as being reliable and operational tools that have greatly facilitated practice, teaching, and research by providing better delineation of syndromes (Üstün, Chatterji & Andrews 2002) and have provided a common language for mental health clinicians and researchers to communicate about mental disorders (Regier, First, Marshall & Narrow 2002). The DSM was developed as a classification system to be used for the diagnosis of mental illness, and it has now become the lingua franca for the entire culture and economy of the mental health establishment (Wylie 1995). Its development went hand in hand with the development of psychiatry and clinical psychology as professions, and in some ways helped to justify their psychological therapist existence. As Bentall (2004: 62) highlights:

> In the USA, the manual was widely embraced both by psychiatrists and psychologists fearful that, without a DSM-III diagnosis for each of their patients, payment from health insurance companies would not be forthcoming. Many journals would not accept papers for publication unless investigators could reassure their readers that the patients studied had been diagnosed according to the DSM-III system, thus ensuring that the criteria became the standard among researchers, not only in America but also elsewhere in the world.

The use of the DSM became firmly entrenched in the world of mental health theory and practice; and in the case of psychiatry and psychology, the DSM became a justification for existence as it anchored their practice in the medical world, ensuring funding and respectability as professions; it was psychiatry and psychology as a form of industrialization.

Theories, assumptions, and methods do not exist independently of those who use them in their activities; mainstream psychologists, and others whose activities depend upon psychology's status quo, will often have a psychological therapist interest in supporting and maintain particular forms of knowledge (Nightingale & Neilands 2001). This industrialization worked alongside the pharmacological approach to mental health problems, leading to the argument that "Pharmaceutical companies are actively involved in sponsoring the definition of diseases and promoting them to both prescribers and consumers. The social construction of illness is being replaced by the corporate construction of disease" (Moynihan, Heath & Henry 2002: 886).

The use of these manuals has come under fierce criticism, particularly the DSM, due to its regular use in mental health practice, with arguments targeting the idea of "diagnosing" mental health problems as if they were "diseases", "illnesses", or "disorders":

> These claims are suspect because they smuggle into existence the problematic terms "disease" and "illness" and give the false impression that there exist "out there" readily recognizable phenomena called diseases which naturally form the subject matter of psychiatry.
>
> (Boyle 2005: 86–87)

Diagnostic categories have been accused of being little more than attempts to confirm current psychiatric practice rather than classifications based on empirical studies (Scheff 1999). The greatest problem with diagnostic categories is that they end up creating their own objectivity, when to the contrary they are largely socially constructed (Pérez-Álvarez & García-Montes 2007). Service users have also criticized the use of diagnostic categories to describe their difficulties, whereby there is a feeling that diagnoses are value judgements that serve to alienate the individual diagnosed leading to a sense of powerlessness and victimization (Campbell 2007). People who hear voices have started challenging the medical model of "schizophrenia" and have attempted to develop new coping strategies that exclude the extensive use of medication (e.g., May 2007; Romme & Escher 1993). An attempt to integrate the DSM with counselling psychology has been argued as being incongruent with the developmental and contextual identity of the profession

(Eriksen & Kress 2006); however, it has also been argued that opposing the DSM is futile due to its political nature (Sequeira & van Scoyoc 2002), and by doing this counselling psychologists are in danger of becoming marginalized psychological therapeutically and financially within the mental health system. This issue is crucial to counselling psychologists as they are confronted with a moral-political choice about where their allegiance should lie, while at the same time avoiding being located themselves within a diagnostic system due to their own resistance to diagnostic categories (Parker 1999).

The medical model is the dominant conceptual model for the understanding of "schizophrenia"; individuals diagnosed with "schizophrenia" are "in most cases called 'patients', reside in 'hospitals', and are 'diagnosed', given a 'prognosis', and 'treated', all a reflection of this dominance" (Furnham & Bower 1992: 201). The medical concept of "schizophrenia" is justified and maintained through the use of medical discourse; discourse refers to patterns or regularities in the way we talk or write (and, by implication, think) about particular phenomena; the idea of "schizophrenia" is written and spoken about by mental health psychological therapists as if it reflected a reality already discovered, or just about to be discovered (Boyle 2005). Discourse is not simply about words; instead, the way we speak or write about an "object" in a particular way is to "construct" and make seem reasonable a particular version of reality (e.g., "schizophrenia" is a biological disorder and can be diagnosed), and this invites or makes reasonable particular kinds of actions or responses (e.g., individuals diagnosed with "schizophrenia" should therefore be treated with medication) (Boyle 2005).

Through discourse, "schizophrenia" is often presented as the last bastion of mental illness with a neurobiological basis; however, it is problematic to assume that there are essences or inherent qualities that would represent the truth of his or her abnormality, as far from being an a human essence, abnormality is considered a construction (Pérez-Álvarez & García-Montes 2007); as Zachar (2001, 2003) states, mental disorders such as "schizophrenia" are not natural kinds, but rather practical kinds constructed on a pragmatic basis. Available discourses on conditions such as "schizophrenia" are not equal in power, with some being more hegemonic or unitary; that is they assume the status of facts and they are considered true and accurate descriptions of the world (Turner 1995). Medical discourse, and the use of diagnoses in particular, has been shown to be a powerful hegemonic discourse that serves to determine the criteria for normality, to define what is considered valid knowledge, who has access to this knowledge, and how this knowledge can be communicated and to whom (Samson 1995). The use of psychiatric diagnoses objectifies the individual who has been diagnosed, provides subject positions that are constraining, pathologizes and disempowers, and limits the individual's freedom to position themselves in relation to other discourses (Sampson 1993). Similarly, counselling psychologists might also find themselves constrained by the same medical discourse that constrains the individual who has been diagnosed, whereby they "fall victim to the mystification of medical knowledge in psychiatric vocabulary and discourse" (Hook & Parker 2002: 52).

Dominant discourses privilege versions of social reality that accord with and reinforce existing social structures and the networks of power relations associated with them. Analysts study the availability of discursive resources within a culture and the implications that this carries for those living within that culture (Coyle 2006). While discourses legitimate and reinforce existing social and institutional structures, these structures, in turn, also support and validate the discourses (Willig 2008); Foucault took the position that discourse has no inside (in thought, ideas, opinions) and no outside (in things that words refer to) (Kendall & Wickham 1999). Discourses have no "truth value". They are not true or false. "Schizophrenia" is not an idea that exists in the minds of psychiatrists or outside in the bodies of people. Rather, it appears (is inscribed) historically, and intangibly, as something that lies on the surface of an interconnected web of statements and techniques. Thus, "schizophrenia" becomes visible (and changing) through statements (the sayable) about the nature of "schizophrenia" (for example, as biological dysfunction or psychological disturbance) and statements are produced through the visibilities of techniques (for example, medication or psychotherapy).

As Gergen (1999) argued, "structures of language are used to build favored realities" (p. 64), which are then supported through the desirability of "conditions" such as "schizophrenia". Boyle (2005) pointed out that this maintenance is pursued by both psychiatry and the public, whereby the idea of "schizophrenia" as a medical condition helps in maintaining links between psychiatry and the medical profession, thus legitimizing the pursuit of "schizophrenia" as a hallmark of psychological therapist identity. For the public, the concept of "schizophrenia" as a biological disorder helps to absolve the "victim", their relatives, and society in general:

> ... by providing a name, a label, psychological therapists convey the powerful and comforting message that they are familiar with these behaviours and experiences, that they have seen them before and (it is implied) have some understanding of them. "Schizophrenia" is therefore a highly seductive label, for psychological therapists, for relatives, for the public and for those whose behaviour has given cause for concern.

> (Boyle 2005: 242)

This draws attention to how the power constituted by discursive and institutional bases is productive of psychological therapist positions, and illuminates how a certain discursive/institutional domain delimits the way in which such problems may be understood (Hook & Parker 2002).

Counselling psychology and psychiatric diagnoses

Douglas (2010) argued that the location of counselling psychology practice has changed since the 1990s, with a move towards working in statutory organizations and mental health services within the NHS. One of the questions raised because of this move, she suggests, is how to retain counselling psychology's,

> ... value base within a framework dominated by a medical model of distress in which treatment guidelines focus on disorder, in which the burgeoning industry of manualized, protocol-based therapy for specific disorder and is promulgated, and in which therapy could be argued to be the adjunct to the politics of employment. Within such a framework therapies, and their research bases, are premised on the notion of disorder and its classification.

> (p. 24)

This appears to be one of the central questions when considering counselling psychology's relationships with diagnostic categories such as "schizophrenia", and was also asked by Bury & Strauss

(2006), Strawbridge & James (2001), Sequeria & van Scoyoc (2002), Turner-Young (2003), Golsworthy (2004), and Lane & Corrie (2006).

Strawbridge & James (2001) raised issues regarding the questionable nature of diagnostic categories, the power of labelling, the pathologizing of distress, the appropriate use of psychiatric categories within specific contexts, practitioners working within their competence in relation to the categories, lack of informed consent, the potential discouragement of service users, and the financial consequences of the use of psychiatric language particularly related to funding and insurance. They argued that because we exist in a climate in which we are forced to claim and justify our expertise, we might be drawn into a medicalized framework because the use of psychiatric categories: "are seen as offering an interdisciplinary and international language as well as enhancing a 'psychological therapist' image in a highly competitive market" (p. 4). They argued for the use of formulation rather than diagnosis, which are specific to the client and context-dependent. These comments appear to view the field of psychology as situated within a labour market, where psychiatric diagnoses, and the labelled individuals, have become products to buy and sell in the name of psychological therapist identity.

Sequeira & van Scoyoc's (2002) round table on the DSM-IV and psychiatric testing raised similar issues relating to the maintenance of a psychological therapist identity grounded in humanism while at the same time being able to compete in a "market" where psychiatric discourse is dominant. Contributors from the floor appeared to have more radical views, including: "We should stand against the DSM-IV as it is not grounded in any psychological or even medical categories … it is political"; "Once we know a language, e.g., DSM, we tend to use it and can't see through different lenses. We need to stay peripheral so we can stay critical"; and "There is a problem with people not having access to second opinions. For example people of colour frequently labelled with schizophrenia. With DSM no thought is given to alternative theories about experience" (p. 46). There were also more cautionary comments of attempting to include the use of psychiatric diagnoses into practice, as well as the consequences of not using them, including: "It is futile to wage war against the DSM …. The problem or question we should be addressing is HOW ..[emphasis in original].. it should be used, not whether it should be used"; "If I have a client with a wrong diagnosis, I can use my knowledge to argue against it"; "What I am feeling throughout this process is FEAR ..[emphasis in original] … I fear I can't use these. It is the fear of not knowing"; and "This has brought up in me a fear of judgement. I am judging the clients and I am being judged by colleagues" (pp. 46–47). The comments in Sequeira & van Scoyoc's article present a variety of responses to the use of psychiatric diagnoses and the DSM, ranging from protest to using the DSM against itself. Unfortunately, the article does not go into much depth about whether any of these approaches were successful when actually situated within an environment dominated by the medical model.

Turner-Young (2003) questioned the growth rate of diagnostic categories and argued that the increase of the categories leads to an increase of pathological normal human behaviour. She relates the use of diagnostic categories to Mahrer's (2000) belief in the philosophical values underpinning psychotherapeutic endeavours, including: "Scientific research on psychotherapy is to test and thus confirm or disconfirm testable hypotheses"; "Biological, neurological, physiological, and chemical events and variables are basic to psychological events and variables"; and "There are mental illnesses, diseases and disorders" (p. 1117).

Golsworthy (2004) argued that:

> It is not enough for Counselling Psychologists to say that, for example "I don't work in that way", any more than to blindly accept such a classification and the limitations in conceptualizing individual concerns that it fosters. It is essential to be able to engage actively with this system, to be knowledgeable about it, and to understand both its strengths and limitations. Counselling Psychologists need to be able to reflect on the questions raised by the categorization of suffering, as well as considering the ways in which diagnostic systems influence our practice, for good and bad, implicitly and explicitly.
>
> (p. 23)

Golsworthy states that it is our societal duty to challenge psychiatric categories and diagnoses even though this may lead to forms of psychological therapist conflict. He points out that through the use of the therapeutic relationship counselling psychologists must question their own assumptions and any supposed supremacy of any particular form of knowledge.

Cooper (2009) stated that the issue of diagnoses in counselling psychology has been extensively debated in the literature, however, as demonstrated above this appears to have been relegated more to discussion and debate surrounding the issue. Although Cooper's arguments about working with individuals with diagnoses that are considered severe should be welcomed, perhaps a further step needs to be taken in relation to this issue. The relationship between counselling psychology's philosophical position and its position in practice raises difficult questions for the profession, and there appears to be a form of dissonance between the two.

Post-existentialism and counselling psychology

As presented by Loewenthal (2008a, 2008b) and in Chapter One, post-existentialism is influenced by Heidegger's ideas of "being" in the world with others and is a mixture of existentialism, phenomenology, and post-modernism. It aims to find a place between the natural and social sciences by starting with notions of existence and the historical and cultural aspects of the social, with a greater awareness of the political. This would include turning to ideas developed by individuals such as Levinas, Derrida, Foucault, Wittgenstein, and Laing. However, it is warned that the ideas of these individuals should be embraced without the need to totalize their approaches, and like any other theory or approach, their political nature requires a reflexive awareness of their application. Loewenthal (2008a) stated that Foucault's place within post-existentialism relates to the questioning of psychiatry as a science and its political status.

Along with individuals such as Laing (1990), issues have been raised regarding the nature of mental illness and how mental health psychological therapists have approached the experiences of individuals with mental health problems. Laing argued that: "The mad things said and done by the schizophrenic will remain essentially a closed book if one does not understand their existential context" (Laing 1990: 17). However, how, if at all, can Foucault's and Laing's ideas be combined with the philosophical position of counselling psychology and post-existentialism? As argued previously, counselling psychology's respect for and emphasis on the subjective experience of the client appears to fall close to Laing's notion of appreciating the client's phenomenological world.

In relation to counselling psychology, Cooper (2009) places this value within the ethics of Levinas (2006) and welcoming the Other. Cooper goes on to argue that recognizing the Other is an acknowledgement of the their uniqueness and "unknowability", and privileging their human face beyond the "psychagogic rhetoric" of psychological theories and assumptions. The intention of this seems to be an attempt to remove the dichotomy that is created through the use of labelling into those who are sick and those who are well (Pilgrim 2000). However, Cooper also asks what implications this approach may have for counselling psychologists working in the NHS: "On the one hand, it might be argued that this would take the profession further outside the NHS, with its specific emphasis on treating psychopathological conditions."

On the other hand, within both national health and wider policy circles, there are clear indications of a move towards more potentiality-based models of psychological functioning" (Cooper 2009: 124). Recent movements within mental health have focused on the recovery model (e.g., Deegan 1988) of rehabilitation. Some proponents of the recovery model draw on the philosophy of Foucault (Fardella 2008). Fardella argues that the recovery model utilizes Foucault's philosophy as a means of challenging psychological therapist discourse which limits the possibilities for client self-expression. Recovery is seen as a deeply human experience, which is facilitated by the human response to others (Anthony 1993), and as such participants in the recovery model reflect the anti-reductionist concerns of post-modern thought (Fardella 2008). However, there appears to be a difficulty when considering that even though recovery, much like counselling psychology, was founded on the assumptions of facilitating growth, actualization, empowerment, and respect for the individual's experience (Cooper 2009), it appears to have been hijacked by the very same evidence-based rhetoric (e.g., Frese, Stanley, Kress & Vogel-Scibilia 2001) to which counselling psychology has fallen prey to in the name of psychological therapistization and political power. This can be positioned within counselling psychology's own ontological insecurity (Laing 1990) in relation to psychiatric categories such as "schizophrenia".

Williams & Irving (1996) argued that counselling psychology has a "conflicted conceptual framework" (p. 4), which is grounded in both a logical empiricist framework and a phenomenological one. This places counselling psychology between two different epistemological positions: one that would advocate the use of diagnostic categories such as "schizophrenia", and another that would endeavour to understand clients in their own terms, without the use of labels; this appears to be an epistemological contradiction (e.g., Brown 2002).

An attempt to integrate these two stances results in what Williams & Irving (1996) called a "logical absurdity" (p. 6), however, this is what has been attempted by counselling psychology in both research and practice by adopting a scientist-practitioner model. This model was conceived as a marriage between therapeutic practice and scientific psychology at the Boulder conference, Colorado, in 1949. The scientist-practitioner model was intended to provide a framework for training and psychological therapist practice, particularly within the emerging field of clinical psychology (Corrie & Callahan 2000), and was intended to serve the dual function of safeguarding the public against poor practice and furnishing the profession with a clear identity and direction (Long & Hollin 1997). With this model being adopted by a counselling psychology striving for psychological therapist identity (Lane & Corrie 2006), it has come under attack as being untenable for the practice of counselling psychology, and that the different priorities of "scientist" and "practitioner" lead to an insurmountable rift between activity and function (Rennie 1994; Williams & Irving 1996).

Particularly within counselling psychology, the appropriateness of trying to integrate research and practice within a single training model has been questioned, and appears to directly contradict the notion of counselling psychology privileging the "respect for the personal, subjective experience of the client over and above notions of diagnosis, assessment and treatment, as well as the pursuit of innovative, phenomenological methods for understanding human experience" (Lane & Corrie 2006: 17). As van Deurzen-Smith (1990) argued, the very philosophical underpinnings of counselling psychology emerged in a response to a psychology that was too preoccupied with scientism to be able to inform our understanding of the dilemmas of human existence.

This issue was explored in research conducted by one of the authors, where interviews were held with counselling psychologists who had experience of working with individuals diagnosed with "schizophrenia" (and in some cases other diagnoses). The aim of the research was to critically explore how counselling psychologists managed the conflict between a phenomenological or context-based understanding of the client and the medical model. The epistemological position taken to this research was a critical-realist approach and the method of analysis was discourse analysis, which is the study of language in use, and adopts a view of language as context-bound, functional, and constructive (Avdi & Georgaca 2007). Discourse analysis draws on a tradition in British social psychology influenced by the fields of linguistics, hermeneutics, and ethnomethodology (Potter & Wetherell 1987) and Marxism, feminism, and critical psychology (Fox & Prilleltensky 1997), and the writings of Foucault (Parker 1992). It allows for the exploration of descriptions or constructions of the world and how these descriptions sustain some patterns of social action and exclude others (Burr 2003). The use of discourse analysis was fuelled by an interest in "practical deconstruction" (Parker 1999), which "reverses the priority given to certain concepts, locates those concepts in certain relations of power and supports resistance on the part of those subjected to them" (p. 105). Using discourse analysis to this end is appropriate as it takes a political approach to the research process, and raises questions about whose interests are served and whose interests are marginalized by the discourses that gain hegemony and authority (Cosgrove & McHugh 2008).

Parker (1992) has argued that some versions of discourse analysis suggest that discursive constructions are entirely independent of the material world, and that they attribute primacy to ideas as expressed in language, as opposed to matter, which may be manifested in structures that exist independently of what we may say or think about them. Instead, Parker advocates a "critical-realist" (e.g., Bhaskar 1978, 1986) position which acknowledges that the knowledge we have of the world is mediated by, and constructed through, language, while also maintaining that there are underlying structures which generate phenomena, versions of which we construct through language. This means that discursive constructions of reality are anchored in social and material structures, such as institutions and their practices. Therefore, Parker argues that "discourse analysis needs to attend to the conditions which make the meanings of texts possible" (p. 28), or as Willig (1999) explains, there must be an analysis of the conditions (historical, social, and economic) that give rise and/or make possible the accounts of participants and the discourses that constitute them: "Particular meanings are made possible by some conditions and not others" (p. 40). The critical-realist ontology and epistemology argues for a reality, but that this reality is reflected in the oppressive influences of social, political, and historical factors.

There have been objections to this approach of discourse analysis, noticeably from Edwards, Ashmore & Potter (1995) and Speer (2007), who argue that material structures can always be reduced to discursive practices; and that critical-realists have no systematic method of distinguishing between the discursive and the non-discursive. Due to this, the constructing factor which constitutes the one and not the other comes down to a choice driven by the researcher's political standpoint (Sims-Schouten, Riley & Willig, 2007).

Research findings

The comments presented below are intended to give a flavour of some of the experiences counselling psychologists have in working with individuals with a diagnosis of "schizophrenia", and are by no means representative.

> Participant A: "I mean, certainly that's the approach ... I've then taken, kind of, individually is to try to think about the voices as being a manifestation of something as opposed to it being a symptom that needs to be got rid of, which I guess is very different to your psychiatric view of things, you know, which is medication to suppress the thoughts, to get rid of, whereas actually I was taking a more relationship style with things ..."

Here, Participant A talks about how approaching a client's difficulties by trying to understanding the contextual and relational aspect of their presentation may sometimes clash with a more "psychiatric" approach that favours medication. The dominance of the medical model and the conceptualization of mental health problems as biological disorders has resulted in an exclusion of the importance of the therapeutic relationship and denied the possibility that psychotherapy can be useful to serious mental health problems (Repper 2002). Using the relationship to be with clients diagnosed with, for example, "schizophrenia" has been criticized as being indefinable and irrelevant to mental health practice (Coleman & Jenkins 1998), and the absence of randomized controlled trials and controlled evidence in the role of the therapeutic relationship has been seen as proof of its lack of efficacy (Lambert & Gournay 1999).

> Participant B: "The problem in my mind comes when we create more distance and separation which I think is one of the, you know, possible downsides to, kind of, diagnostic labelling, you create that separation between

yourself as the psychologist and this other person, somebody who has this supposed thing called schizophrenia, which again is open to debate."

In this extract, Participant B reflects on how the label itself creates a distance between the psychologist and the client. This mirrors what Cooper (2009) refers to as the "trans-diagnostic" aspect of the individual, which looks beyond a particular label or category, and how a diagnostic category with all of its discourse creates a space between the two.

Participant B: "… and a lot of the time, you know, the person who's been positioned and who's been labelled as being schizophrenic, that might not be an issue for them. They don't care, you know, they might just want to get off the ward or get home or that's not their issues, you know, that's me as a middle-class white guy who likes thinking about these things and is grappling with those concepts in quite an abstract kind of way really. It, you know, it matters to me. You know, it's always led to me questioning my role and I suppose questioning the industry, the discipline that I'm involved with as well because I think it's at the heart of what we do, what we're about."

Here, Participant B also talks about his own approach to diagnostic categories, and how as a psychologist positioned within the debate on the value of diagnoses, he sees it as a political matter to challenge. This echoes Golsworthy's (2004) statement that it is our psychological therapist duty to challenge psychiatric categories and diagnoses even though this may lead to forms of psychological therapist conflict.

Participant C: "I feel a bit alone at times … but feel like it is a constant struggle to change stigma and perception, guiding the way we work with people and not so much for me psychiatry interestingly, but nurses and, well you got nurses, social workers in the team but probably more nurses really that struggle to formulate and to understand the importance of relationships sometimes and are quite scared of some relationships with some clients … you know, really struggle with that and revert back to kind of medical models and ways of working at times when they are struggling with relationships I think, so I think as a counselling psychologist … you have to network quite well really to keep your links outside with your profession because you can feel like going into battle sometimes, but there are individuals that you have been helping to develop and helping them to think differently, but it can be a struggle at times to do that, perceptions."

Participant C: *"There is still a lot of stigma within the staff that I am working with the enduring mental health problems."*

Participant C reflects on the difficulties of being positioned within a medical environment as a counselling psychologist, and some of the challenges inherent to trying to look at clients from a different view. Gallagher, Gemez & Baker (1991) found that in a study of 150 psychologists' beliefs about their role in the treatment of "schizophrenia", there was a 91 per cent disagreement with the statement that "schizophrenia" is too severe a condition for psychologists to work with. Instead, they found that clients labelled with "schizophrenia" were thought to be unrewarding to work with, and that working with "neurotic" clients was found to generate more success. Similarly, Servais & Saunders' (2007) survey of 306 clinical psychologists' perceptions of individuals with mental illness found that individuals with the "schizophrenic" label were viewed as being ineffective or incomprehensible to work with.

The discourses surrounding working with individuals diagnosed with "schizophrenia" creates a barrier between the client and the practitioner, and as observed by Participant C, it is sometimes easier to revert to the medical model and the space it creates between the two than actually face the "inexpressible irreversibility" of the Other (Cooper 2009). However, there is also an indication that Participant C, as a counselling psychologist, also experiences stigma due psychological therapist identity in that they have been positioned as a psychological therapist who cannot work with individuals with mental health problems considered severe. This was reported in Lewis & Bor's (1998) study of how counselling psychologists are perceived by clinical psychologists, in which it was found that 60 per cent (97) of the respondents did not feel that psychotic individuals should be referred to counselling psychologists, and that counselling psychologists would be best suited to work with adjustment problems (such as marital problems, bereavement, relationship difficulties).

Conclusion

It is hoped that this chapter has presented a picture of counselling psychology in relation to psychiatric diagnoses and that this has contributed further to the literature pertaining to this issue. Through the lens of post-existentialism, this chapter has argued that counselling psychology can "wake up" from its march towards a medicalized future by being brave enough to challenge particular forms of knowledge. Post-existentialism argues that we should accept, rather than escape, who we are (Loewenthal 2008a), and there appears to be a danger that counselling psychology is in the process of escaping from its philosophical foundations due to political pressure and a need to adapt to the current networks of power. These questions were raised by Goldstein (2009) concerning the future of counselling psychology. In it, he asked: "Perhaps the key questions for all of us now are which identity, why, and for whom do we wish to project this identity into the future?" If counselling psychology is to retain a critical stance towards taken-for-granted knowledge and avoid being incorporated in clinical psychology, as suggested by Kinderman (2009), it will have to start challenging the discourses that make it vulnerable to this type of future.

CHAPTER EIGHT

A training in post-existentialism: placing Rogers and psychoanalysis

Del Loewenthal and Robert Snell

Introduction

This chapter describes a model of a training in post-existentialism. It is argued that much of the emerging dominant training model of today is unbalanced, with too great an emphasis on CBT and short-term cost-effectiveness, rather than on the provision of a sound understanding based on learning from lived experience. There is concern at the extent to which the authors are concerned about how the depths of thinking and feeling can be brushed aside, and with this a focus on the relationship and understanding of people's experiences. The authors provide an analysis of their chosen training model, a Professional Doctorate/ MSc in Psychotherapy and Counselling through locating it historically in trends within European philosophy. After the MSc (out of which has come Chapter Six), it is also possible to do a PhD programme (out of which has come Chapter Three, Four, and Five). We are also involved with a BSc in integrative counselling which has come out of the Psy-chD/MSc described in this chapter; as well as PsychD in counselling psychology (out of which has come Chapter Seven) which has been influenced by what is described here.

Theoretical background

Within some areas of Europe, state provision of psychoanalysis is used as a means of cost reduction in medicine, for example in Germany (Hardt 2006); whereas in the United Kingdom (Layard 2005, 2006b, c), evidence presented on the effectiveness of becoming more thoughtful, reflective practitioners than would be the case if the focus were just on the application of technique and measurable results. The programme discussed here, at Roehampton University in the United Kingdom, attempts to counteract this narrowing of focus. The programme, which has been running since the 1980s, is founded on a learning community model. In terms of academic and philosophical content, students follow phenomenology through to post-phenomenology, and along the way learn from humanistic/existential philosophy and psychoanalytic and European post-modernist thought. It is an emotional as well as an intellectual journey. The course raises critical questions about the humanistic idea that the human being is essentially whole ("holism") and that successful therapy necessarily leads to integration. This can be so challenging to some students as to lead to them leaving. However, those who do complete typically report how much they value and appreciate the learning experience. The authors argue that the programme puts people on the road to becoming thoughtful, reflective practitioners in a way that might be considered to be of a better quality than if the focus were just on the application of technique and measurable results.

This study is the first stage in a larger international comparative project, coordinated through the International Association of Counselling, on policy determinants in the education of psychological therapists. A case study approach is used (see Chapter Four, and Greenwood & Loewenthal 2005) that asks what are the important features of the therapeutic learning experience provided by different programmes. Notions of evidence can be questioned both within a European tradition, as we attempt on the Roehampton programme, and from cultures with very different roots.

A note about style must be made here. As discussed below, the authors carry out different roles during the programme, including being both tutors and members of the core experiential group. They are also the authors here, and one of them (Loewenthal) is coordinating the international comparative project. This complexity is reflected in the changes of voice that are required in the present chapter in order to convey the flavour of the programme as well as its key principles and outcomes.

In this chapter, the authors argue that the learning community is a container for growth and development. At the same time, they take a post-existential view that, influenced by post-modernism, questions a fixed or stable centre. This can allow for a primacy on lived experience, and the emergence of new ways of speaking about it—speaking the new, rather than speaking what has already been said. On the postgraduate training programme at the Centre for Therapeutic Education at Roehampton University, the learning community group is involved in a training that stretches over a minimum of three years. Learning is experientially based, rather than primarily skills- or knowledge-based, and it begins with questioning what it means to be in the world of and with others.

The training moves from an emphasis to feeling, to experience, to the unconscious and repressed, to our being subject to language, and to each other, with ethical implications flowing from this (Levinas 1969). As in the practice of psychological therapy in other settings, the mutual encounter can feel like it brings about an expansion of all our potentialities as people. We as staff are also subject, as one student recently put it, to "something so big you can't see it". We are stretched to our limits, in varying ways, with each student group: angered, frustrated, despairing, moved in different ways. But it is just this rawness, if the higher education system can still enable it, that seems to be required for new experience and learning, both in ourselves and in the students.

How does one train psychological therapists/therapists in the relational? The idea of emotional labour (Hochschild 2003), and the emotional learning required for this, promises to be helpful for our thinking about such training. How do we prepare trainees to facilitate emotional learning in their clients? It involves the trainees, and it involves us as staff, in their and our own emotional labour—how do we help them and ourselves with the emotional labour of the training, and that which the students will need to undertake with their clients?

What emotional learning is needed? One definition of emotional learning is that it is something personal to the individual with a focus on intentional psychological change (Quigley & Barrett 1999). It can be considered in terms of learning to allow feelings through a process of facing and alleviating anxiety, which involves reparative work too, for the wear and tear of previous emotional labour. Should trainers, therefore, be reclassified as conductors of emotional learning? Or does "conductor" carry too strong a connotation that we ourselves are somehow outside the process?

Learning communities are associated with humanism. The modernist notion of holism and the autonomy and wisdom of the organism, derived from thinkers such as Rogers (2003) and applied to the individual and the group, still has currency in some fields. Yet for many, humanism is a failed project; crucially, to quote Heidegger: "... every humanism remains metaphysical. In defining the humanity of man [sic] ... humanism not only does not ask about the relation of Being to the essence of man [sic]; because of its metaphysical origin humanism even impedes the question by neither recognizing nor understanding it" (Heidegger 1993: 226). It is hard to see humanism, as it was once widely regarded, as a key to personal and social transformation (the idea of a "key", post-deconstruction, is itself questionable). Does this mean that learning communities are dead, and that the learning community model must be replaced, within education in general and therapeutic education in particular, by modular learning? Such that all that is left is learning as commodity, and an experience of post-humanist, postmodern fragmentation and decentring? Another argument against the learning community model has been cost effectiveness, an argument that has also supported the rise of CBT in public health; a form of therapy whose "effectiveness" can supposedly be seen and measured. Yet the modular and the behavioural, divorced from the humanistic, do not seem to lead to a sense of community. Just because we are decentred, does this mean we cannot have a sense of community?

The Roehampton programme has evolved over a period of more than thirty years and its design was influenced from the start by the work of Heron (1999), Rogers & Freiburg (1994), Rogers (2003), and Laing (1990). Our experience is that Heron and Rogers help open up the register of feelings for our students and ourselves. Heron's work has been key to helping shape the particular facilitative environment of the learning community. Heron also usefully analysed some of the hidden assumptions behind the kinds of interventions people make with each other, and he opened up questions about where people in general, and therapists in particular, may be coming from when we and they speak (Heron 1999). The influence of Rogers was and is important for thinking about how feelings link to teaching and learning (Rogers & Freiburg 1994):

if people are aware of where they are they will automatically know the next place to go. For Rogers, this is an inherent capacity of the human organism; however, a certain conscious reparative work needs to happen first: in order for feelings to come into current awareness, there needs to be a facilitating—non-directive, non-judgemental, empathic, genuine, and congruent—other (Rogers 2003). R. D. Laing's emphasis on intersubjectivity and on learning to speak from experience (e.g., Laing 1990) derived from existentialist thinkers such as Sartre (1943) and Binswanger (1963) is also valuable here.

While Heron and Rogers came from humanism and Laing from an existential-analytic tradition, what they have as a common background is phenomenology (for example, the implicit emphasis in Rogers on description rather than explanation), and it is phenomenology that the Roehampton programme brings into focus. The programme aims to model a notion of psychological therapy as a means of learning from experience. It is based on an exploration of major phenomenological currents in European twentieth- and twenty-first-century therapeutic thinking (Loewenthal & Snell 2003), as manifest, in particular, in humanism, psychoanalysis, and post-modernism, and of how phenomenology has developed within these areas of theory and practice.

Post-existential programme

Central to our understanding of the learning community is the idea that it is a place in which we might learn to be less caught up and immobilized, as groups and as individuals, in past patterns, and as a result be clearer that we are responding to and for our clients rather than just ourselves. The programme is founded in a study of what emerges between people. It starts by inviting students to identify issues cognitively (areas they are conscious of wanting to develop), and leads to a lived enquiry, through experience, into relationship. The learning community passes through a kind of progression of anxiety—each stage of the course raises different kinds and levels of anxiety—and there is inevitably overlap between stages. Thus there is the opportunity for revisiting and working through, over the course of the four years, earlier stages of the course. These might include scenes of trauma from the life of the group. This might be thought about in terms of what Freud came to call *"Nachträglichkeit"*—"effect of afterwardsness"—where previous experiences that may not have been felt as traumatic at the time are later, when revisited, felt as such (Freud 1896: 233).

The learning community spends lengthy continuous stretches of time together; seven hours weekly (including breaks) over three thirty-week years, in addition to five-day blocks at the start of each of the first two years and two full assessment days at the end of year one. The programme challenges the culture of modularization and discreetly packaged learning, opening up instead the possibility of an experience of learning together. There are typically, in any given week during the programme, hour-long large and small, agenda-free groups.

The large experiential group, which includes the tutors, is an opportunity for students to speak about and process experiences on and off the course, as well as being a forum in which members might reflect on their experiences of being in the group. The experiential groups are often felt to be very challenging, by students and by tutors; at the same time, they can function as the most important vehicles for emotional labour and learning. An aim of this emotional labour and learning is to bring to awareness ways in which students' responses may be driven by their own way of being, which affords them the capacity to choose to attend in a more focused way to what their clients bring to therapy sessions. There are other activities undertaken collectively; for example, in years one and two, case presentations, business meetings, lecture/seminar and practice workshop groups, and group tutorials with regard to the written assignments the students produce during the year. The students are, with the support of the learning community, also responsible for arranging their own therapy, practice placements, and external supervision. To enable individuals and their peers to judge when they are ready to practise is a key part of the peer learning process: in year one, there is a final two-day peer and tutor assessment, in which students are required to read, respond to, and assess each other's writing about their development on the programme.

In itself, the process of writing, especially writing about oneself, seems inevitably to generate anxiety. It can mean facing in oneself tremendous loss—of one's idealized or infantile sense of one's own grandeur and potency, and a fear that can paralyse (for a useful account of this process, from a psychodynamic perspective, see Barwick 2003). Combined with the two-day assessment, writing on the course requires the emotional labour of trying to think clearly while mastering anxieties around having one's own profound vulnerabilities exposed, in a way that can free and open participants to further learning from experience—provided that they and we are able to manage the persecutory possibilities, phanta-sized or real, inherent in the process.

In terms of content, the training starts, in the first year, by aiming to open up people's feelings, through an examination of Rogers and phe-nomenology and, inevitably, through an exposure to the anxiety that can be provoked by speaking about feelings. We would consider Rogers & Freiburg's (1994) *Freedom to Learn* to be of particular importance. We would, however, bring the role of anxiety into sharper focus than Rogers did. Phenomenology encourages us to try to stay close to expe-rience, and to learn to speak about the struggle to do this. In encourag-ing students to stay with their anxieties—to acknowledge and describe them in words rather than attempt to dissipate them through action—we are, hopefully, helping them to see the benefit that emotional work undertaken for oneself (in the group, in therapy) can have for the com-munity and the other. Staying with anxiety involves emotional labour for both students and tutors; in contrast to labour as Marx & Engels (1878) understood it, as purely for someone else's gain, or that produces learning purely for one's own gain. The emotional labour on the pro-gramme is potentially of benefit both for the labourer(s) and for the community's learning.

What we do in year one is to demonstrate in theory and practice how, at its best, phenomenological listening, which we consider to be inherent in Rogers' thinking, is fundamental and mandatory for the practice of psychological therapy, whatever the theoretical label. The programme invites students to question humanistic notions, of "core" self or identity, of the achievement of "autonomy" as the main goal of therapy; rather, it aims to open students up to an ethic in which our "subjecthood", both as clients and therapists, consists of our being subject to the other.

At the start of the second year, we chart a phenomenological tradition through the existentialism of prominent European philosophers, includ-ing Kierkegaard (1944, 1954a, b), Heidegger (1993), Merleau-Ponty (1962), Sartre (1956), and others; all of which underpins a reading of Levinas (1989) in the third term. Students pursue a critical reading of these existentialist thinkers, with their characteristic emphasis on anxi-ety and dread as part of the human condition.

The second term of year two we embark on a reading of Freud (1995) and some major post-Freudian psychoanalytic theorists: Winnicott (1958), Klein (1930, 1946), and Laplanche (1992), for example. We try to speak with students about the anxiety that emerges when unconscious feelings and thoughts, the erotic and the repressed, are touched upon. In addition, our experience, and that of many of the students, is that from the very start of the course we find we are subject to our aggressive and hate-filled impulses as well as loving ones. The possibility of speaking further about this experience in terms of transference, positive and negative, is facilitated by this psychotherapeutic learning. With regard to theorizing emotional learning, we draw on Bion's (1984b) recognition, derived from the work of Klein (1930), that feeling and thinking are in the last analysis inseparable: cognition cannot be separated from unconscious phantasy. Failures of thought can be understood as attacks on emotional linking (Bion 1984a), damage that is potentially reparable through the kind of "learning from experience" (Bion 1984b) that can take place in an analysis. The process of mitigating unconscious anxiety and primitive defences founded in experiences of trauma is initiated in the training.

In term three of year two, we explore some post-modern, post-phenomenological thinkers, including Lacan (1977, 1988a, b, 1993), Derrida (1998), and Levinas (1989; see also Loewenthal & Snell 2003). The work of post-modern European philosophers can help students to an appreciation of how much the different layers of anxiety community members pass through are culturally as well as individually determined. The meanings we generate are regarded as all finally stemming from the unconscious, which, it can be argued, is "structured like a language" (Lacan 1993: 167). The post-modern, post-phenomenological turn to language underlines how much words speak us—how we are subject to language. This is part of the impetus behind Lacan's and Derrida's radical insistence on resisting closure and certainties—for meanings are relative and shifting—and on the attempt to stay phenomenologically open to our always and already language-mediated experience. Levinas points to the ethical importance of staying open to each other, given that we are, in the last analysis, subject to the other (Levinas 1989).

The third, MSc, year is devoted to developing and writing a substantial piece of research, with the philosophical readings of the previous two years in mind, and this work too is substantially undertaken in a group setting. This research can be developed into a Practioner Doctorate or a PhD.

The different kinds of meetings—from tutorials, to business meetings, to large groups—within which the programme is undertaken can help participants to a lived awareness of language-mediated experience and the need for phenomenological openness; each setting requiring a different kind of engagement and focus, and the passage from, say, large experiential group (for an exploration of issues regarding the leader and the group in this context, please see Loewenthal & Snell 2006), to tutorial, to business meeting can foster a student's ability to move from one kind of engagement or focus to another. Overall, in terms of emotional learning, the programme's aims might be summarized as developing members' abilities to make use of the programme as a container for anxieties, in order to help them both to be subject-to(o) and to find their voices; to develop means for assessing emotional learning; to exploring what needs to take place before learning from experience can happen. Such learning is difficult if your current experience is too confused with past experience.

Emotional learning from experience: some vignettes

In this section, we attempt to explore emotional learning as we attempt to facilitate it on the programme. It would be consistent with the emphasis placed on the experiential to start by trying to give a flavour of the students' and the tutors' struggles on the programme; the lived experience. "I never realized I hated my mother so much for dying. It came to me as a complete revelation." This could have come from a client in psychological therapy, but in fact was said by a student at the end of the first year. This was a student who had throughout the year appeared very intransigent and resistant to learning. The tutors—who, perhaps controversially, take the role of group facilitators in the large, agenda-free group that is a central feature of the programme—had experienced the student up to this point as attacking and aggressive. What was important was that she seemed to change into someone who could be insightful. Her ability to think and feel seemed to increase, and with it her openness to others and, therefore, in our view, her capacity to become a therapist. What was the process and what was the nature of the labour that may have facilitated this emotional learning, enabling her to develop her ability to think?

The first year, and the first days of the programme, are often critically important. In the first experiential group of one year of the course, a group member spoke of how the silence left him feeling he was "bursting … stifling … crying … breathing". He and others voiced anger with the tutors for "dropping us in it". "I don't want to play the tutors' game", said one. She continued: "I am determined to keep it down because Robert [tutor] said I couldn't"—a response to the tutor's suggesting that her need to speak might be in order to prove she was at second-year, Diploma, level and that she was above the other students. She was trying to prove him wrong, trying to show she could repress what in fact she was showing she could not repress. A great deal seemed to be opened up in twenty minutes with regard to her emotional constrictions.

At the next meeting, there was some discussion of a previous group that a member had been in. The theme of "unfinished business" emerged, something that might constrain learning in the present group. If the group task, as the tutors formulated it, was "to look at our experience of being in a group … experience that is beyond our experience", what else might stop people learning from this? A member mentioned "the black holes in the carpet pattern", which he found himself counting—order, a tutor wondered to him, to keep emerging feelings in check? An infinite black hole was perhaps being made finite, countable. He also noticed what he said was a bricked-up door outside, in the building opposite. Someone else pointed out that it was not a bricked-up door at all, but just a recess in the wall—he was, perhaps, internally bricking up doors that were not bricked up. Perhaps there was something he feared that needed to be blocked out, a potential in him? Someone else said that he himself was "listing people's names" in his head. Another member in the same meeting kept her diary on her lap, as someone irritably pointed out to her.

Defences against and blocks to learning, to listening to the emotional experience of being in the group, take different forms. If there is too much anxiety about what was, it is difficult to stay with what is. If learning is beyond a person's experience, it is hard for them to feel they can go beyond their experience. Defences against learning are defences against fear of an unknown. "I haven't got my diary today", commented the group member with the diary during the next meeting: people can start to learn that they do things that are about their own defences and not about the other person. Later in the meeting, someone commented: "perhaps there could be something good here"—meaning, as we understood it, something of value to be found in the group. Learning about how anxiety is defended against can work as an invitation to come alive—like the invitation "to go mad" at South West London College, where both tutors trained in the 1970s and 1980s.

What, someone asked, was "appropriate" material or behaviour for the group? What may be thought to be appropriate, however, may be an inappropriate way of being. What might be most appropriate would be for the group to explore what its members considered appropriate.

For example, it might seem appropriate for group members to express concern over an absent colleague, as happened within the same training group six months later, at the end of the second term. This particular member had hitherto been almost completely silent in the group. The previous week, a far more talkative group member had used the analogy of the group as a forest, in which some members went in search of food while others waited to be fed. When the silent member did return after a week's absence, he spoke about how bad he felt about being got at and accused, as he felt it, of being a parasite, waiting to be fed. The tutors posed the question in the group as to how much people's concern for the absent member (particularly perhaps that of the student who had made the "forest" analogy) was not for the absent, silent member at all, but for themselves. How much, the tutors asked, were group members using the absent member as a receptacle for their own projected anxieties about being "got at" in the group by the tutors? Speaking in the group, as some members report, can often be experienced as dangerous for this reason.

The incident described was the occasion for a wide variety of learning—for example, personal learning for the silent member about the anxieties he brought to the group from his past experience, and group learning about rivalry and competition over scarce resources. The silent member was able to put into words how pinioned and silenced he had up to now felt in the group, a possible result, a tutor suggested, not only of his personal history but also of an interpersonal phenomenon, the group members' projections of their painful past experiences of having been silenced. The student who coined the analogy of the forest had in fact recently shared with the group how much she felt her talkativeness was to make up for having felt crushed and reduced to silence in her original family.

Crucially, what was opened up was a question about members' motives for becoming psychological therapists/therapists at all. Did this come from a wish to help people? How much might this wish be a kind of cover story for getting help with one's own damage, potentially leading to unconscious persecution of one's clients? This seems to us to be a fundamental and mandatory question for any programme claiming to offer training in psychological therapy, and we do not know of a more potent way of opening it up than through the shared emotional labour, students' and tutors', of an experiential group within a learning community.

Discussion

In our thinking about learning on the programme, we do not give priority to a developmental model, with its idea that development can be arrested at some stage and that there is stage-appropriate behaviour. Rather, we use Freudian ideas, particularly the idea of the compulsion to repeat (Freud 1914), to inform a more phenomenological approach: our concern is with what is specific to the individual. For example, a course member may be so busy protecting himself from once more having something bad being done to him that he cannot learn. We go through a process with our students that is designed to help them be able to help their clients go through a similar process.

A danger of the groups is that people learn a new line of defence, and perhaps the tutors too have learned some robust defences. Early in a new group's life, someone made this raw comment to the facilitators: "you don't speak, you don't care". Other members picked this up. Of course, it felt important for us to register the real possibility that we did not care nor want to listen; equally, it felt important to consider that by focusing on the facilitators, the students may have been protecting themselves against the possibility of their being angry with each other. "I'm not anxious about this, just trying to work it out logically", said one. After a while, people seem to learn not to say things like the above. An opening up and a closing down typically happens—the early group sessions are the most intense. There is a process of getting in touch with rawness, and speaking about something new. Then the group learns to protect itself again, to close down, and re-socialize in a way that is probably not helpful to emotional development. Feelings may open up again later in the life of the group, but often in a more measured, far less raw way.

What about those group members who do not get through? A danger for us as tutors is that we merely rationalize this by claiming, for example, that they were not ready for emotional learning. Another viewpoint might be that we are not prepared to jump through the hoops of our own psychopathology. As tutors, we feel we should try to stay as open as we possibly can to this possibility, and, in managing the emotional tension in us that this involves, model something very important for students. This might be summarized thus: that there is no final court of appeal as regards our efforts to treat each other ethically, except perhaps, as Levinas would say, the face of the other (Levinas 1985: 86).

A psychoanalytic way of formulating our task would be to say that it is to interpret group members' defences in the hope of keeping members emotionally open. It is true that we are tutors, not outside facilitator therapists, and our changes of role certainly carry powerful meanings and present potential difficulties. This is something that we attempt to take very seriously, and continue to offer our work to the academic community for scrutiny. There are those who might wish to argue philosophically and theoretically against the potential role-blurring suggested here. An example: one of us had the strong sense, in a routine business meeting, that he had actually "hit" a group member when he (the tutor) had said "no" to the student's practical but unmeetable request. Had there once been, the tutors reflected to each other later, a father's verbal "no" that had long ago traumatized the student and was now being re-enacted? And how much might the tutor have been caught up, and unable to process in the heat of the business meeting, in the echoes of a father's "no" in his own development, a "no" he was now passing on to the hapless student? Was the aggression that the tutors experienced as coming from the student perhaps based on the student's identification with the aggressor—with the tutor's real aggression? The issue of multiple, boundaried roles and the difficulties of sustaining therapeutic pedagogy within them is something we have addressed in another paper (Loewenthal & Snell 2006).

It is, however, also worth noting here that much of what happens in the experiential group sessions feeds into the emotional language of the learning community and into its other activities—into what is "sayable". The point is that as tutors, we are involved with the students. The tutor might eventually say to this student, "I felt I hit you", for example, in the peer review at the end of the Certificate year. While each role and setting has its own boundaries, each also offers a new opportunity and context for speaking something, including the tutors' thoughts and feelings about our own personal involvement. At best, the whole course can be like what Bion (1984a) called a container: a boundaried maternal space in which strong and frightening feelings can be experienced, shared, linked up, and translated into words.

A draft of this chapter was given to a group of doctoral students, all of whom had been through the programme, for their comments, and one question they raised was indeed about our own emotional involvement, labour, and learning. They felt we had downplayed this. Reflecting on this, we feel ourselves to be in a dilemma that maps onto a dilemma we live with on the programme, an inherent tension in our role. Do we interpret the doctoral students' feedback in terms of, for example, a demand for reassurance that they mattered and matter to us, that they have an effect on us? Or in terms of an anxiety that they have been too much for us? Or, is to interpret it in this way a defensive position we take up, under the guise of an "analytic" stance? Might we also see ourselves and our labour as integral, in the sense that we are co-labourers, ourselves challenged and changed? The question of how and when it might be appropriate to convey and explore this with students would then be an important part of our emotional labour—a labour that continues now in this writing. We thus refuse to take up either a purely "humanist" or a purely "psychoanalytic" stance; if we must have one, we prefer the label "existential/analytic" or "post-existential".

The philosophy and ethics of Levinas (1989) are a very important influence for us, and for the programme and its emphasis on the relational. For Rogers, the key question, in the practice of psychotherapy and the training of therapists, might be: can I get in touch with what you are feeling and what you are making me feel? For a post-Freudian, it might be: how might what I am feeling be an unconscious communication from you, conceptualized in terms of counter-transference, or projective identification? For Levinas, the question would be: is my expression of what I am feeling a way of putting you first? Levinas' concern with individual emotion is in specific regard to how one might put the other first, and this, as we have argued elsewhere (Loewenthal & Snell 2003), is for Levinas a phenomenological rather than a moral necessity. Deriving some of his thought from Heidegger, Levinas argued that just as we are born into a world of others, who precede us, so must the other come first, before us, ethically. Levinas' thinking can be seen as less egoic than Rogers', in that his starting point is not the self but the other, and it is arguably less egoic than Freud's, in so far as when psychoanalysts speak of the id or the unconscious (*das Andere*), it tends to be of a personal unconscious or id, as if a personal possession, rather than an outside, not-me, other (*der Andere*). Levinas' ethics are also very different from Christian ethics, from the idea of doing to the other as one would be done to. The Christian starting point is still the "I". The Lacanian unconscious ("structured like a language") (Lacan 1993: 167), and in some ways the Jungian "collective" unconscious (Jung 1921), are less personal, more "other", although what both Lacanian and Jungian theory may be said to lack is the intensity of the Levinasian focus on the primacy of the other.

In terms of actual practice, within a Levinasian way of thinking, we would need to keep reminding ourselves that we need to be clear about how we are feeling, as therapists/tutors/students of counselling and psychotherapy, in order to be helpful. Christianity appears at times to say: put oneself aside, give up the ego. A humanist position would be: "me first, then I can help you too to achieve autonomy". Psychoanalysis has generated much debate around unconscious communication and counter-transference; but this does not need to arise for Levinas: the unconscious is merely part of the infinite, an unknown. Levinas' writings might lead us to say: "I am only attending to myself in order to be helpful to you; I need to have some sense of myself in order to put you first—to be in touch with my own concern with death and my own violence, in order to see it in your face." One of Levinas' most important ethical formulations is: "don't let me die alone, don't do violence to me" (for example, see Levinas 1985: 86). I can only be responsible for your responsibility if I am responsible, able to speak in a way that is embodied (Rogers might say "genuine" or "congruent"). At the same time, Levinas thoroughly critiqued the notion of "autonomy". For him, the end product is not "autonomy" but "heteronomy", other-centredness, and he argued this at length (see Chapter Two, and Loewenthal & Snell 2003: 154–159). The distinction is central to his philosophy. From this perspective, to think of therapy as primarily to do with autonomy and self-knowledge is to start in the wrong place; one can never know oneself, or the other.

Levinas argued against Heidegger's emphasis on questions of being: "The ego is the very crisis of the being of a being ... because I begin to ask myself if my being is justified, if the Da of my Dasein [the "there" of my being there] is not already the usurpation of someone else's place" (Levinas 1989: 85). Nor can Levinasian emotional learning be skills-based, founded in the idea that we can somehow have the knowledge and skills to help us know how to be therapists. It is something we need to live in perpetual crisis about. One cannot get rid of the crisis by learning some skills or theory. The appeal, rather, is to responsibility, "which is not a practical stopgap measure designed to console knowledge in its failure to match being" (Levinas 1989: 85). It is a question of learning not to know—not to colonize, appropriate, or reduce the other to the same, from the standpoint of one's own questing "autonomy".

Conclusion

What do we learn? We are challenged to re-examine our assumptions about therapeutic theory and practice from the ground up, as it were. As in the practice of psychological therapy in other settings, the encounter with our students can feel like it brings about an expansion of our potentialities as people. Subject to "something so big you can't see it", we too as tutors are, as we have suggested above, often stretched to our emotional limits. But, we argue, this rawness is mandatory for new experience and learning, in ourselves and our students. Both of us tutors notice shifts in our perceptions of individual students that also seem to mark genuine shifts in the particular individual; these shifts can often seem more dramatic than those we experience in our private practices. We are left with a sense of wonder at people's differences. Each group experience seems to lead, for sufficient group members and for ourselves, to something being thought, lived, and worked through, although the notion of "working through" itself might suggest an end point. Rather, there can develop a sense of being constantly on the edge—of "edginess".

We are conscious too of wanting to protect the community and our students from the culture of consumerism, including from the occasional intrusions of the institution, in so far as it too is subject to the pressures of managerialism and modularization. The space that opens up between people on the programme can be invaded in all kinds of ways. The battle is also sometimes fought out on the terrains both of the learning community and the institution itself: the appeal to "consumer rights" is one that is alluringly available to students who are, necessarily, facing disappointments and anxieties as a result of the programme. For Levinas, emotional learning would be about being able to be open to the other and to one's own otherness. It is about developing responsibility for the other's responsibility: emotional learning in the training of psychological therapists/therapists consists in helping them to help clients with their emotional learning. The "how" of this is not to do with "knowledge", in the university sense. The ethical must precede the search for knowledge and self-knowledge. The learning community aims to facilitate a return to learning from experience, and to learning as living.

We are arguing for the learning community as a container for growth and learning at the same time as taking a post-modern view that there is no fixed or stable centre. We position ourselves between totalitarian humanism and anarchy. We support not modularization—little containers that structurally don't come together—but a coming together, in the consulting room as on the psychological therapy training programme, in which primacy is given to the experiential, in the sense of a meeting between people and the new saying (rather than a dwelling on the already said: see Levinas 1985: 88) that can emerge from a meeting between people. Learning from experience is difficult, however, because the world is such a scary place, and to varying extents, we have all been traumatized by it. To categorize learning into self-contained modules can work to shield learners and teachers from the anxieties of experience. There is, of course, some argument that universities are not the best places wherein to run psychological therapy training (Parker 2002). In further and higher education, it is hard to get lecturers to spend six hours a day with students when there is no module, category, or economic justification for this.

Modularization is allied to managerialism. Education—including some psychological therapy trainings—becomes something to be packaged and consumed, a commodity, and as such lends itself as a defence against, rather than an opening onto, the complexities of shared experience (a phenomenon that was becoming evident even three decades ago—see Toffler 1973). Similarly, in the wider society, people are further and further away from being contained, except in little parts of the day—for example, when watching TV, or in the pub—in modules. The value of psychological therapy, we would argue, is precisely that, as a shared activity, it is not about seeing experience as modular, and learning as commodity.

In talking about the learning community of the programme, and its values, we are talking about the wider community too, and giving a primacy to questions of value. In different ways, we all belong to learning communities. Argyris & Schon (1995), for example, wrote about the learning organization in terms of business values. An essential question is about the value of a community in which business values might play a part but not a dominant part.

We conclude this chapter by offering some thoughts about psychological therapy in training and ethics. In our understanding, the pursuit of self-knowledge, through such approaches as the humanistic, behavioural, or psychoanalytic, must come second to something else. Emotional learning on the programme is not primarily skills- or knowledge-based, but begins with questioning what it means to be in the world of and with others. Some ethical implications for emotional learning might, we have argued, be found in the work of the French philosopher Emmanuel Levinas (1905–1995). However, as Levinas questions our cultural assumptions about giving a primacy to autonomy, by arguing that we should privilege heteronomy, so it is expected that what appears right for a society, and hence influences how we train psychological therapists, will be even more challenged when we explore what is taken as evidence in other cultures where Western ideas of authenticity and psychological depth—as well as such aspects as the acceptability to reveal emotion—may lead to a very different training that is more culturally appropriate. Such clashes in culture have been explored on a larger scale by those such as Hofstede (2001) who suggested that we might consider "intercultural management" in terms of individualism versus collectivism (which could include competitiveness versus caring), high and low respect for authority, masculinity versus femininity, and short-term versus long-term orientation. Lichia & Raymond (1985) and Lago (2006), amongst others, have used Hofstede's framework to explore value dimensions and issues of race and intercultural therapy; but would such concepts also be helpful in exploring the appropriateness of a therapeutic culture for the communities it serves?

The place taken up by teachers and therapists might also be considered abusive in terms of the teachers'/therapists' personal power because of their compliance to the dominant discourse. There are many questions concerning the training of psychological therapists. Who determines whether the training of therapists meets the need of the population(s)? When is the course culture (regarding both what is learned and how) something for the broader society to aspire to; and who decides this? Yet are "market forces" not another form of state control? When is a therapy oppressive, and when is it liberating? How does what we offer fit the different perspectives of our culture; and should it? When do we successfully adapt to what is good, and when do we successfully resist the bad? When is therapy a form of social control attempting to regulate our identity, particularly in a multi-cultural society?

In order to establish the suitability of the policy determinants in the education of psychological therapists, it is clear that the issues are complex, involving, for example, questions of identity for therapeutic communities, as well as larger dominant and minority communities. There are also questions of individual and collective identity that post-modernism has thrown some light on—even though it may initially cause more disturbance. On a visit to New Zealand by one of the authors (Loewenthal), these questions arose in terms of post-colonialism. Pakeha (European), Maori, Samoan, or Asian, there is no simple way out—which "language" does one use? Who "interculturally" manages whom? Which experience does one privilege? Will wherever one comes from lead to some form of cultural domination? Perhaps such questions are becoming increasingly problematic for all of us in the so-called global village with its apparent opportunities and problematics. It is hoped that post-existentialism can provide another way of keeping open that which our dominant managerialist culture attempts to keep out.

CHAPTER NINE

Research, ideology, and the evolution of intersubjectivity in a post-existential culture

Del Loewenthal

Introduction

Freud and Rogers would both seem to suggest that it is important, for what in the UK we now term the "psychological therapies", to keep up to date with cultural changes/fashions in what is taken to be research (and evidence). But is keeping up to date in terms of coming alongside different to doing it, let alone believing in it? It would appear that both Freud and Rogers did actually attempt to carry out what was in vogue in terms of research and evidence. So, would it be futile to attempt to convince our society of the need to consider other forms of evidence and research which may be more suited to the psychological therapies, yet contradict the current dominant evidence/research discourse? This does seem to have happened in, for example, France, whereas previously, as reported in the *European Journal of Psychotherapy and Counselling*, the French Minister for Health proposed that psychoanalysis should not be subject to prevailing notions of evidence-based practice, but should be allowed to develop in its own way (Snell, 2007). It is suggested in this chapter that in considering what we should take as evidence and research in the psychological therapies, one fundamental question is "what is the ideology we bring in exploring the nature of psychological therapeutic knowledge"? Particularly as it would appear that we don't really know how such therapies work. Furthermore, notwithstanding the phenomenological arguments against theory (Heidegger; Merleau-Ponty), it is increasingly being questioned as to the usefulness of the various competing theories (Craib 1987; Heaton 2000; House 2008). Perhaps they are there more to take the psychological therapists' minds off their problems than necessarily to be of any direct benefit to their clients/patients !!

A further interesting development is the idea that there may be some common factors (Bergin, 1982; Orlinsky & Howard, 1987) that are helpful to all these therapies, the relationship being foremost among them (Beutler & Harwood 2002). Yet, how are such "facts" arrived at? It is finally being recognized that Randomized Control Trials (RCTs) are frequently idiotic in looking at the effectiveness of psychological therapies (as if it were possible to keep everything constant except for one variable!).

In the UK, the Medical Research Council is currently funding research in order to examine approaches other than RCTs that bodies such as the National Institute of Clinical Excellence might consider (MRC Methodology Research Programme). However, it would also appear that most people involved in psychological therapeutic research aren't so much interested in research as proving that their particular approach is a winner (see, for example, Winter 2010, on "The Allegiance Effect").

In contrast, however, there are arguments that the current directions of research in the psychological therapies are helpful. Furthermore, Mick Cooper suggests 'the facts are friendly" (Cooper 2008). Both BACP and UKCP have recently published examples of research that they think to be of particular help to practitioners and are increasingly running conferences partly in order to encourage the use of research and show the government that they can talk this language. (Indeed, I have both contributed to one of these publications and have been conference chair for such an event.) What does all this say? Perhaps, what is particularly important is to show what we don't know in questioning claims made but again in saying this, where am I coming from?

In the UK, at the time of writing, psychological therapy bodies are prioritizing research within their organizations and within their training courses in an attempt to stay in the game at least until (and if) the government reduces their influence through their plan (though watered down by the subsequent coalition government) for the

Health Professions Council (HPC) to take over statutory regulation of the various psychological therapies, and the Department of Health through a policy entitled "Skills for Health" approve only those therapeutic approaches in the public services which are deemed "evidence-based". And, as if this wasn't enough state regulation, there is also the funding of the government's new "Improving Access to Psychological Therapies" programme which avoids existing umbrella psychological therapist bodies and is mainly based on cognitive behavioural therapy (CBT).

One aspect of the rapid development of CBT which is highly seductive is its apparent ability to incorporate anything that research has proven to work. There are, of course, many other reasons for CBT's popularity, including the fact that it is cheaper to train therapists and that both therapists and, more importantly, society can condone and indeed encourage the prevention of thoughts coming to them. So, are we are now so alienated that we can no longer experience our alienation? (Loewenthal 2009).

Again, at the time of writing, another major body, the British Psychological Society, in a last-ditch stand has recently attempted to influence the HPC (who are again taking over statutory regulation from them) that entry level for counselling and clinical psychologists will be at practitioner doctorate level. They will also continue to award their own members an accolade through conferring the title "Chartered Scientist". Meanwhile, there is great danger that both the attempts in many areas of the psychological therapies to make entry increasingly at doctoral level will lead to a few thousand more words on the Masters dissertations previously often just focusing on applying a technique for research methods and that this research will do little good. Indeed, there is a danger that it will harm practice, not only in terms of its so-called "findings", but doing for research what the American psychoanalyst Otto Kernberg (1996), termed "thirty methods to destroy the creativity of psychoanalytic candidates". Yet, there remain such questions as: How are potential clients/patients, and indeed governments, to determine which therapist to go for? Can there be something better than word of mouth?

It is also, of course, possible for good to come out of this work, particularly for the individual research practitioner, but there are many pitfalls to be overcome if it is to optimize thoughtful practice; for a start, the whole idea of the practitioner researcher which Freud warned us against. For carrying out research on our own clients leads us to having an agenda which takes away from being attentive (though, it could be argued that Freud himself was a practitioner researcher).

What is being suggested here is that there is a need to come alongside current fashions in research, but that we should still be sceptical about its relationship with truth and consider more where we are coming from. We could, as mentioned in Chapter One, at least pay far more attention to what the founding fathers of psychology took to be essential: the marrying of empirical research with the cultural and historical (Wundt, 1904). There is, of course, a need sometimes to just do empirical research but this should not necessarily be the norm. Indeed, there may also be a case that in order to be clear, what may be called for is a non-empirical research approach. For example, Cioffi (1998) asks when is it a mistake to take our interest in a phenomenon in the direction of an enquiry into its cause and conditions, rather than be concerned with the impression that it has on us or the ruminations that it produces in us? He argues that it is at least sometimes a mistake to proceed as if a phenomenon calls for empirical enquiry when what is really wanted with respect to it is "clarity as to the sources of our preoccupation and, where appropriate, untroubled contemplation of it" (Cioffi, 1998, p. 1). He claims that Freud makes this mistake: he tries to explain when what is needed is "clarification" of the significance for us of these phenomena. Perhaps Cioffi is arguing less against empirical research and more about questioning of its appropriateness, and in particular with our difficulty with seeing when this is not what we need. Thus, issues of ideological dominance, through establishing a form of research by ensuring the way in which it is questioned is within pre-described parameters, should be essential aspects of research.

Doctoral-level research can be helpful in developing thoughtful practice in the psychological therapist, but this cannot be achieved with narrow notions of evidence as its basis. (How indeed does one explore, let alone measure, evidence of love, intimacy, friendship—how stupid can we get if we think the quality of our lives can be assessed by measuring this just quantitatively, let alone qualitatively attempting to ape the quantitative?) Instead, we need to open up theories and methods, both in the psychological therapies and in the way we attempt to research them, not only epistemologically, ontologically, and methodologically, but also ideologically, in order sometimes to enable that which we cannot and may not ever be able to measure, so that it can flourish. Currently, our positivistic research seems concerned with not only narrow notions of evidence, but narrow notions of method.

But Freud and Rogers would not have necessarily argued that what they were doing was a special case which would not fit the prevailing notions of research; though, importantly, their work was not constrained by this. So, should we do the same and carry out RCTs (however absurd they may often seem in this context) but not let our thoughts be censored by this? The danger is that the use of research as an attempt at psychological therapistization and political game-playing in the name of psychological therapist survival will in fact constrict the nature of the psychotherapeutic endeavour. Furthermore, is there no possibility that we could work and genuinely search for truth with all its problematics—to look at whether what we are doing is helpful and how we might improve—rather than attempting to prove that what we are doing works?!

Traditionally, such endeavours have been the province of clinical supervision—though this has usually been done within the ideology of a particular modality. In order to be able to think how we might be more helpful, we need to perhaps consider more the relationship between truth and method (Gadamer, 1975) and in particular how the current dominant cultural ideology, as well as the underlying modality ideologies, attempt to set up research methods which wrongly appear as independent.

We now have governments involved in significantly funding the psychological therapies and questionably involved in statutory regulation (Parker & Revelli 2008). There are many concerns here, including that the state, through regulating psychological therapies, is conveniently focusing on symptoms rather than societal causes (Loewenthal 2009). There is also, within the managerial language of accountability and transparency and suchlike (delightful concepts for surreptitious ideological manipulation), the need for the use of research methods that will legitimize this way of thinking. And while, on the one hand, I have some sympathies with policy makers who wish to make the best use of their resources, how can we do this if we don't really know how psychotherapy works? What seems to have happened is that the research methods which have come to the forefront are those that sustain this managerialist ideology in favouring those modalities which are the cheapest to provide and take our minds both individually and as a society off the causes of our problems. As with other modalities, this may be right for some of the people some of the time, but it can't be right, as the state now seems to hope, for all of the people all of the time.

At least starting with practice can be seen to be of increasing importance as a reaction to technological and managerialist approaches. Perhaps by starting to explore the practice-based research, this might play a part in the emergence of a new form of cultural capital whereby psychotherapists and others can use their abilities in a slightly different way to influence what they regard as important. But what then are our underlying values in researching therapeutic relations? What, for example, has happened to intersubjectivity after post-modernism?

Post-modern discourses have been on the fringe of a scientific/empirical tradition and logic that dominate research in the United Kingdom, unlike in continental Europe. However, post-modernism, whilst dated, is still perhaps foremost amongst a cluster of approaches constituting the mainstream of contemporary debate (as shown, for example, in current cultural discourses on film, architecture, and literary criticism). Furthermore, whilst the term "post-existential" will be used here, it is argued that there is still a good deal of rigour in aspects of post-modernism which can usefully inform our practice.

Research from the post-modern to the post-existential

The post-modern challenged the modern narrative: those we research as tellers of stories would have us believe that as narrators, they tell us what is real as it happens. However, from a post-modern perspective, this would be a naive approach. Respondents operate like movie directors: they are editing, have biases, can toe the party line, etc. Thus there are histories and not history—it is also more problematic for us to see our jobs as researchers as just facilitating the researched to tell a story, as if it were the story with our respondent centre stage and most probably subject to little.

As researchers, one important question, in which many claim to have a particular interest, concerns where our values lie. When are perversions intolerable? When in imposing standards are we treating others as puppets? Post-modernism and its method, deconstruction, has again been useful here, as it is concerned with studying standards. Sometime in our history, Christianity formed the standards. Later, the scientific method came to prominence. But then it became clearer that there are different scientific methods and, as with other cultural practices, at any given time there are certain standards which are valued and those that are not valued.

One aspect we are interested in at the Research Centre for Therapeutic Education is the psychological therapies as a form of learning. To what extent has the development of psychological therapy, and indeed research, been emerging in an era of individualism when the standards are centred on the person—for example, self-directed learning and person-centred counselling (or even "I Did It My Way"!). So we move from God to science to the person—so is the person the new God, and which person is it: the researcher or the researched? It is argued here that researchers will still be subject to what emerges in the research interview and, through it, the way we experience such aspects as language and ethics.

Therapeutic theory

Whilst it is assumed that all schools of the psychological therapies have potentially useful implications for research, post-modernism has challenged all of them. As researchers, what do we consider it means to be human? Humanistic approaches have the self at the centre. In fact, a behavioural, humanistic, existential, and, in most cases, psychoanalytic orientation can create delusional systems, in that they would have a client/those we research believe that they are the core, the centre, the subject. If we attempt to see ourselves as subjects, then do we treat everybody else as an object? We are all subject too.

The subjectification process has been written about in a variety of ways—for example, linguistically by Derrida (1978) and Lacan (1966), pragmatically by Deleuze (1990), genealogically by Foucault (1980), and ethically by Levinas (1969). Let us take Lacan and Levinas as writers who are sometimes associated with the post-modern but who may still be helpful in our thinking about research. Lacan was particularly interested in language and psychoanalysis. For Lacan, Freud (1900) was really saying that the unconscious is our ruler, and this is one of the reasons why, for Lacan, "words speak us". Lacan continues to have a worldwide influence on psychoanalysis and feminism (Irigaray 1985; Kristeva 1969, 1986).

Lacan talks of the baby looking at itself in the mirror (which could be the mother's eyes) wanting to be told that it is masterful and the centre of the world whilst in fact it is clumsy and dependent. To what extent do researchers attempt to bring about such a re-provided service for those they research, and ultimately for themselves? Is this delusional, as the situation never really did exist, or is it at best a form of nostalgia (Oakley 1990)? Lacan pointed out that Freud's followers tamed his radicalism and subversiveness so that not only did their approach become more technique-orientated but they minimized the effect of the unconscious—it wasn't OK that it ruled—and many then sold psychoanalysis on the idea that the ego could really be in charge (e.g., Hartmann 1958). In contrast, behaviourists assume that rationality will win the day whether it's the therapist or client who knows best. Humanistic approaches can be seen as similar in that individuals are the centre of their world and, through therapy, it is sometimes claimed that they can be in charge of changing into the people they want to become. Furthermore, a post-modern analysis would suggest that we can never be a "whole" person, and that such attempts to incorporate everything that is good and different are often selfish, and can be driven by the wish not to face death (see Chapter Three and Blanchot 1993). Thus, Rogers (1967) is modern, with grand narratives being written by the client.

Furthermore, as researchers, should we be attempting empathy? To attempt to know the other can not only be impossible but can also be violent. Would it be better to accept the other as different not even in comparison with our school and ourselves but from a different difference (Derrida 1978; Levinas 1969)? Existentialism can help us explore our experience of relationships, but it can also be seen as being modern, for whilst there is a disillusionment with reason, it is still egocentric— the person is at the centre. Perhaps if we are interested in meaning emerging between people after the post-modern era, yet being influenced by it, might this lead to what has been suggested in this book as the post-existential?

Implications of post-existentialism for research

Post-modernism has blown the whistle on scientific intellectualism as one more form of Victorian morality which inappropriately tries to establish itself with reference to people.

Again, as has been argued elsewhere (Loewenthal 1996, 2003), one then has to move the parameters of science beyond the quantifiable to the qualitative. This is not intellectual and rational but possibly ethical in a new tradition, one that is yet to really emerge. The science of quality would regard the ethical as arbiter—it is the wellbeing for one's fellow person/humanity. Could this emerge, albeit with difficulty, from the current two cultures of the scientific and non-scientific?

Much of qualitative research involves relationships, not only in its conclusions but particularly in the way it is carried out. Yet how can we carry this out? Existing qualitative research methods mimic quantitative approaches for their legitimacy. Thus "phenomenological" research attempts to show it is scientific, yet if it stuck to Husserl's (1960) intentions, then the word "research" would be redundant and notions of meaning units and so on (Colaizzi 1973; Giorgi 1985) could be seen to be psychologisms that technologize thinking, preventing the phenomenological from emerging. Such "phenomenological research" does, however, attempt to examine what emerges in the between but still assumes that words come from the things themselves; and developments such as those in structural linguistics are not considered.

Other qualitative research is modern, assuming either interviewee or interviewer as the one who truly speaks, with the message sent being the one received. Questionably, grounded theory (Glaser & Strauss 1967) assumes that the interviewees are at the centre and that the researcher can remove their own being from the relationship. This in many ways has similarities with much narrative research (McLeod, 1997), with the focus on the researched being centre stage. In contrast, Heuristic research (Moustakas 1994) puts the researcher centre stage, and the researched are used to convince the reader of the legitimacy of the researcher's own experience. Again, this is modern. A more recent development is discourse analysis (Potter & Wetherell 1987) which gives a primacy to language and attempts to allow the research "to be subject to", though there is something like a modern procedure for achieving this! Whereas, feminist-post-modern research (Bungay & Keddy 1996) has the problem of transferring its approach into action whilst being true to its underlying philosophy. There again, case study method and action research (Gummesson 2000; Yin 1984) have possibilities in the moment but are problematic when it comes to generalization.

Hollway's (1989) work on subjectivity, with her criticism of "the almost intentional blindness of psychology to its own conditions of production", is applicable. Some further questions of the implications of post-modernism for research are explored in Scheurich (1997) and Kvale (1992). For example, Scheurich (1997) points out how research is presented as if researcher and researched assumed understanding is fixed in time, and therefore does not take into account how what we think can change, sometimes in the next instant. Post-modernism has therefore shown us how problematic it is both to attempt to synthesize research involving people and how difficult it is to research another as other. Yet it is becoming more apparent that if we were entirely caught up in post-modernism, we wouldn't be able to have any understanding of each other. Could post-existentialism enable us sometimes to reach a truth whilst being subject to?

The psychologizing of therapeutic research

From some post-modern perspectives, research, from which so many psychological therapist bodies, universities, and research students hope so much will flow, can also be seen to be about images which are images of images (like Warhol's *Campbell's Soup*). Nevertheless, the design of the soup can make people buy it. Researchers, along with psychological therapists' professional bodies, have therefore become far more concerned with image management. However, as has been previously mentioned, modernism is always attempting to capture post-modernism. *Campbell's Soup* doesn't have a core; one can only have a core from a subjective perspective, that is, from a modern rather than a post-modern reading. Typically, "research-speak" as well as "psycho-therapy-speak" is modern, with the productive subject at the centre. Evidence-based practice and quantification both suit approaches like the cognitive behavioural, and can produce useful results (despite "evidence" often being too narrowly defined—Loewenthal 2006), but as a dominant discourse can provide dangerous cover stories to replace the human rather than allowing it to come first.

Previously, it was suggested that one would be creating a delusional system if one were to believe in the client as having a "core". However, could Levinas (1969), who brought phenomenology to France and greatly influenced the post-modernism of the likes of Lyotard and Derrida, and who talks of "justice" and "responsibility" rather than psychologisms, be both, as has been argued here, less delusional and a good example of post-existentialism? What has been argued in Chapter Two in terms of the relationship between psychological therapist and client patient, it is suggested, occurs in the relationship between researcher and researched. The argument in that chapter comparing Buber and Levinas has implications for the practice of research as well.

I have devised a framework summarizing the previous discussion on the implications of Levinasian ethics for research. This can be used to discuss specific theories and methods in research (and counselling and psychotherapy) in terms of the ethics of the ontological:

A researcher's ethical window

	Researched puts Researched first	Researched puts Researcher first
Researcher puts Researcher first	*Theories and methods*	*Theories and methods*
Researcher puts Researched first	*Theories and methods*	*Theories and methods*

The researcher's ethical window is typically a two-dimensional model; the main axis concerns whether the researcher puts the researcher or the researched first. The other axis is whether the researched puts the researched or the researcher first. In bringing this second dimension, reciprocity is not intended; "I'll put you first if you put me first." However, both dimensions seem needed for responsible relatedness (Gans 1989) to exist. For the researcher to put the researched first is a complex notion: it does not necessarily mean doing what the researched wants, or denying the researcher's desire, as both would not necessarily be putting the other first. Moreover, if speaking of the other as other is yet another technique of seduction, in the name of putting the other first, then is it not "me first", yet again? There is the concern that such notions as Levinas' ethical practice might be used as the new, ever more subtle, seduction. Perhaps Hegel's fable of master–slave, where we have no choice but to be either master or slave (Sarup 1993), is always inevitable—both in the macro sense, with regard to the position between countries as explored below, and in the micro sense, within the consulting room. If this is the case, then the seducer must always only appear to be open and never really reveal the thinking behind what is happening.

An implication of Levinas' writing is that if we put our individualistic theories first, rather than the other, we are at best privileging a position that gives primacy to autonomy at the expense of others, and our society in general. It is hoped that the researcher's ethical window will help an evaluation of theories of research methods and the psychological therapies. But what about the world beyond the dyad of researcher and researched? What, for example, of the politics of society; and our place in it as a researcher? What exploration is allowed of cultural values that we are, often unknowingly, expounding and the values regarding cultures in conflict? Below is an exploration of one way of responding to these questions. Others who are also interested in implications of such ethics for research will, I hope, wish to open up other ways.

Research and cultural contexts: what is the ideology of research?

In order to explore how our ideology as researchers may reinforce through our practices the conflicts outlined above, I wish to describe what might be taken as a spoof, a story amongst stories. In Bram Stoker's *Dracula*, the victims are identified by a mark caused by Dracula's embrace (Stoker 1994). Dracula was someone else who came from Central Europe (besides Freud and Husserl). In Europe and elsewhere, is there also a consistent mark left on trainees and through them their clients/patients?

I once saw a mark on a French provincial town wall; it read "G8 ASSASSINS". This reflects concern that the rich countries of the world meet in order to sustain and enhance their position in *relation* to the "third world", which we are being asked to refer to as "less economically developed countries". Within these eight rich countries, there is also a *relational* economic pecking order that has been called a class system. All these countries also have psychological therapists and psychotherapists examining their *relationships* with their clients in order to help these clients with their *relationships* with others. What connection, if any, is there between these macro and micro situations?

If one accepts that the privileged few, in terms of world economies, are living from the added value generated through the manipulation of third-world economies, then is this mirrored both in research and in the consulting room? Through various colonial and post-colonial policies, countries in Europe and North America have been able to generate and preserve an economic advantage for their people over many others.

Have such policies attempted to put their populations' minds at rest through developing an ideology where ideology is a dirty word? For sure, many Europeans and North Americans would reach into their pockets if they were to meet for more than a fleeting moment a young child making, for example, sports shoes for us Westerners; but then, would our economy as we know it collapse? Yet the mark-up from such products allows that we, the purchasers, gain both the shoes and a well-heeled system.

What, then, of the relationship between researcher and researched—is it not a microcosm of the global economy? Is it in any way possible that research is encouraged to collude with bids for dominance, maintaining and enhancing privilege through a form of Dracula-like blood-sucking whereby the researcher instructs others in the ever-changing cultural forms of seduction within our own social order? For the behaviourist, conceptually, "demand" was the buzz word: would one be assertive enough to take one's shoes back to the shop and get them changed, without really much notion of the shop assistant as "other"? The humanists seemed more interested in need, where the individual primarily puts him- or herself first as the subject, with the associated danger of putting the other second as object.

Furthermore, is the analyst's interest, in, for example, wishes or desires, any less selfish? Deleuze & Guattari (1977) describe various ways in which the seductions of power, status, and money encourage the repression of non-conforming revolutionary desire. Deleuze & Guattari oppose themselves to the Freudian and Lacanian emphases on Oedipus and Signifier, and therefore the psychoanalytic priesthood. (It is perhaps to be expected that such texts seem rarely to appear in psychological therapy training.) Psychotherapeutic researchers continue to make political choices without necessarily being aware that all the time there is a translation or mediation of something between the researched and the culture we are in. Perhaps one aspect influencing the fashions of and in schools of psychological therapy research (and not given the attention it perhaps deserves) is that change is required when the manipulative elements of the current dominant schools become overt. In all these systems of thought, and for any management ideology, is a manipulative seduction essential? People are taught to show that they appear to listen, but if they were really to listen, they would be brought face to face with the potential exploitation in their relationships; or in their societies, and in that third-world child making those shoes. What is fostered instead is a way of thinking whereby an examination of the way we think politically throughout our society, including conducting research, is taboo.

There are a few examinations of politics and social responsibility in the therapies, of which Samuels (2001) is an erudite example. It can be argued that these attempts are continually necessary, for, as with the drops of blood at the end of those *Dracula* films, everyone knows that this means that the monster within has not been eradicated but only suppressed, and needs always to be fought again. Indeed, it may be considered too grandiose a thought for what we as researchers can do (if it did not have the further backing of Deleuze & Guattari); for it was an operation launched from a "lunatic asylum" (a place familiar to many of us) that "destroyed" Count Dracula. Deleuze & Guattari stress the collective nature of desire, with "no separation between the personal and the social, the individual and the collective" (Sarup 1993: 93). Following Reich's interest in the mass psychology of fascism, they believe that "the unconscious is a political force and that fascism dwells in it as much as on the historical stage or in political parties" (Sarup 1993: 93). Deleuze & Guattari argue that there are two types of desire: the paranoid (a reactionary desire—based on the authoritative structure of the hierarchical state) and the schizophrenic (a real desire—centred on flight). These correspond respectively, in social terms, to: the authoritarian (insistence on centralized power) and the libertarian (loose organizations without territorial limits or a system of hierarchy). For Deleuze & Guattari, Freudian psychoanalysis is an example of interpretation as impoverishment. It is when a patient's life has been rewritten according to the terms of Freud's family romance. Yet our students rarely seem permitted to consider such far-reaching alternatives. There is thus less chance that we can fight and leave a different mark, even if only for a while. Or is such talk just a minor safety valve in the process of globalization creating the illusion of free speech?

So ends this story. What has been presented is not typical of therapeutic research training. Similarly, the main streams of research (as well as psychoanalysis, counselling, psychotherapy, psychology, and psychiatry) lack much in the way of radical ideological challenges. It would thus appear that research students of the psychological therapies learn little about politics and ideology through their formal training. Whilst it is widely acknowledged that this lack of radicalized modernism is apparent in all forms of cultural practice (Lyotard 1984; Parker 1997), it is, interestingly, particularly pronounced in the psychological therapies. An important and complex question for researchers (following from the work of a photographer) concerns the encouragement of "tradition and continuity rather than rupture and change" (Bolton 1989). Related questions include: How individually, and particularly collectively, do we orchestrate meaning? What other ways of understanding have been dismantled and destroyed? With the success of late modernism, has the political basis of modernism been pushed aside so that we think of our practice as apolitical? Has modernism therefore re-structured knowledge? And what effects have our classification systems and psychological therapizing processes had on meaning?

Mainstream psychological therapy research literature appears apolitical. Where change for the individual is examined, the social consequences in terms of notions of how we view "the good", "health", or "madness", let alone changing fashions in research and the legitimization of knowledge, are not left open to close scrutiny for long. How is research used to promote class, and national interests? Do claims of lifting repression lift off the chains of oppression, or do they become part of a more sophisticated oppression? Mainstream psychological therapy research practice appears to offer little by way of analysis of the effects of power in representation, generally encouraging the reverse and implying that what is discussed (in the consulting room) is neutral and above ideology. This tendency is expressed in the frequent refusal of psychological therapy to consider anything other than to incorporate all that is said into an uncritical history of psychotherapy (which is self-contained, self-referential, and self-justifying). This potentially strengthens the role of psychotherapy and psychological therapy as the voice for the status quo. Furthermore, there is now the hope, indirectly supported by governments, that the teaching of research will strengthen the professions. So where are the critical histories of psychological therapy; and what place will the researcher take up?

What are the politics of the psychological therapy truth(s)? Danto (1998) uses archival and oral history in attempting to show that Freud proposed the creation of clinics providing free treatment. We could, for example, ask, "What is the importance of this article appearing, opening up what is claimed to be a "little known aspect of the history of psychoanalysis" in terms of changes in the economics of private practice?" In fact, does research of any therapeutic truth require in turn an analysis of power, which in turn depends upon our understanding of the social and political aims of the psychological therapies? Thus, for example, the expectation of what is psychological therapy in itself confines psychotherapy into a particular discursive space. There again, what are the effects of notions of liberalism and objectivity on psychotherapeutic practice? Can they actually supplement social activism and, if so, is this a legitimate aim? To raise such questions is to call into question the ideological closure that would appear to generally characterize psychological therapy training and research.

To choose a final example from Bolton's book on photography, research "can be used to honour or repress its subjects, to either compliment the 'ceremonial presentation of the bourgeois self' or 'establish and delimit the terrain of the other' ". In this way, research can be seen to aid in "the construction of social and moral hierarchies". Derrida (1996) has argued how the concept of the archive is fundamental to our understanding of meaning. Yet can such developments find their way into research through our psychological therapy programmes?

The questions raised here, to borrow from Bolton yet again, are "intended to be productive rather than exhaustive". Behind the above questions is perhaps a whole further set of assumptions, arguments for change in the psychological therapies and for change in the history of history and interpretation of interpretations, arguments for acknowledging the changing relationships within society. Is it too grandiose to consider how research can best change society? Is it something that just happens? In other words, do we simply accept the attempted separation of culture and society promoted by late modernism? Perhaps the most important question is why (with the possible exception of sexual difference) such questions have so seldom explicitly been researched.

This chapter has started to examine some implications of post-existentialism for research in the context of the psychological therapies in the twenty-first century. Post-existentialism has been put forward as a possible way of exploring what, for example, the implications are of claims of the death of God, science, and the subject for how we research human experience in the clinical encounter. It has been argued that, despite criticisms, it may be essential that the implications of post-existentialism are considered for all existing (modern) modalities of therapy. Through post-existentialism, as introduced in Chapter Two, such questions arise for the researcher as for the therapist as to: What is the place of psychotherapeutic theory in examining how we research human experience through psychotherapeutic discourse? Is it possible to have both justice and action? Are, for example, behavioural, humanistic, existential, and most of psychoanalytic theories merely perpetuating unintentional violence? Has traditional thinking been replaced by theories with fields of knowledge, territories, and ownership of psychotherapeutic subject disciplines policed by economic licensing arrangements, which in turn attempt to control language and thought—appropriating difference in the name of difference? How can we research human experience within the context of the clinical encounter in terms of ideas of truth, justice, and responsibility? Are there ethical implications through which we can assist as researchers in an embodied way so that we help others not to do violence to others? Indeed, is it possible for researchers (and therapists) not to interrupt their own and others' continuity, not to play roles in which they no longer recognize themselves and whereby they betray not only their commitments but their own substance? A post-existential exploration of the above questions in terms of relational ontologies still has to be developed, and perhaps this will be made through those such as Derrida, Lacan, and in particular Levinas' injunction to put the other first and be responsible for the other's responsibility.

In another sense, this chapter is arguing for the development of phenomenology through post-modernism, and argues that whatever the cultural changes we are currently in, that post-existentialism may be a useful (and even perhaps necessary) way of thinking about starting with practice and the relational. How can we research "what is", and phenomenologically open up aspects of psychoanalysis such as the unconscious and aspects of post-modernism, which have in part been built on phenomenology? We are subject to these cultural views, yet human agency is possible and can be enhanced, but neither if we think we can be fully in charge, nor if we think we are completely subject to aspects such as language.

To conclude, the post-existential may help us to be more thoughtful in and about our practice. For example, being cast into the role of the psychological therapist researcher could be a self-deceptive language. One imagines one is concerned about the other person. Where we want to appear concerned we set up the stage (Gans 1989) to look like the good relational researcher, psychological therapist, psychotherapist, psychologist—but do we really acknowledge the other? Also, in our attempts for such agency, is the potency and potentiality of our own lives diminished? Furthermore, how do we prepare researchers for putting the other first, in a way that is not about self/psychological therapist image and privilege? How do we know when they are ready? Perhaps, a Levinasian implication would be to aim towards (as with issues of psychological therapist ethics) not determining our responsibility as teachers of research for our trainee researcher's responsibility to those they research, by application of a set of rules. Instead of being primarily concerned with systems of power and knowledge, we should be more concerned with justice on a case by case basis—for real justice cannot be appropriated or territorialized—the researcher has to be just in the moment with another. Such justice may enable us more to explore the "what is" and not end up being driven by an unthinking cultural (often technical) response. Levinas shows us one way in which we might examine the "what is" which is influenced by our changing cultural practices, bringing about different fashions in theories and research methods. The post-existential, in also including the possibility of such aspects as the unconscious and developments in structural linguistics, shows that our way of thinking is inevitably caught up with our socio-cultural setting, but that relational research of aspects of human agency, which we can never fully be in charge of, is, as both Kierkegaard (for existentialism) and Derrida (for post-modernism) have pointed out, more than enough to make us "tremble".

CHAPTER TEN

Towards a therapy without foundations

Del Loewenthal

In this book, we have argued for the place of practice at the heart of psychotherapy. This aim can be seen as stretching from the time of Pyrrhonian scepticism to, more recently, the writings of Wittgenstein, where post-existentialism can be understood to be more about the activities in which we participate with our clients/patients. There is therefore an increasing body of opinion showing the futility of theory as the basis of the psychological therapies and, with it, what is currently regarded as research. But the psychological therapies are also cultural practices, and this book is an attempt to reformulate an understanding of meaning as contextual and emerging through psychological therapists and patients having social intercourse.

Thus, how we understand such emerging meaning will be mediated by cultural practices through the mixture of ideas that permeate our society in any period. This book is therefore an attempt to put the case for what is termed "post-existentialism", by defining a potential cultural moment in contrast to the positivistic, managerialist, audit culture that currently pervades. The hope is that the implications of examining meaning, through post-existentialism, show how such enterprises can never have a foundation. The book is therefore written to increase the possibility that what is termed "post-existentialism" will help psychological therapists start with practice and will enable them to help their patients/clients. Thus, not only CBT, but any therapies whether they be humanistic, existential, or psychoanalytic, which become total-izing moves, are potentially violent. At best, such theories are second-ary and, whilst they may have implications, they can never provide a foundation to the primacy of practice.

There is, of course, the danger that in attempting to give a cultural moment a name, it becomes a modality rather than a passing moment. Those authors whose names regularly appear in these chapters more frequently use non-technical, ordinary language, though sometimes they, and particularly their followers, have been tempted to provide a theoretical foundation for practice. It is clearly a danger for which those involved with post-existentialism will have to be mindful.

But first to briefly summarize this book. In Chapter One on "The very idea of post-existentialism", I attempt to explore a way of giving a pri-macy to practice through re-opening existentialism in the name of post-existentialism. I follow this in Chapter Two on "From existentialism to post-existentialism: from Buber to Levinas" by privileging the work of Levinas. Yet, as with post-existentialism of which Levinas' influence is currently such an important part, his work can never be a basis of practice but can hopefully lead us, better than most, to not giving a primacy to theory. In attempting to start with practice, one needs to let go of any Levinasian mantra. Again, with Julia Cayne in Chapter Three "Post-phenomenology and the between as unknown", we attempt to re-open phenomenology in the name of post-phenomenology through an exploration of questions of an unknown. With Dennis Greenwood in Chapter Four "On learning to work with someone with a label: some post-existential implications for practice, theory, and research", we particulalry explore through a case study a possible way, influenced by post-existentialism, of researching the psychological therapies as well as considering Levinas' important notion of the non-intentional. In Chapter Five, "Language, experience, and representation: a re-examination of the case of Lola Voss", with Rhiannon Thomas, we explore the suggested elliptical relationship between language and experience by revisiting the existentialist Binswanger's patient Lola Voss and providing an exploration from a post-existential perspective. With Tom Cotton in Chapter Six, "Laing and the treatment is the way we treat people", we reassess Laing's pioneering therapeutic commu-nity at Kingsley Hall from which post-existentialism could be seen as one development. In Chapter Seven, "Post-existentialism, counselling psychology, and the diagnosis of schizophrenia", with Patrick Larsson, we look at the emerging profession of counselling psychology and consider how from a post-existential perspective these psychologists are having to appear to work within a medical model, which may be unhealthy for them as well as their clients. With Robert Snell in Chapter Eight, "A training in post-existentialism: placing Rogers and psychoanalysis", we provide an example of the trainings that I have been involved for over thirty years in developing, many of them with Robert. Then, in Chapter Nine, I return to one of the preoccupations of this book, as there is currently a strong demand for a particular variant of it in our audit culture which has from at least a post-existential perspective little to do with thoughtful practice, namely research (another related preoccupation is the rise of manualized therapies). The authors of these chapters have backgrounds in art history, education, management, nursing, philosophy, and psychology—all of which have directly or indirectly contributed to and could be influenced by post-existentialism. All this takes me to this chapter, which is attempting to put the case for using post-existentialism to move towards a therapy without foundations.

Throughout this book, the main problem would appear to be reification. For to take these chapters again: in Chapter Two, it is suggested from Levinas that ethics are not a moral but a phenomenological necessity for practice (Loewenthal & Snell 2003). Even here, it is so easy for this to become a totalizing move—where "otherness" becomes a commodity. Again, in Chapter Three on post-phenomenology, Merleau-Ponty's "the between" can become a thing, as can "the relational". Chapter Four may have similar difficulties when referring to the "non-intentional", although this chapter does provide a possible way of reconsidering research that would be similar to the psychological therapist taking his/her thoughts to supervision and possibly publishing them afterwards, hopefully so that the thoughts coming out of the practice are modified as the result of these further consultations.

Chapter Six explores what are taken to be the very important interrelationships between language and experience, which we encounter in Chapter Seven, where besides hopefully providing a useful reassessment of R. D. Laing and colleagues' establishment at Kingsley Hall, the language of research may show in this case that the "treatment is how we treat people" can work against itself, such that this so-called phenomenological research ends up taking what people say out of context. The "treatment is how we treat people" refers just as much to the practice of research as it does to therapeutic practice. Unfortunately, the language of research is generally technical and unable to reflect the nature of the human soul which it purports to be understanding whilst simultaneously, wrongly legitimizing its violent methods. This forced use of inappropriate language is also reported in Chapter Eight, where it was found that counselling psychologists had to disguise relational ways of working through using medical terminology, but where also, as previously quoted, Vykovsky states that the subject "is shaped by the tools and instruments that he comes to use".

This raises questions with regard to where one should place post-existentialism with regard to current approaches to research and evidence-based practice. What we have to date attempted to do is to come alongside and if necessary carry out normally qualitative research as an attempt to research relationships and then be critical of this from, for example, the continental philosophy literature. This strategy of attempting to take part in current discourse has its dangers, for example in terms of the energy and space it takes up that could be more fruitfully directed elsewhere. An alarming account of this process is given by another doctoral student and colleague, Val Todd, when "examining questioning practitioner research". Here, she discovers that psychological therapists who, whilst in her initial research were alarmed by the way in which carrying out pre- and post-evaluations of the therapy they provided affected their practice, now, when asked similar questions do not argue against the use of such evaluations but only suggest that the evaluation questions asked should be modified.

Again, Chapters Eight and Nine attempt to skate around these problems of reification but inevitably get trapped by them. It is as if each psychological therapy session has to be reinvented for each client/patient in such a way that it is unique and, whilst far from denying client's and therapist's previous experience, minimizes theoretical and technical shorthand. Otherwise what is said in this way is already dead and can rarely revive the patient or the psychological therapist.

Yet despite all these concerns, without a name to mobilize another possibility, we are left with the influence of engineered market forces and increasingly weakened contrasting forces such as the family, community, and religion to counter these. As has already been mentioned, there would seem to be a growing body of thought questioning the primacy of theory, with the increasing importance of the work of Wittgenstein

(Heaton 2010) and the growth of the relational school (Frie & Orange 2009) and psychology in general (Brown & Stenner 2009). The place of theory is further significantly questioned from a more humanistic tradition by the writings of my colleague Richard House, in for example "Therapist's Modernist 'Regime of Truth'" (House 2010), and initially from a more psychoanalytic position from Peter Lomas (see King 2011). There is at least the call for pluralism (Cooper & McLeod 2010), and also a growing interest, as reported earlier, in common factors in the psychological therapies (Beutler 2009). In research, this is not the only book returning to case studies (McLeod 2010) and the politics of practice-based research (Lee & Freshwater 2008).

Post-existentialism, we have argued, opens up another possibility for returning to practice, as this is the essence of a re-examination of phenomenology. Furthermore, existentialism, when it is revisited, without its self-centredness, can also help us to think about meaning within its context from the writings of those such as Heidegger and Kierkegaard.

REFERENCES

Adityanjee, Aderibigbe, Y. A., Theodoridis, D. & Vieweg, W. V. R. (1999). Dementia praecox to schizophrenia: the first 100 years. *Psychiatry and Clinical Neurosciences, 53*: 437–448.

American Psychiatric Association (2000). *Diagnostic and Statistical Manual of Mental Disorders* (Fourth Edition). Washington, DC: APA.

Andreasen, N. C. (1997). The evolving concept of schizophrenia: from Kraepelin to the present and future. *Schizophrenia Research, 28*: 105–109.

Anthony, W. A. (1993). Recovery from mental illness: the guiding vision of the mental health service system in the 1990s. *Psychosocial Rehabilitation Journal, 16(4)*: 11–23.

Argyris, C. & Schon, D. (1995). *Organizational Learning: Theory, Method and Practice.* [Organization Development Series.] Boston: Addison-Wesley.

Ashworth, P. (2004). The origins of qualitative psychology. In: J. A. Smith (Ed.), *Qualitative Psychology: A Practical Guide to Research Methods* (pp. 4–24). London: Sage.

Askay, R. & Farquhar, J. (2006). *Apprehending the Inaccessible: Freudian Psychoanalysis and Existential Phenomenology.* Evanston, IL: Northwestern University Press.

Auerbach, A. (Ed.) (1959). *Schizophrenia: An Integrated Approach.* New York: Ronald Press.

Avdi, E. & Georgaca, E. (2007). Discourse analysis and psychotherapy: a critical review. *European Journal of Psychotherapy and Counselling, 9(2)*: 157–176.

Barber, B. (2000, October 20). Ballots versus bullets. *Financial Times*, p. 1.

Barkham, M. (1990). Counselling psychology: in search of an identity. *The Psychologist, 12*: 536–539.

Barlow, D. H. (2005). Clarification on psychological treatments and psychotherapy. *American Psychologist, 60(7)*: 734–735.

Barthes, R. (1984). *Image, Music, Text*. New York: Hill and Wang.

Barwick, N. (2003). Mad desire and feverish melancholy: reflections on the psychodynamics of writing and presenting. *British Journal of Psychotherapy, 20(1)*: 59–71.

Bateson, G. (1958). Cultural problems found by a study of schizophrenic process. In A. Auerbach (Ed.), *Schizophrenia: An Integrated Approach*. New York: Ronald Press.

Becker, C. & Becker, L. (Eds.) (1992a). *A History of Western Ethics*. New York: Garland.

Becker, L. & Becker, C. (Eds.) (1992b). *Encyclopedia of Ethics*. New York: Garland.

Bentall, R. P. (2004). *Madness Explained*. London: Penguin.

Bentall, R. P. (2005). R. D. Laing: an appraisal in the light of recent research. In S. Raschid (Ed.), *R. D. Laing: Contemporary Perspectives*. London: Free Association Books.

Beutler, L. E. (2009). Making science matter in clinical practice: Redefining psychotherapy. *Clinical Psychology: Science and Practice, 16*: 301–16317.

Bhaskar, R. (1978). *A Realist Theory of Science* (2nd ed.). Brighton: Harvester Press.

Bhaskar, R. (1986). *Scientific Realism and Human Emancipation*. London: Verso.

Binswanger, L. (1957). The case of Lola Voss. In J. Needleman (Ed.), *Being in the World: The Selected Papers of Ludvig Binswanger*. New York: Basic Books.

Bion, W. R. (1984a). *Second Thoughts: Selected Papers on Psychoanalysis*. London: Karnac.

Bion, W. R. (1984b). *Learning from Experience*. London: Karnac.

Black, M. (1993). More about metaphor. In A. Ortony (Ed.), *Metaphor and Thought* (2nd ed.) (pp. 19–41). Cambridge: Cambridge University Press.

Blanchot, M. (1993). *The Infinite Conversation*. London: University of Minnesota Press.

Bleicher, J. (1980). *Contemporary Hermeneutics*. London: Routledge & Kegan Paul.

Bleuler, E., In R. P. Bentall (2004) *Madness Explained*. London: Penguin.

Bolton, R. (1989). *The Contest of Meaning*. Cambridge, MA: MIT Press.

Bond, T. (2000). *Standards and Ethics for Counselling in Action* (2nd ed.). London: Sage.

Bor, R. & du Plessis, P. (1997). Counselling psychology research in health care settings. *Counselling Psychology Review, 12*: 19–22.

Borch-Jacobsen, M. (1991). *Lacan: The Absolute Master*. Stanford, CA: Stanford University Press.

Bowie, M. (1991). *Lacan*. London: Fontana Press.

Boyle, M. (1999). Diagnosis. In: C. Newnes, G. Holmes & C. Dunn (Eds.), *This Is Madness: A Critical Look at Psychiatry and the Future of Mental Health Services* (pp. 75–90). Ross-on-Wye: PCCS Books.

Boyle, M. (2005). *Schizophrenia: A Scientific Delusion?* (2nd ed.). London: Routledge.

Bracken, P. (2002). *Trauma, Culture, Meaning and Philosophy*. London: Whurr.

Brentano, F. (1995a). *Descriptive Psychology*. London: Routledge.

Brentano, F. (1995b). *Psychology from an Empirical Standpoint*. London: Routledge.

British Psychological Society (2006). *Division of Counselling Psychology: Psychological Therapist Practice Guidelines*. Leicester: British Psychological Society.

Brown, J. F. (2002). Epistemological differences within psychological science: a philosophical perspective on the validity of psychiatric diagnoses. *Psychology and Psychotherapy: Theory, Research and Practice, 75*: 239–250.

Brown, S. & Stenner, P. (2009). *Psychology without Foundations: History, Philosophy and Psychological Theory*. London: Sage.

Buber, M. (1922). *I and Thou*. New York: Scribner.

Bungay, V. & Keddy, B. (1996). Experiential analysis as a feminist methodology for health psychological therapists. *Qualitative Health Research 6(3)*: 442–452.

Burr, V. (2003). *Social Constructionism* (2nd ed.). London: Routledge.

Burston, D. (1996). *The Wing of Madness*. Cambridge, MA: Harvard University Press.

Bury, D. & Strauss, S. M. (2006). The scientist practitioner in a counselling psychology setting. In: D. A. Lane & S. Corrie (Eds.), *The Modern Scientist-Practitioner: A Guide to Practice in Psychology* (pp. 119–129). Hove: Routledge.

Campbell, P. (2007). Hearing my voice. *The Psychologist, 20(5)*: 298–299.

Caramelli, P., Poissant, A., Gauthier, S., Bellavance, A., Gauvreau, D., Lecours, A. R. & Joanette, Y. (1997). Educational level and neuropsychological heterogeneity in dementia of the Alzheimer type. *Alzheimer's Disease and Associated Disorders, 11*: 9–15.

Carmack, S. & Glucksberg, M. (1984). Metaphors do not use associations between concepts: they are used to create them. *Journal of Psycholinguistic Research, 13*: 443–455.

Carroll, N. (1984). Visual Metaphor. In: J. Hintkikka (Ed.), *Aspect of Metaphor.* London: Kluwer, 189–218.

Carter, J. A. (2002). Integrating science and practice: reclaiming the science in practice. *Journal of Clinical Psychology, 58(10)*: 1285–1290.

Cayne, J. & Loewenthal, D. (2007). The unknown in learning to be a psychotherapist. *European Journal of Psychotherapy and Counselling, 9(4)*: 373–387

Chessick, R. D. (1992). Phenomenology of the emerging sense of self. *Psychoanalysis and Contemporary Thought, 15*: 57–88.

Clegg, J. W. & Slife, B. D. (2004). Epistemology on the hither side. *The European Journal of Psychotherapy, Counselling and Health, 7*, 65–76.

Cohen, C. I. (1993). The biomedicalization of psychiatry: a critical overview. *Community Mental Health Journal, 29*: 508–521.

Cohen, L. J. (2003). The semantics of metaphor. In: A. Ortony (Ed.), *Metaphor and Thought* (2nd ed.) (pp. 58–70). Cambridge: Cambridge University Press.

Colaizzi, P. F. (1973). *Reflection and Research in Psychology: A Phenomenological Study of Learning.* Dubuque, IA: Kendall Hunt Publishing.

Coleman, M. & Jenkins, E. (1998). "Mental health nursing policy: a critical voice", *Journal of Psychiatric and Mental Health Nursing*, Vol. 5 pp. 355–359.

Cooper, D. E. (1990). *Existentialism: A Reconstruction.* Oxford: Blackwell.

Cooper, M. (2003). *Existential Therapies.* London: Routledge.

Cooper, M. (2008). *Essential Research Findings in Counselling and Psychotherapy: The Facts Are Friendly.* London: Sage.

Cooper, M. (2009). Welcoming the Other: actualising the humanistic ethic at the core of counselling psychology practice. *Counselling Psychology Review, (24)3&4*: 119–129.

Cooper, M. & McLeod, J. (2010). *Pluralistic Counselling and Psychotherapy.* London: Sage.

Cooper, R. (2004). What is wrong with the DSM? *History of Psychiatry, 15(1)*: 5–25.

Corrie, S. & Callahan, M. M. (2000). A review of the scientist-practitioner model: reflections on its potential contribution to counselling psychology within the context of current health care trends. *British Journal of Medical Psychology, 73*: 413–427.

Cosgrove, L. (2005). When labels mask oppression: implications for teaching psychiatric taxonomy to mental health psychological therapists. *Journal of Mental Health Counselling, 27(4)*: 283–296.

Cosgrove, L. & McHugh, M. (2008). A post-Newtonian, post-modern approach to science: new methods in social action research. In: S. N. Hesse-Bibber & P. Leavy (Eds.), *Handbook of Emergent Methods* (pp. 73–86). London: Guildford Press.

Cotton, T. (2008). What relationship, if any, is there between the way we treat people and "the treatment" in psychotherapy? (unpublished MSc research paper).

Coyle, A. (2006). Discourse analysis. In: G. M. Breakwell, C. Fife-Schaw, S. Hammond & J. A. Smith (Eds.), *Research Methods in Psychology* (3rd ed.) (pp. 366–387). London: Sage.

Cushman, R. (2001). *Therapeia: Plato's Conception of Philosophy.* Piscataway, NJ: Transaction.

Danto, A. (1998). The ambulatorium: Freud's free clinic in Vienna. *International Journal of Psychoanalysis, 79*: 287–300.

De Beauvoir, S. (1972 [1949]). *The Second Sex* (Trans. H. M. Parshley). London: Penguin.

Deegan, P. E. (1988). Recovery: the lived experience of rehabilitation. *Psychosocial Rehabilitation Journal, 11*: 11–19.

Deleuze, G. (1990). *The Logic of Sense.* London: Athlone Press.

Deleuze, G. & Guattari, F. (1977). *Anti-Oedipus: Capitalism and Schizophrenia.* Minneapolis: University of Minnesota Press.

Department of Health (2006). *Mental Health Bill 2006 Summary Guide,* Retrieved April, 2011 http://www.dh.gov.uk/en/Publicationsandstatistics/Publications/PublicationsLegislation/DH_062926

Derrida, J. (1978). *Writing and Difference.* London: Routledge.

Derrida, J. (1990). *Resistances to Psychoanalysis.* Stanford: Stanford University Press.

Derrida, J. (1996). *Archive Fever.* Chicago: The University of Chicago Press.

Derrida, J. (1998). *Of Grammatology.* transl. by Gayatri Chakravorty Spivak Baltimore: The Johns Hopkins University Press.

Dewey, J. (1960). *The Quest for Certainty.* New York: Putnam.

Dillon, J. (2009). Jacqui Dillon. In: M. Romme, S. Escher, J. Dillon, D. Corstens & M. Morris, *Living with Voices: 50 Stories of Recovery.* Ross-on-Wye: PCCS Books.

Double, D. B. (1990). What would Adolf Meyer have thought of the neo-Kraepelinian approach? *Psychiatric Bulletin, 14*: 472–474.

Douglas, B. (2010). Disorder and its discontents. In: R. Woolfe, S. Strawbridge, B. Douglas & W. Dryden (Eds.), *Handbook of Counselling Psychology* (3rd ed.) (pp. 23–43). London: Sage.

Dryden, W., Mearns, D. & Thorne, B. (2000). Counselling in the United Kingdom: past, present and future. *British Journal of Guidance and Counselling, 28(4)*: 467–483.

Eagleton, T. (1996). *The Illusions of Post-Modernism*. Oxford: Blackwell.

Ecclestone, K. (2004). Learning or therapy? The demoralisation of education. *British Journal of Educational Studies, 52*: 112–137.

Ecclestone, K. & Hayes, D. (2007). *Dangerous Rise of Therapeutic Education*. London: Routledge.

Edwards, D., Ashmore, M. & Potter, P. (1995). Death and furniture: the rhetoric, politics and theology of bottom line arguments against relativism. *History of the Human Sciences, 8(2)*: 25–49.

Egan, G. (1990). *The Skilled Helper: A Systematic Approach to Effective Helping* (4th ed.). Pacific Grove, CA: Brooks/Cole.

Elliott, R., Fischer, C. & Rennie, D. (1999) Evolving guidelines for publication of qualitative research studies in psychology and related fields. *British Journal of Clinical Psychology, 38*: 215–229.

Eriksen, K. & Kress, V. E. (2006). The DSM and the psychological therapist counseling identity: bridging the gap. *Journal of Mental Health Counseling, 28(3)*: 202–217.

Fardella, J. A. (2008). The recovery model: discourse ethics and the retrieval of the self. *Journal of Medical Humanities, 29(2)*: 111–126.

Felman, S. (1987). *Jacques Lacan and the Adventure of Insight: Psychoanalysis in Contemporary Culture*. Cambridge, MA: Harvard University Press.

Ferenczi, S. (1900). Two errors in diagnosis. In: J. Borossa (Ed.), *Selected Writings: Sandor Ferenczi*. London: Penguin, 1999.

Fink, B. (1996). *A Clinical Introduction to Lacanian Psychoanalysis*. Cambridge, MA: Harvard University Press.

Foucault, M. (1974 [1954]). *The Psychological Dimensions of Mental Illness* (Trans. A. M. Sheridan-Smith). New York: Harper and Row.

Foucault, M. (1980). *Power/Knowledge: Selected Interview and Other Writings 1972–1977*. Hassocks: Sussex Harvester Press.

Fox, D. & Prilleltensky, I. (Eds.) (1997). *Critical Psychology: An Introduction*. London: Sage.

Frese, F. J., Stanley, J., Kress, K. & Vogel-Scibilia, S. (2001). Integrating evidence-based practices and the recovery model. *Psychiatric Service, 52(11)*: 1462–1468.

Freud, S. (1896). Letter to Wilhelm Fliess. *Standard Edition* (Vol. 1, p. 223). London: Hogarth Press and the Institute of Psycho-Analysis, 1966.

Freud, S. (1900). *The Interpretation of Dreams. The Standard Edition of the Complete Psychological Works of Sigmund Freud* (Vol. 5, 2nd part). London: Hogarth Press.

Freud, S. (1911). Recommendations to Physician Practising Psycho-Analysis. In: P. Gay (Ed.), *The Freud Reader* (pp. 356–362). London: Vantage, 1995.

Freud, S. (1914). *On Narcissism: An Introduction. Standard Edition* (Vol. 14, pp. 67–102). London: Hogarth Press, 1957.

Freud, S. (1927). The Future of an Illusion. In: P. Gay (Ed.), *The Freud Reader* (pp. 685–722). London: Vantage, 1995.

Frie, R. (2003). "Understanding experience: Psychotherapy and post-modernism" London: Routledge

Frie, R. & Orange, D. (Eds.) (2009). *Beyond Postmodernism: New Dimensions in Clinical Theory and Practice*. New York and London: Routledge.

Friedman, M. (1964). *The Worlds of Existentialism*. London: Humanities Press.

Friedman, M. (1991). *The Worlds of Existentialism: A Critical Reader* (pp. 414, 426). New York: Delmar Publishers.

Fuchs, T. (2005). Psychiatry and phenomenology today. In: S. Raschid (Ed.), *R. D. Laing: Contemporary Perspectives*. London: Free Association Books, 113–149.

Furedi, F. (2006, May 7). Politicians, economists, teachers … why are they so desperate to make us happy? *The Sunday Telegraph*, http://www.telegraph.co.uk/opinion/main.html?xml=/opinion/2006/05/07do0706.xml.URL accessed on 25/04/07.150 D. Loewenthal Downloaded By: [Roehampton University] At: 17: 09 26 October 2007.

Furnham, A. & Bower, P. (1992). A comparison of academic and lay theories of schizophrenia. *British Journal of Psychiatry, 161*: 201–210.

Gallagher, A. G., Gemez, T. & Baker, L. J. V. (1991). Beliefs of psychologists about schizophrenia and their role in its treatment. *The Irish Journal of Psychology, 12(4)*: 393–405.

Gans, S. (1989). Levinas and Pontalis. In: R. Bernasconi & S. Wood (Eds.), *The Provocation of Levinas: Rethinking the Other*. London: Routledge.

Gans, S. (1997). Lacan and Levinas: towards an ethical psychoanalysis. *British Journal of Phenomenology, 28(1)*: 30–48.

Gans, S. (2006). Paper presented to the Research Centre for Therapeutic Education.

Gelso, C. & Carter, J. A. (1994). Components of the psychotherapy relationship: their interaction and unfolding during treatment. *Journal of Counseling Psychology, 41(3)*: 296–306.

Gelvin, M. (1989). *A Commentary on Heidegger's Being and Time* (revised ed.). Illinois: Northern University Press.

Gergen, K. (1999). *An Invitation to Social Construction*. London: Sage.

Gilbert, M. & Evans, K. (2000). *Psychotherapy Supervision*. Buckingham: Open University Press.

Giorgi, A. (1985). *Phenomenology and Psychological Research*. Pittsbugh: Duquesne University Press.

Glaser, B. & Strauss, A. (1967). *The Discovery of Grounded Theory*. Chicago: Aldine.

Goldstein, R. (2009). The future of counselling psychology: a view from the inside. *Counselling Psychology Review, 24(1)*: 35–37.

Golsworthy, R. (2004). Counselling psychology and psychiatric classification: clash or co-existence? *Counselling Psychology Review, 19(3)*: 23–28.

Gombrich, E. H. (1960). *Art and Illusion*. Woodstock, Oxford: Princeton University Press.

Gravey, N. & Braun, V. (1997). Ethics and the publication of case material. Professional. *Psychology: Research and Practice*, 28, 399–404.

Greenwood, D. (2003). The Possibility of Psychotherapy with a Person Diagnosed with Dementia. Unpublished PhD dissertation, University of Surrey.

Greenwood, D. (2008). Recognizing the "non-intentional"—some implications for practitioner education. *The Humanistic Psychologist*, 36: 19–30.

Greenwood, D. & Loewenthal, D. (1998). Psychotherapy with an older person suffering from dementia. *European Journal of Psychotherapy, Counselling, and Health, 1*: 281–294.

Greenwood, D. & Loewenthal, D. (2005). The use of "Case Study" in psychotherapy research and education. *Journal of Psychoanalytic Psychotherapy, 19(1)*: 1–13.

Greenwood, D., Loewenthal, D. & Rose, T. (2001). A relational approach to providing care for a person suffering dementia. *Journal of Advanced Nursing, 36(4)*: 583–590.

Grosz, E. (1986). Language and the limits of the body: Kristeva and abjection. In: E. Grosz, T. Threadgold & D. Kelly (Eds.),. *Excursions into Post-Modernity*. Sydney, Australia: Power Institute Publications, 116–129.

Gummesson, E. (2000). *Qualitative Methods in Management Research*. Thousand Oaks, CA: Sage.

Haack, S. (1984). Dry truth and real knowledge: epistemologies of metaphor and metaphors of epistemology (pp. 1–22). In: J. Hintkikka (Ed.), *Aspect of Metaphor*. London: Kluwer Academic.

Hage, S. M. (2002). Reaffirming the unique identity of counseling psychology: opting for the "Road Less Travelled By". *The Counseling Psychologist, 31(5)*: 555–563.

Hand, S. (Ed.) (1989). *The Levinas Reader*. Oxford: Blackwell.

Hardt, J. (2006). Psychoanalytic and therapeutic training in Germany: "After" Freud. *The European Journal of Psychotherapy and Counselling, 8(4)*: 375–385.

Hare-Mustin, R. T. & Marecek, J. (2001). Abnormal and clinical psychology: the politics of madness. In: D. Fox & I. Prilleltensky (Eds.), *Critical Psychology: An Introduction* (pp. 104–120). London: Sage.

Hayek, F. A. (1979). *The Counter-Revolution of Science: Studies on the Abuse of Reason* (2nd ed.). Indianapolis, IN: Liberty Fund.

Heartfield, J. (2002). *The "Death of the Subject" Explained*. Sheffield: Sheffield Hallam University Press.

Heaton, J. M. (1993). The sceptical tradition in psychotherapy. In: L. Spurling (Ed.), *From the Words of My Mouth: Tradition in Psychotherapy*. London: Routledge.

Heaton, J. M. (2010). *The Talking Cure: Wittgenstein's Therapeutic Method for Psychotherapy*. London: Palgrave Macmillan.

Heidegger, M. (1927). *Being and Time* (Trans. J. Macquarrie and E. S. Robinson). London and New York: Harper and Row, 1962.

Heidegger, M. (1971) *Poetry, Language, Thought*. New York: Harper and Row.

Heidegger, M. (1993). Letter on humanism. In: D. F. Krell (Ed.), *Basic Writing: From Being and Time (1927) to the Task of Thinking (1964)* (p. 226). London: Routledge.

Heron, J. (1999). *The Complete Facilitator's Handbook*. London: Kogan Page.

Hochschild, A. R. (2003). *The Managed Heart: Commercialisation of Human Feeling*. Berkeley: University of California Press.

Hoeller, K. (1986). Editor's Foreword—Dream and existence. *Special Issue of Review of Existential Psychology and Psychiatry*: 7–17.

Hofstede, G. (2001). *Culture's Consequences: Comparing Values, Behaviours, Institutions and Organizations across Nations*. Thousand Oaks, CA: Sage.

Hollway, W. (1989). *Subjectivity and Method in Psychology*. London: Sage.

Hook, D. & Parker, I. (2002). Deconstruction, psychopathology and dialectics. *South African Journal of Psychology, 32(2)*: 49–54.

House, R. (2010). In: *Against and Beyond Therapy: Critical Essays towards a Post-Professional Era*. Ross-on-Wye: PCCS Books.

House, R. & Loewenthal, D. (2007). *Against and For CBT*. Ross-on-Wye: PCCS Books.

House, R. & Loewenthal, D. (2009). *Childhood, Well-Being and a Therapeutic Ethos*. London: Karnac Books.

Husserl, E. (1960). *Cartesian Meditation: An Introduction to Phenomenology* (Trans. D. Cairns). The Hague: Martinus Nijhoff.

Husserl, E. (1977). *Phenomenological Psychology* (Trans. J. Scanlon). The Hague: Martinus Nijhoff.

Husserl, E. (1983). *Ideas Pertaining to a Pure Phenomenology and to a Phenomenological Philosophy* (Trans. F. Kersten). The Hague: Martinus Nijhoff.

Indurkhya, B. (1984). Metaphor as change of representation: an interaction theory of cognition and metaphor. In: J. Hintkikka (Ed.), *Aspect of Metaphor* (pp. 95–150). London: Kluwer Academic.

Irigaray, L. (1985). *The Sex Which Is Not One*. Ithaca, NY: Cornell University Press.

Jacobs, M. (2000). Psychotherapy in the United Kingdom: past, present and future. *British Journal of Guidance and Counselling, 28(4)*: 451–466.

James, H. (2004). *The Real Thing and Other Tales*. Whitefish, MT: Kessinger.

James, P. E. & Bellamy, A. (2010). Counselling psychology in the NHS. In: R. Woolfe, S. Strawbridge, B. Douglas & W. Dryden (Eds.), *Handbook of Counselling Psychology* (3rd ed.) (pp. 397–415). London: Sage.

Jarvis, P. (1999). *The Practitioner Researcher: Developing Theory from Practice*. San Francisco: Jossey Bass. Joseph, J. (2003). *The Gene Illusion*. Ross-on-Wye: PCCS Books.

Jung, C. G. (1921). *Psychological Types (Collected Works of C. G. Jung*, Vol. 6). Princeton, NJ: Bollingen.

Kanellakis, P. (Ed.) (2003). Counselling psychology and psychological testing. *Counselling Psychology Review, 19(4)*: 4–44.

Kazdin, A. (1982). *Single-Case Research Designs—Methods for Clinical and Applied Settings*. Oxford: Oxford University Press.

Kearney, R. & Rainwater, M. (Eds.) (1996). *The Continental Philosophy Reader*. London: Routledge.

Kemp, R. (2006). Towards a phenomenological reading of Lacan. *Indo-Pacific Journal of Phenomenology, 6.1*: 1–9.

Kendall, G. & Wickham, G. (1999). *Using Foucault's Methods*. London: Sage.

Kierkegaard, S. (1843). *Fear and Trembling* (Trans. W. Lowrie). New York: Doubleday Anchor, 1954.

Kierkegaard, S. (1844). *The Concept of Anxiety* (Trans. R. Thomte). Princeton: Princeton University Press, 1980.

Kierkegaard, S. (1848). *The Concept of Dread* (Trans. W. Lowrie). In: M. Friedan (Ed.), *The Worlds of Existentialism: A Critical Reader* (pp. 369–71). New York: Random House, 1964.

Kierkegaard, S. (1855). *The Sickness unto Death* (Trans. W. Lowrie). Princeton: Princeton University Press, 1941.

Kierkegaard, S. (1944). *Concluding Unscientific Postscript* (D. Swenson and W. Lowrie). Princeton: Princeton University Press.

Kinderman, P. (2009). The future of counselling psychology: a view from the outside. *Counselling Psychology Review, 24(1)*: 16–21.

King, L. (2011). Special Issue on the works of Peter Lomas. *European Journal of Psychotherapy and Counselling 13(1)*: 3–10.

Kirsch, I. (2009). *The Emperor's New Drugs: Exploding the Anti-Depressant Myth*. London: The Bodley House.

Klein, M. (1930). The importance of symbol formation in the development of the ego. *International Journal of Psychoanalysis, 11*: 24–39.

Klein, M. (1946). Notes on some schizoid mechanisms. *International Journal of Psychoanalysis, 27*: 99–110.

Kristeva, J. (1969). *Semeiotike: Recherches pour une sémanalyse*. Paris: Éditions du Seuil.

Kristeva, J. (1974). *Revolution in Poetic Language*. In: T. Moi (Ed.), *The Kristeva Reader*. Oxford: Blackwell, 1986.

Kristeva, J. (1975). *The System and the Speaking Subject*. In: T. Moi (Ed.), *The Kristeva Reader*. Oxford: Blackwell, 1986.

Kristeva, J. (1983). *Freud and Love: Treatment and Its Discontents*. In: T. Moi (Ed.), *The Kristeva Reader*. Oxford: Blackwell, 1986.

Kvale, S. (Ed.) (1992). *Psychology and Post-Modernism*. London: Sage.

Kyzirdis, T. C. (2005). Notes on the history of schizophrenia. *German Journal of Psychiatry, 8(3)*: 42–48.

Lacan, J. (1966). *Écrits*. Paris: Éditions du Seuil.

Lacan, J. (1977). *Écrits: A Selection* (Trans. A. Sheridan). London: Routledge.

Lacan, J. (1977 [1958]). The direction of the treatment and the principles of its power. In: *Écrits*. London: Routledge.

Lacan, J. (1988a). The topic of the imaginary. In: J. Alain-Miller (Ed.) & J. Forrester (Trans.), *The Seminar of Jacques Lacan*, Book 1, *Freud's Papers on Technique 1953–1954* (pp. 73–88). Cambridge: Cambridge University Press.

Lacan, J. (1988b). Overture to the seminar. In: J. Alain-Miller (Ed.) & J. Forrester (Trans.), *The Seminar of Jacques Lacan*, Book 1, *Freud's Papers on Technique 1953–1954* (pp. 1–3, 73–80). Cambridge: Cambridge University Press.

Lacan, J. (1993). *The Seminar of Jacques Lacan*. Book III, *The Psychoses, 1955–1956* (Ed. J. Alain-Miller & Trans. R. Grigg). London: Routledge.

Lafont, C. (2002). Pre'cis of Heidegger, language, and world-disclosure. *Inquiry, 45*: 185–90.

Lago, C. (2006). *Race, Culture and Counselling*. Maidenhead: Open University Press.

Laing, R. D. (1965). *The Divided Self: An Existential Study in Sanity and Madness*. London: Penguin.

Laing, R. D. (1967). *The Politics of Experience and the Bird of Paradise*. London: Tavistock Publications.

Laing, R. D. (1969). *Self and Others* (2nd ed.). London: Routledge.

Laing, R. D. (1970). *Knots*. Aylesbury: Hazell Watson and Viney.

Laing, R. D., Philipson, H. & Lee, A. R. (1969). *Interpersonal Perception: A Theory and a Method of Research*. London: Tavistock Publications.

Lakoff, G. & Johnson, M. (1980). *Metaphors We Live By*. London: University of Chicago Press.

Lambert, G. & Gournay, K. (1999). Training for the mental health workforce: a review of developments in the United Kingdom. *Australian and New Zealand Journal of Psychiatry, 33*: 694–700.

Lane, D. A. & Corrie, S. (2006). Counselling psychology: its influences and future. *Counselling Psychology Review, 21(1)*: 12–24.

Laplanche, J. (1992). *Seduction, Translation, Drives* (Ed. J. Fletcher & M. Stanton & Trans. M. Stanton). London: Institute of Contemporary Arts.

Laplanche, J. (1999). *Essays on Otherness*. Luke Thurston, Philip Slotkin, and Leslie Hill, Trans.). London: Routledge.

Laungani, P. (2002). Mindless psychiatry and dubious ethics. *Counselling Psychology Quarterly, 15(1)*: 23–33.

Layard, R. (2005). Mental health: Britain's biggest social problem? Retrieved 22 August 2007, from http://www.cabinetoffice.gov.uk/strategy/downloads/files/mh-layard.pdf

Layard, R. (2006a). *Happiness: Lessons from a New Science*. London: Penguin.

Layard, R. (2006b). *The Depression Report: A New Deal for Depression and Anxiety Disorders*, internet: <http://cep.lse.ac.uk/research/mentalhealth>

Layard, R. (2006c). The case for psychological treatment centres. *British Medical Journal, 332(7548)*: 1030–1032.

Leader, D. (2008). *The New Black: Mourning, Melancholia and Depression*, Hamish Hamilton.

Lee, J. & Freshwater, D. (2008). *Practitioner Based Research*. London: Karnac.

Levinas, E. (1961). *Totality and Infinity: An Essay on Exteriority* (Trans. A. Lingis). Pittsburgh, PA: Duquesne University Press.

Levinas, E. (1967). *Martin Buber and the Theory of Knowledge*. In: S. Hand (Ed.), *The Levinas Reader*. Oxford: Blackwell, 1989.

Levinas, E. (1981). *Substitution*. In: S. Hand (Ed.), *The Levinas Reader*. Oxford: Blackwell, 1989. Levinas, E. (1984). *Ethics as First Philosophy*. In: S. Hand (Ed.), *The Levinas Reader*. Oxford: Blackwell, 1989. Levinas, E. (1985). *Ethics and Infinity: Conversations with Philippe Nemo* (Trans. R. Cohen). Pittsburgh, PA: Duquesne University Press.

Levinas, E. (1989). *Time and the Other*. In: S. Hand (Ed.), *The Levinas Reader*. Oxford: Blackwell, 1989. Levinas, E. (1995). Ethics of the infinite. In: R. Kearney (Ed.), *States of Mind: Dialogues with Contemporary Thinkers on the European Mind*. Manchester: Manchester University Press.

Levinas, E. (1997). *Otherwise than Being; or Beyond Essence*. Pittsburgh, PA: Dusquesne University Press.

Levinas, E. (2006). *Humanism of the Other*. Chicago: University of Illinois Press.

Lewis, S. & Bor, R. (1998). How counselling psychologists are perceived by NHS clinical psychologists. *Counselling Psychology Quarterly, 11(4)*: 427–437.

Lichia, Y. & Raymond, S.-U. (1985). Value dimensions in American counseling: a Taiwanese-American comparison. *International Association for Counselling, 8(2)*: 137–146.

Loewenthal, D. (1996). The postmodern counsellor: Some implications for practice, theory, research and professionalism *Counselling Psychology Quarterly, 9 (4)*: 373–381.

Loewenthal, D. (1998). The attack on European thought. *European Journal of Psychotherapy, Counselling and Health, 1 (3)* (editorial).

Loewenthal, D. (2002). Involvement and Emotional Labour, *Soundings, Issue 20*: 151–162.

Loewenthal, D. (2003). The other in educational research: some post-modern implications for educational practice, theory, research and psychological therapistism. *Research in Post-Compulsory Education, 8(3)*: 367–377.

Loewenthal, D. (2004). Should either psychology or psychiatry be the basis of psychotherapy? *International Journal of Critical Psychology, 4.4*: 214–222.

Loewenthal, D. (2005a). Cultural conflict, values, and relational learning in psychotherapy. In: L. Hoshmand (Ed.), *Culture, Psychotherapy, and Counseling: Critical and Integrative Perspectives*. Thousand Oaks, CA: Sage.

Loewenthal, D. (2005b). Case studies in relational person centred care. In: P. Vaarama & R. Piper (Eds.), *Managing Integrated Care for Older Persons in Europe* (pp. 153–179). Helsinki: European Healthcare Management Association.

Loewenthal, D. (2006a). Questioning psychotherapeutic "evidence" (and research). In: D. Loewenthal & D. Winter (Eds), *What Is Psychotherapeutic Research?* London: Karnac.

Loewenthal, D. (2006b). Psychotherapy, ethics and the relational. In: L. Hoshmand (Ed.), *Culture, Psychotherapy and Counseling: Critical and Integrative Perspectives* (pp. 205–226). Thousand Oaks, CA: Sage.

Loewenthal, D. (2007a). Relational research, ideology and the evolution of intersubjectivity in a post-existential culture. In D. Loewenthal (Ed.), *Case Studies in Relational Research* (pp. 221–240). London: Palgrave Macmillan.

Loewenthal, D. (2007b). *Case Studies in Relational Research*. Basingstoke: Palgrave Macmillan.

Loewenthal, D. (2008a). Introducing post-existential practice: an approach to well-being in the 21st century. *Philosophical Practice, 3(3)*: 316–321.

Loewenthal, D. (2008b). Post-existentialism as a reaction to CBT? In: R. House & D. Loewenthal (Eds.), *Against and For CBT: Towards a Constructive Dialogue?* (pp. 146–155). Ross-on-Wye: PCCS Books.

Loewenthal, D. (2010). Post-existentialism instead of CBT. *Journal of Existential Analysis, 21.2*

Loewenthal, D. & House, R. (Eds.) (2010). *Critically Engaging CBT*. Maidenhead: Open University Press.

Loewenthal, D. & Snell, R. (2001). Psychotherapy as the practice of ethics. In: F. Palmer-Barnes & L. Murdin (Eds.), *Values and Ethics in the Practice of Psychotherapy and Counselling* (pp. 23–31). Buckingham: Open University Press.

Loewenthal, D. & Snell, R. (2003). *Post-Modernism for Psychotherapists.* London: Routledge.

Loewenthal, D. & Snell, R. (2006). The learning community, the trainee and the leader. *European Journal of Psychotherapy and Counselling, 8(1)*: 61–77.

Long, C. G. & Hollin, C. R. (1997). The scientist-practitioner model in clinical psychology: a critique. *Clinical Psychology and Psychotherapy, 4(2)*: 75–83.

Løvlie, L. (1993) Post-modernism and subjectivity. In: S. Kvale (Ed.), *Psychology and Post-Modernism* (pp. 119–134). London: Sage.

Lyotard, J.-F. (1984). *The Post-Modern Condition: A Report on Knowledge.* Manchester: Manchester University Press.

MacCabe, J. (2006). *Beyond Nature and Nurture in Psychiatry: Genes, the Environment, and Their Interplay.* Abingdon, Oxon: Informa Healthcare.

Macquarrie, J. (1973). *Existentialism.* Harmondsworth: Penguin Books.

Mahrer, A. R. (2000). Philosophy of science and the foundations of psychotherapy. *American Psychologist, 55(10)*: 1117–1125.

Marshall, S. (2004). *Difference and Discrimination in Psychotherapy and Counselling.* London: Sage.

Marx, K. & Engels, F. (1848). *Manifesto of the Communist Party.* In: R. Tucker (Ed.), *The Marx–Engels Reader* (pp. 473–483). London: W. W. Norton, 1978.

May, R. (1950). *The Meaning of Anxiety* (revised ed.). New York: W. W. Norton, 1996.

May, R. (2007). Working outside the diagnostic frame. *The Psychologist, 20(5)*: 300–301.

McCabe, J., O'Daly, O., Murray, R. M., McGuffing, P. & Wright, P. (Eds.) *Nature and Nurture in Psychiatry.* Abingdon, Oxon: Informa Healthcare.

McLeod, J. (1994). *Doing Counselling Research.* London: Sage.

McLeod, J. (1997). *Narrative and Psychotherapy.* London: Sage.

McLeod, J. (2001). *Qualitative Research in Counselling and Psychotherapy.* London: Sage.

McLeod, J. (2003). The humanistic paradigm. In: R. Woolfe, W. Dryden & S. Strawbridge (Eds.), *Handbook of Counselling Psychology* (2nd ed.) (pp. 140–160). London: Sage.

McLeod, J. (2010). *Case Study Research in Counselling and Psychotherapy.* London: Sage.

Merleau-Ponty, M. (1945). *The Phenomenology of Perception* (Trans. C. Smith). London: Routledge Kegan-Paul.

Merleau-Ponty, M. (1962). *The Phenomenology of Perception* (Trans. C. Smith). London: Routledge Kegan-Paul.

Merleau-Ponty, M. (1964). *The Primacy of Perception*. Evanston, IL: Northwestern University Press.

Milton, M. (Ed.) (2003). Evidence-based practice. *Counselling Psychology Review, 18(3)*: 3–35.

Moran, D. (2000). *Introduction to Phenomenology*. London: Routledge.

Morris, M. (2009). *Living with Voices: 50 Stories of Recovery*. Ross-on-Wye: PCCS Books.

Morton, A. (2003). *A Guide through the Theory of Knowledge* (3rd ed.).Oxford: Oxford University Press.

Moustakas, C. (1990). *Heuristic Research: Design, Methodology, and Applications*. Thousand Oaks, CA: Sage.

Moustakas, C. (1994). *Phenomenological Research Methods*. London: Sage.

Moynihan, R., Heath, I. & Henry, D. (2002). Selling sickness: the pharmaceutical industry and disease mongering. *British Medical Journal, 324*: 886–890.

Nietzsche, F. (1883). *Thus Spoke Zarathustra* (Trans. A. Tille). New York: Dutton, 1933.

Nietzsche, F. (1888). *The Gay Science* (Trans. W. Kaufman). New York: Vintage Books, 1974

Nightingale, D. & Neilands, T. (2001). Understanding and practising critical psychology. In: D. Fox & I. Prilleltensky (Eds.), *Critical Psychology: An Introduction* (pp. 68–84). London: Sage.

O'Brien, M. (2010). Towards integration. In: R. Woolfe, S. Strawbridge, B. Douglas & W. Dryden (Eds.), *Handbook of Counselling Psychology* (3rd ed.) (pp. 173–192). London: Sage.

Oakeshott, M. (1991). *Rationalism in Politics and Other Essays*. Indianapolis: Liberty Fund.

Oakley, C. (1990). An account of the first conference of the society for existential analysis. *Journal of the Society for Existential Analysis, 1*: 38–45.

Parker, I. (1992). *Discourse Dynamics: Critical Analysis for Social and Individual Psychology*. London: Routledge.

Parker, I. (1997). *Psychoanalytic Culture: Psychoanalytic Discourse in Western Society*. London: Sage.

Parker, I. (1999). Deconstructing diagnosis: psychopathological practice. In: C. Feltham (Ed.), *Controversies in Psychotherapy and Counselling* (pp. 104–112). London: Sage.

Parker, I. (2002). Universities are not a good place for psychotherapy and counselling training. *European Journal of Psychotherapy and Counselling, 5(4)*: 331–346.

Peperzak, A. (1992). *To the Other: An Introduction to the Philosophy of Emmanuel Levinas*. Indiana, IN: Purdoe University Press.

Pérez-Álvarez, M. & García-Montes, J. M. (2007). The Charcot effect: the invention of mental illness. *Journal of Constructivist Psychology, 20*: 309–336.

Pilgrim, D. (1990). Competing histories of madness: some implications for modern psychiatry. In: R. Bentall (Ed.), *Reconstructing Schizophrenia*. London: Routledge, pp. 211–233.

Pilgrim, D. (2000). Psychiatric diagnosis: more questions than answers. *The Psychologist, 13(6)*: 302–305.

Pilgrim, D. (2007). The survival of psychiatric diagnosis. *Social Science and Medicine, 65*: 536–547.

Polyani, M. (1966). *The Tacit Dimension*. Gloucester, MA: Peter Smith, 1983.

Porter, R. (2002). *Madness: A Brief History*. Oxford: Oxford University Press.

Potter, J. & Wetherell, M. (1987). *Discourse and Social Psychology: Beyond Attitudes and Behaviour*. London: Sage.

Pugh, D. & Coyle, A. (2000). The construction of counselling psychology in Britain: a discourse analysis of counselling psychology texts. *Counselling Psychology Quarterly, 13(1)*: 85–98.

Quigley, K. S. & Barrett, L. F. (1999). Emotional learning and mechanisms of intentional psychological change. In: J. Brandtstädter & R. M. Lerner (Eds.), *Action and Self-Development: Theory and Research through the Life Span* (pp. 435–464). Thousand Oaks, CA: Sage.

Radley, A. & Chamberlain, K. (2001). Health psychology and the study of the case: from method to analytic concern. *Social Science and Medicine, 53(3)*: 321–332.

Ramon, S., Healy, B. & Renouf, N. (2007). Recovery from mental illness as an emergent concept and practice in Australia and the UK. *International Journal of Social Psychiatry, 53*: 108–122.

Raschid, S. (Ed.) (2005). *R. D. Laing: Contemporary Perspectives*. London: Free Association Books.

Read, J., Goodman, L., Morrison, A. P., Ross, C. A. & Aderhold, V. (2004). Childhood trauma, loss and stress. In: J. Read, L. R. Mosher & R. P. Bentall (Eds.), *Models of Madness*. London: Routledge, 925–935.

Read, J., Mosher, L. R. & Bentall, R. P. (Eds.). (2004). *Models of Madness*. London: Routledge.

Regier, D. A., First, M., Marshall, T. & Narrow, T. E. (2002). The American Psychiatric Association (APA) classification of mental disorders: strengths, limitations and future perspectives. In: M. Maj, W. Gaebel, J. J. López-Ibor & N. Sartorius (Eds.), *Psychiatric Diagnosis and Classification* (pp. 47–78). New York: Wiley.

Rennie, D. (1994). Human science and counselling psychology: closing the gap between research and practice. *Counselling Psychology Quarterly, 7(3)*: 235–250.

Repper, J. (2002). The helping relationship. In: N. Harris, S. Williams & T. Bradshaw (Eds.), *Psychosocial Interventions for People with Schizophrenia* (pp. 39–52). Hampshire: Palgrave.

Richardson, W. (2003). Truth and freedom in psychoanalysis. In: R. Frie (Ed.), *Understanding Experience: Psychotherapy and Post-Modernism* (pp. 77–99). London: Routledge.

Rizq, R. (2007). Tread softly: counselling psychology and neuroscience. *Counselling Psychology Review, 22(4)*: 5–18.

Rizq, R. (2008). Psychoanalysis revisited: a psychologist's view. *Counselling Psychology Review, 23(1)*: 6–19.

Robertson, M. (2006). Power and knowledge in psychiatry and the troubling case of Dr Osheroff. *Australasian Psychiatry* 13:343–350.

Rogers, C. (1967). *A Therapist's View of Psychotherapy: On Becoming a Person*. London: Constable.

Rogers, C. (2003). *Client-Centred Therapy: Its Current Practice, Implications and Theory*. London: Constable and Robinson.

Rogers, C. & Freiburg, H. J. (1994). *Freedom to Learn* (3rd ed.). New Jersey: Prentice Hall.

Romme, M. (2009). The disease concept of hearing voices and its harmful aspects. In: M. Romme, S. Escher, J. Dillon, D. Corstens & M. Morris (Eds.), *Living with Voices: 50 Stories of Recovery*. Ross-on-Wye: PCCS Books.

Romme, M. & Escher, S. (1993). *Accepting Voices*. London: Mind Publications.

Rorty, R. (1989). *Contingency, Irony and Solidarity*. Cambridge: Cambridge University Press.

Rose, S. (2005). *The Future of the Brain: The Promise and Perils of Tomorrow's Neuroscience*. New York: Oxford University Press.

Sampson, E. E. (1993). Identity politics: challenges to psychology's understandings. *American Psychologist, 48(12)*: 1219–1230.

Samson, C. (1995). Madness and psychiatry. In: B. S. Turner (Ed.), *Medical Power and Social Knowledge* (2nd ed.) (pp. 55–83). London: Sage.

Samuels, A. (2001). *Politics on the Couch*. London: Profile Books.

Sartre, J.-P. (1943). *Being and Nothingness: An Essay on Phenomenological Ontology* (Trans. H. Barnes). New York: Philosophical Library, 1956.

Sarup, M. (1993). *An Introductory Guide to Post-Structuralism and Post-Modernism*. New York: Harvester Wheatsheaf.

Saussure de, F. (1959). *Course in General Linguistics*. London: Fontana.

Scheff, T. (1999). *Being Mentally Ill* (3rd ed.). Hawthorne, NY: Aldine de Gruyter.

Schelling, T. C. (1960). *The Strategy of Conflict*. Cambridge, MA: Harvard University Press.

Scheurich, J. J. (1997). *Research Method in the Post-Modern*. Bristol, USA: The Falmer Press.

Schwartz, S. & Susser, E. (2006). The myth of the heritability index. In: J. McCabe, O. O'Daly, R. M. Murray, P. McGuffing & P. Wright (Eds.), *Beyond Nature and Nurture in Psychiatry*. Abingdon, Oxon: Informa Healthcare.

Seligman, M. (1995). The effectiveness of psychotherapy: the Consumer Reports Study. *American Psychologist, 50(12)*: 965–974.

Sequeira, H. & van Scoyoc, S. (2002). Division Round Table 2001: should counselling psychologists oppose the use of DSM-IV and testing? *Counselling Psychology Review, 16(4)*: 44–48.

Servais, L. M. & Saunders, S. M. (2007). Clinical psychologists' perceptions of persons with mental illness. *Psychology: Research and Practice, 38(2)*: 214–219.

Silverman, K. (2000). *World Spectators: Cultural Memory in the Present*. California: Stanford University Press.

Sims-Schouten, W., Riley, S. C. E. & Willig, C. (2007). Critical realism in discourse analysis: a presentation of a systematic method of analysis using women's talk of motherhood, childcare and female employment as an example. *Theory and Psychology, 17(1)*: 101–124.

Smail, D. (2007). *Power Interest and Psychology: Elements of a Social Materialist Understanding of Distress*. Ross-on-Wye: PCCS Books.

Snell, D. (2009). (book review) Beyond postmodernism: new dimensions in clinical theory and practice, by R. Frie and D. Orange. *European Journal of Counselling and Psychotherapy, 11.4*: 425–430.

Speer, S. A. (2007). On recruiting conversation analysis for critical realist purposes. *Theory and Psychology, 17(1)*: 125–135.

Spinelli, E. (2005). *The Interpreted World: An Introduction to Phenomenological Psychology* (2nd ed.). London : Sage.

Spinelli, E. (2007). *Practising Existential Psychotherapy: The Relational World*. London: Sage.

Stoker, B. (1994). *Dracula*. Harmondsworth: Penguin.

Strawbridge, S. & James, P. (2001). Issues relating to the use of psychiatric diagnostic categories in counselling psychology, counselling and psychotherapy: what do you think? *Counselling Psychology Review, 16(1)*: 4–6.

Symington, N. (1986). *The Analytic Experience—Lectures from the Tavistock*. London: Free Association.

Szasz, T. (1973). *The Second Sin*. Garden City, NY: Doubleday Anchor.

Szasz, T. (1988). *The Myth of Psychotherapy*. New York: Syracuse University Press.

Thomas, P. & Bracken, P. (2005). *Postpsychiatry*. Oxford: Oxford University Press.

Toffler, A. (1973). *Future Shock*. London: Pan.

Turner, B. S. (1995). *Medical Power and Social Knowledge* (2nd ed.). London: Sage.

Turner-Young, L. (2003). Counselling psychology and diagnostic systems: do they have a place in our philosophy? *Counselling Psychology Review, 18(1)*: 53–55.

Üstün, T. B., Chatterji, S. & Andrews, G. (2002). International classifications and the diagnosis of mental disorders: strengths, limitations and future perspectives. In: M. Maj, W. Gaebel, J. J. López-Ibor & N. Sartorius (Eds.), *Psychiatric Diagnosis and Classification* (pp. 25–46). New York: Wiley.

Van Deurzen-Smith, E. (1990). Philosophical underpinnings of counselling psychology. *Counselling Psychology Review, 5(2)*: 8–12.

Van Deurzen, E. (1997). *Everyday Mysteries: Existential Dimensions of Psychotherapy*. London: Routledge.

Van Deurzen, E. & Kenward, R. (2005). *Dictionary of Existential Psychotherapy and Counselling*. London: Sage.

Vygotsky, L. (1962). *Thought and Language*. New York: MIT Press.

Wallerstein, R. (1993). Psychoanalysis as science: challenges to the data of psychoanalytic research. In: N. Miller, L. Luborsky, J. Barber & J. Docherty (Eds.), *Psychodynamic Treatment Research – A Handbook for Clinical Practice*. New York: Basic Books.

Wampold, B. E. (2001a). Contextualizing psychotherapy as a healing practice: culture, history, and methods. *Applied and Preventive Psychology, 10*: 69–86.

Wampold, B. E. (2001b). *The Great Psychotherapy Debate: Models, Methods, and Findings*. Mahwah, NJ: L. Erlbaum.

Wertz, F. J. (2005). Phenomenological research methods for *Journal of Counseling Psychology. Qualitative Methods in Counseling Psychology Research.* Special Issue: *Knowledge in Context, 52(2)*: 167–177.

Williams, D. J. & Irving, J. A. (1996). Counselling psychology: a conflation of paradigms. *Counselling Psychology Review, 11(2)*: 4–7.

Willig, C. (1999). Beyond appearances: a critical realist approach to social constructionist work. In: D. J. Nightingale & J. Cromby (Eds.), *Social Constructionist Psychology: A Critical Analysis of Theory and Practice* (pp. 37–51). Buckingham: Open University Press.

Willig, C. (2008). *Introducing Qualitative Research Methods in Psychology* (2nd ed.). Maidenhead: McGraw-Hill/Open University Press.

Winnicott, D. W. (1958). Transitional objects and transitional phenomena. In: D. W. Winnicott (Ed.), *Through Paediatrics to Psychoanalysis: Collected Papers* (pp. 229–242). London: Tavistock.

Winnicott, D. W. (1971). *Playing and Reality*. London: Routledge.

Winnicott, D. W. (1986). *Home Is Where We Start From*. Harmondsworth: Penguin.

Winter, D. (2010) (editorial). Introduction to Special Issue on "Researcher Allegiance in the Psychological Therapies." *European Journal of Counselling and Psychotherapy, 12.1*: 3–9.

Wolfreys, J. L. (Ed.) (1998). *The Derrida Reader: Writing Performances.* Edinburgh: Edinburgh University Press.

Woolfe, R. (1996). Counselling psychology in Britain: past, present and future. *Counselling Psychology Review, 11(2)*: 7–18.

World Health Organization (1994). *International Statistical Classification of Diseases and Related Health Problems.* Geneva: WHO.

Wundt, W. (1874). *Principles of Physiological Psychology* (Trans. E. B. Tichener). London: Allen, 1904.

Wylie, M. S. (1995). Diagnosis for dollars? *The Family Therapy Networker, May/June*: 23–34, 65–69.

Yalom, I. D. (1980). *Existential Psychotherapy.* New York: Basic Books.

Yalom, I. D. (1989). *Love's Executioner, and Other Tales of Psychotherapy.* New York: Harper Perennial.

Yin, R. (1984). *Case Study Research: Design and Method.* London: Sage.

Young, R. M. (1994). *Mental Space.* London: Process Press.

Zachar, P. (2001). Psychiatric disorders are not natural kinds. *Philosophy, Psychiatry, and Psychology, 7(3)*: 167–182.

Zachar, P. (2003). The practical kinds model as a pragmatist theory of classification. *Philosophy, Psychiatry, and Psychology, 9(3)*: 219–227.

INDEX